THE $7 A MEAL PRESSURE COOKER COOKBOOK

FEED A FAMILY FOR $7 OR LESS

301 DELICIOUS MEALS YOU CAN PREPARE QUICKLY FOR THE WHOLE FAMILY!

Chef Susan Irby
the Bikini Chef

Acknowledgments

To fans of Susan Irby, the Bikini Chef, thank you for your continued support! Keep those recipe comments and questions coming. Thank you to my mom for many nutritious and delicious home-cooked, pressure-cooked meals. And thanks to everyone at Adams Media for their dedication to the *$7 Meal* series and the Bikini Chef.

Contains material adapted and abridged from *The Everything® Pressure Cooker Cookbook*, by Pamela Rice Hahn, copyright © 2009 by F+W Media, Inc., ISBN 10: 1-4405-0017-7, ISBN-13: 978-1-4405-0017-6; and *The $7 a Meal Slow Cooker Cookbook*, by Linda Larsen, copyright © 2009 by F+W Media, Inc., ISBN 10: 1-60550-118-2, ISBN 13: 978-1-60550-118-5.

Published by
Adams Media, a division of F+W Media, Inc.
57 Littlefield Street, Avon, MA 02322. U.S.A.
www.adamsmedia.com

ISBN 10: 1-4405-0654-X
ISBN 13: 978-1-4405-0654-3
eISBN 10: 1-4405-0998-0
eISBN 13: 978-1-4405-0998-8

Printed in the United States of America.

J I H G F E D C B

Library of Congress Cataloging-in-Publication Data
is available from the publisher.

This book is available at quantity discounts for bulk purchases.

For information, please call 1-800-289-0963.

CONTENTS

iv   INTRODUCTION

1   CHAPTER 1: PRESSURE COOKERS 101

10   CHAPTER 2: DIPS, SPREADS, APPETIZERS, AND SAUCES

36   CHAPTER 3: WHAT'S FOR BREAKFAST?

57   CHAPTER 4: CHICKEN AND TURKEY MADE SIMPLE

88   CHAPTER 5: EASY PORK DISHES

116   CHAPTER 6: BEEF AND SPECIALTY DISHES

152   CHAPTER 7: FISH AND SEAFOOD

176   CHAPTER 8: JUST SOUPS

204   CHAPTER 9: STEWS AND CHOWDERS

224   CHAPTER 10: VEGETARIAN FAVORITES

249   CHAPTER 11: PASTA, RICE, BEANS, AND GRAINS

277   CHAPTER 12: SAVORY CASSEROLES AND SIDE DISHES

317   CHAPTER 13: DESSERTS: BUTTERS, GLACÉS, COMPOTES, AND MORE

330   INDEX

INTRODUCTION

When I think of a pressure cooker, I am reminded of watching my mother cook when I was a child. She'd often use a big, heavy silver pot that had a lid that latched onto it. After she put beef, fresh vegetables, and seasonings in the big pot, she locked on the lid, turned on the heat, and then the spout on top would shake and rattle and make all kinds of noise like it was going to explode. I could not imagine what my mom was cooking in there or if, in fact, we could eat it. As a kid, I thought the whole pot, lid and all, was going to take off into orbit like an alien spacecraft. Imagine my surprise when the spacecraft landed. The spout stopped rattling and my mom safely removed the lid and served an entire meal of tender beef and vegetables seasoned to perfection. It was delicious. I honestly could not believe it. One of the greatest parts to those dinners was that Mom was always so happy and relaxed afterward because she had only one pot to clean.

That was the pressure cooker. Fortunately, today's pressure cookers have evolved to the point where even top chefs like Bobby Flay have used them on shows like the Food Network's *Iron Chef*. They are still heavy compared to your average stockpot, (they have to be to hold in all the pressure), but they are not as heavy and cumbersome as the one my mom had. They are also easier to use, easier to latch, and much quieter than they used to be.

If you don't own a pressure cooker yet, not to worry! I'll explain exactly what they are, their many benefits, and how to choose one that will work for you. I think you'll find adding a pressure cooker to your kitchen will have its advantages and save you loads of time and money in the long run. Even if you already own a pressure cooker, you may not know how truly versatile they are in terms of what kinds of foods you can cook in them. In this book, we'll make everything from appetizers to desserts!

When it's time to get cooking, you'll find more than 300 affordable, easy recipes that are so simple and delicious, you will be wondering why it took you so long to get on the pressure cooking bandwagon. With these quick, flavorful recipes, you will be thrilled with how much time you save in the kitchen, leaving you more time to spend together with your family and friends!

CHAPTER 1

PRESSURE COOKERS 101

Ever hear the phrase, "I feel like I'm in a pressure cooker and am about to explode!"? I have heard some of my fans say that out of frustration from life's pressures—careers, family, finances, and so on. You just want to say, "Enough pressure; I'm about to explode." Well, harness all that pressure into your safe, convenient pressure cooker and relieve at least the stress of cooking dinner every night.

WHAT IS A PRESSURE COOKER?

Simply put, a pressure cooker is an aluminum or steel pot that is sealed with a lid. You add a relatively small amount of water to the pot along with the ingredients, then seal with the lid. The lid does not allow moisture to escape below a preset pressure. When placed on the stove top (or if using an electric cooker, when the electric cooker is turned on), the water heats and forms steam, thereby cooking foods faster. This steam process is all held in tightly by the secured pot, which creates pressure. It is this steam-and-pressure combination that holds in the high temperature during the cooking process and beautifully cooks the food in a minimal amount of time.

Cooking with steam is not a new concept and neither is a pressure cooker. Hot steam helps keep food moist and retains nutrients (as opposed to boiling foods) and is thereby a very healthy, flavorful way to cook. With a pressure cooker, the process of steam cooking is made simple while still providing flavorful meals. The secret to the flavor? Adding in your favorite spices! In this book, you will find plenty of flavorful recipes.

To help control the steam and pressure, pressure cookers have a gasket, or regulator, that is built into the lid. This gasket helps to retain and release pressure, or steam, as needed to hold the desired amount of pressure during the cooking time and preventing your pressure cooker from exploding.

WHY SHOULD I COOK WITH A PRESSURE COOKER?

There are so many great reasons to cook in a pressure cooker. Here are just a few:

SAVE TIME!

The most obvious reason to own a pressure cooker is that it saves time. Foods can cook in a pressure cooker in less than half the time—sometimes in just a few minutes—making it the perfect solution at the end of a busy day when you are too tired to cook an entire meal or just don't feel like cooking at all.

They are especially useful when unexpected guests arrive (hungry, of course) and you want to get a healthy meal made quickly.

SAVE MONEY!

Pressure cookers can save you and your family money in a variety of ways:

- Pressure cookers will help you save on energy costs by using less gas and electricity because of their energy efficiency and quick cooking time.
- They are very durable and can last a lifetime, making your $40 or $50 investment cost virtually nothing over a several-year span.
- Pressure cookers can make both small or large meals in virtually minutes with even heat distribution. So, when cooking for your family, why not make twice the meal at

one time? You can enjoy one portion for dinner, then freeze the remaining meal to be enjoyed two weeks later. It's easy to do with a pressure cooker because everything cooks together in one pot. Just put it all in together and minutes later you have a feast (or two)!

- Pressure cookers also cook with such intense steam that less expensive cuts of meats, which are sometimes tough when cooked in a regular oven, are now moist and tender. So, enjoy bottom round, sirloin tips, or a whole chicken tonight and save your money for filet next month or even an occasional night out.

NUTRITIONAL BENEFITS

Pressure cookers use high-heat steam to cook foods, as opposed to more fattening cooking methods such as frying. And, because the foods are steamed and not boiled, essential vitamins and minerals tend to stay with the food rather than cooking out of the food. As an added bonus, foods cooked in a pressure cooker are cooked in a shorter amount of time, thus allowing more nutrients to be retained.

THE WHOLE KITCHEN DOESN'T GET HOT!

Middle of summer and it's too hot to cook? Don't want to heat up the whole house by using your oven? Use your pressure cooker instead! By cooking your meals in a convenient, easy-to-use pressure cooker, you avoid heating up your kitchen and your house by spending hours roasting a chicken, pork roast, or spare ribs. You can cook those hearty foods in half the time or less, saving you not only a hot kitchen but also high energy bills—without sacrificing flavor or texture.

NO FUSS, NO MESS

One of the best benefits of a pressure cooker is that it's often a one-pot cleanup. No more having a sinkful of dirty mixing bowls, pots, pans, and utensils when you are done cooking. Chop your ingredients as needed, clean your knife and your cutting board, toss all the ingredients into the pressure cooker, and secure the lid. That's it (much of the time, anyway). There's nothing worse than enjoying a delicious meal only to have it ruined by a stack full of dirty dishes. Avoid all that; use a pressure cooker.

With pressure cooking, you'll also find you have delicious, healthy, well-balanced meals in minutes, which takes the pressure of cooking off you! You'll find you enjoy cooking more because it's less stressful, less time-consuming, and easier to clean up.

OTHER WAYS TO SAVE MONEY ON GROCERY SHOPPING

Once you've got a pressure cooker, you'll start saving money right away for the reasons mentioned earlier in this chapter. Here are some extra tips on how to keep those meals under $7!

Shopping on a budget begins with determining your family's needs; how much you have to spend each week or each month on groceries; finding the best value for your dollar in shopping for fresh produce, fresh meats, fish, and poultry; and keeping your fresh foods fresh for as long as possible.

One of the first things to do before even thinking about going to the store is to decide what you want to feed your family in the upcoming week (or weeks—sometimes you may find it beneficial to shop for two weeks or more). Preplanning allows you the luxury to choose specific meals, locate the recipes you'd like to cook, and make your shopping list based on the ingredients you need to make those meals. Simply writing down your meal plan and making your shopping list will save you loads of wasted time and food. As a rule of thumb, the more you stick to your list, the less likely you are to overspend!

Before you go to the store, check your cabinets for items you already have or those that you are low on. There's nothing worse than spending money on a spice like cayenne pepper only to find when you get home that you already had a brand-new bottle. That $3 to $5 pricetag could have gone to something like ground beef or a whole chicken.

Don't dismiss saving "only" a few dollars here and there. Those few dollars can make the difference between a big grocery bill that goes beyond your budget and a manageable grocery bill that helps you save money.

Other smart practices to put into use every grocery visit include:

- Eat a healthy snack before you go to the store. If you grocery shop while hungry, you will typically spend more money! You want to buy everything you see because your tummy is talking.

- Take a few extra moments to compare prices. And, don't just compare bottom-line prices; look at the fine print. Compare the price per ounce or per pound. Just because one item is priced a little lower than a competitor's doesn't necessarily mean it's less expensive. It may just have less product in the package! So, compare ounce per ounce or pound per pound to get the true price you are paying.

- Whenever possible, buy protein items in bulk. For example, if whole chickens are at a spectacular price today, buy two instead of one. Use one for dinner tonight and freeze the other one and use it next week.

The same goes for ground beef, ground turkey, chicken breasts, steaks . . . don't be afraid to use your freezer. Frozen foods can be just as fresh as truly fresh foods. Just be sure to use freezer-safe containers and sealable bags and label everything you put in the freezer with the ingredient name and date. Labeling will make it easier for you when you go to cook.

- Buy fresh items like tomatoes, red bell peppers, lettuce, and green onions, as needed and more frequently so they don't go bad before you get to use them. If you've planned out your menu through Saturday and it's only Monday, what's the point of buying the lettuce for Saturday now? Buy it super fresh on Friday, or better yet, Saturday, and enjoy conserving cash for a few extra days. The savings may not sound like much, but if you are really on a budget, sometimes those few extra days can really help out.

WHAT FOODS CAN I COOK IN A PRESSURE COOKER?

Believe it or not, you can throw almost anything that can be cooked with high steam/moisture into a pressure cooker. You can make the pressure-cooker staples such as traditional stews, roasts, and chili,

but today's pressure cookers are also designed to handle casseroles, vegetables, rice, beans, and even desserts such as puddings and custards!

TIPS ON BUYING A PRESSURE COOKER

Pressure cookers come in different styles, such as pressure saucepans, skillets, braisers, stockpots, canners, and electric countertop models. In addition, they come in varying sizes, are made from a variety of materials, feature different ways of releasing pressure, and are priced all over the spectrum.

TYPES OF POTS
- **Stockpots:** Stockpots are the most popular and familiar style of pressure cooker. Available in 4-quart, 6-quart, and 8-quart sizes, they are readily available in both steel and aluminum. Four-quart pressure cookers are perfect for singles, couples, or making one-course family meals. The 6-quart cooker is ideal for a family of two to four, while the 8-quart pressure cooker is the best for large families and if you do a lot of entertaining.
- **Saucepans:** As the name implies, saucepans are used for making sauces or simple items, such as quick-cooking oatmeal and polenta.

This saucepan, however, can double as a pressure cooker through the use of the secure lid and latch. It is ideal for smaller meals and cooking for one or two people.

- **Skillets:** Pressure cooker skillets have a long handle and can double as either a skillet with no pressure or as a small pressure cooker. Use as a skillet without the lid to sauté vegetables and brown meats and proteins like ground beef and ground turkey. Use as a pressure cooker by securing the lid. These are best for smaller meals and recipes, usually available in 2.5-quart sizes.

- **Braisers:** Although similar in function to the skillet style, the braiser pressure cookers have two short side handles as opposed to one long handle. Braisers are versatile in that you can brown meats and then continue with your pressure cooker recipe by attaching the lid. Braisers are available from 2.5-quart up to the 5-quart size.

- **Canners:** Canners are large stockpot-style pressure cookers and are usually used for just that: canning foods such as meats, vegetables, and fruits. They come in 17- and 22-quart styles and can also be used for very large groups and parties. They're not recommended for a typical family of five or more unless you do a large amount of canning or entertain large parties on a regular basis, as they require a lot of storage space.

TYPES OF POT MATERIAL

Aluminum pressure cookers are generally lighter than the steel versions, are good overall heat conductors, and are usually priced at the lower end of the scale. However, because they are made only of aluminum, they tend to be not quite as durable as steel cookers. Still, they are a good place to start if you are working on a tight budget.

Steel pressure cookers are, by contrast, heavier, more durable, and usually more expensive. Stainless steel cookers can have hot and cold spots, or places where there is more or less heat. These hot spots can cause the food to burn.

Therefore, it's best if you use a pressure cooker that is a combination of both aluminum and steel. These tend to conduct heat better and more evenly than just steel and are more durable than the aluminum-only alternatives.

WHICH VALVE WORKS BEST

All pressure cookers have a valve, which is necessary to retain and release the pressure inside the cooker. My mom's pressure cooker had the jiggly, loud, spouting valve—called a weighted valve—that was actually quite scary to watch and listen to as a child. Although those are still available, newer models have less intimidating valves and are, in my opinion, easier to work with. Here are the main types of valves and how each one works:

- **Weighted valves** are the original pressure cooker valve and sit on top of a little vent pipe. As I stated earlier, they jiggle while spouting off steam and you can hear the steam releasing. While these types of pressure cookers work fine, more modern pressure cookers are a little simpler to use and make less noise, and therefore are perhaps not as intimidating.

- **Modified valves** are also attached to the top of the cooker but have a regulator that helps release the steam in shorter bursts. That way, the regulator does not jiggle and it's less noisy.

- **Spring valves** are the newest steam regulators for pressure cookers. A shorter pop-up style valve, spring valves have a built-in viewing regulator by which you can monitor the pressure and adjust the heat higher or lower as necessary. They are quieter than the other valves or regulators and, in my opinion, are a little less intimidating to use. Pressure cookers with spring valves are usually a bit more expensive than those with weighted valves.

WHAT SIZE PRESSURE COOKER IS RIGHT FOR ME?

The size of the pressure cooker you need depends upon how many people you are usually cooking for. Standard pressure cooker sizes are 4-quart, 6-quart, and 8-quart. If you are single and primarily cook for yourself, then a 4-quart cooker is probably fine for you. However, if you are single and you like to entertain, investing in a larger one makes more sense. Likewise, families can make good use of a 6- or 8-quart pressure cooker, as you can cook entire meals in minutes.

Although there are even larger pressure cookers on the market, a 6- or 8-quart cooker can suit most, if not all, your needs. However, a plus to having an 8-quart (or larger) pressure cooker is the ability to make enough for a family of four to enjoy now while at the same time saving some for quick, easy, nutritious meals later by freezing any leftovers.

ELECTRIC PRESSURE COOKERS

Electric countertop pressure cookers are not a bad alternative to stovetop versions—however, they tend to be a little bit more difficult to regulate. Even in general cooking, most chefs, including myself, prefer cooking over a gas stove because adjusting the heat up or down is much more manageable and the heat adjusts more quickly. The same is true for electric pressure cookers. The electric temperature adjustments take longer, which can throw off your recipe either way, making things underdone or overdone. If it fits within your budget and space, use a stovetop pressure cooker instead.

RELEASING THE PRESSURE POST-COOKING

There are a couple of safe ways to release the pressure from the pressure cooker once you're done cooking: natural release or quick release. While either way can be used on most recipes, the natural-release method takes longer to cool down than the quick-release method. Therefore, some recipes are more efficient using the quick-release method or a combination of both. The recipes in this book designate when to use which method. Let's take a look at the methods and benefits of each one.

NATURAL-RELEASE METHOD

The natural-release method is the most simple method and involves removing the pressure cooker from the heat and letting the pressure release gradually as the pot cools on an unused part of the stovetop. The main benefit is that you don't have to lift the cooker from the stovetop and carry it to the sink, risking dropping it. As lightweight as they have become, pressure cookers can still be a little bit heavy and the pan is still hot when removed directly

from the stove. So, by releasing the pressure naturally, the cooker rests on the stove top until the pot has cooled down and the pressure has been released.

QUICK-RELEASE METHOD

Quick-releasing the pressure is as simple as running the entire cooker under cold water. However, it does require lifting a somewhat heavy pot to the sink without dropping it and without burning yourself. While the natural-release method may be a little safer, sometimes you're in a hurry and can't wait. In addition, some recipes involve a two-step process that uses *both* methods, or the recipe will in fact produce a better flavor and texture if you use the quick-release method. Each recipe in this book designates when to use which release method, so there's no guesswork for you. Just read the recipe before you begin to know what to expect.

FINAL TIPS FOR USING PRESSURE COOKERS

- Don't overstuff a pressure cooker— it will throw off the pressure and can result in an explosion of food in your kitchen. Never fill a pressure cooker more than two-thirds full.
- When in doubt about cooking times or other issues, check with the instruction manual that came with your cooker.

- When you have a variety of vegetables, chop them to similar-sized pieces so they cook evenly. Same goes for roasting potatoes and other vegetables. Try to keep the size about the same across the board and distribute evenly on the baking sheet.
- Make sure foods are completely thawed before putting them in your pressure cooker, to ensure even cooking time and a more accurate result.

CHAPTER 2

DIPS, SPREADS, APPETIZERS, AND SAUCES

Tomato Chutney with Fresh Ginger Root / 11

Spiced Apricot Preserves / 12

Jalapeño Mango Chutney / 13

Wild Berry Black Currant Jam / 14

Traditional Louisiana Corn Maque Choux / 15

Medley of Citrus Marmalade / 16

Peach Apricot Preserves with Toasted Almonds / 17

Traditional Hummus / 18

Simple Stuffed Grape Leaves / 19

Pineapple Cilantro Pesto on Crostini / 20

Eggplant Purée in Endive Cups / 21

Spiced Split Pea Purée on Pita Crisps / 22

Purple Cabbage Rolls with Beef, Mint, and Tarragon / 23

Spicy Black Bean Purée with Monterey Jack / 24

Torta of Sun-Dried Tomato / 25

Mexicali Dip of Chicken and Bacon / 26

Fresh Herb Marinara / 27

Plum Tomato Sauce with Spicy Italian Sausage and
    Mushrooms / 28

Fresh Marinara with Beef and Herbs / 30

Barbecue Sauce with Smoked Paprika and Molasses / 31

True Southern-Style Barbecue Sauce / 32

Hearty Bolognese Sauce / 33

Fresh Cranberry Sauce with Apples / 34

Curried Spinach Sauce with Chicken / 35

Tomato Chutney with Fresh Ginger Root

 Makes 3 cups

3 pounds ripe tomatoes, peeled

1 (1") piece fresh ginger root

3 cloves garlic

1¾ cups white sugar

1 cup red wine vinegar

2 onions, diced

¼ cup golden raisins

¾ teaspoon ground cinnamon

½ teaspoon ground coriander

¼ teaspoon ground cloves

¼ teaspoon ground nutmeg

¼ teaspoon ground ginger

1 teaspoon chili powder

1 pinch paprika

1 tablespoon curry paste

Use this recipe as a dip or spread on top of a toasted English muffin with deli-sliced turkey breast for a quick, healthy sandwich. This delicious chutney could also be used on homemade pizzas in place of traditional marinara sauce.

1. Purée the peeled tomatoes and fresh ginger in a blender or food processor.
2. Pour the puréed tomato mixture into the pressure cooker. Stir in the remaining ingredients. Stir to mix, lock the lid into place, and cook at low pressure for 10 minutes. Remove from heat and allow pressure to release naturally. Refrigerate in a covered container until ready to use. Serve chilled or at room temperature.

Easy-Peel Tomatoes

Here's a quick little trick I learned in Italy. Make an "x" on the bottom of the tomato with a small paring knife. Place in boiling water for about a minute or until the skin of the tomato begins to peel away. Drain and cool by running under cold water or plunging into a bowl of water with ice (an ice bath). Peel away remaining skin using your hands, and voilà! You are ready to make any kind of sauce with freshly peeled tomatoes.

Spiced Apricot Preserves

 Makes 7 cups

4 cups dried apricots, chopped

2 cups water

5 black peppercorns

5 cardamom pods

2 (3") cinnamon sticks

2 star anise

½ cup lemon juice

4 cups granulated cane sugar

Create your own preserve recipes by substituting your favorite dried fruits.

1. Add the apricots to a bowl or to the pressure cooker. Pour in the water, cover, and let the apricots soak for 24 hours.
2. Wrap the peppercorns, cardamom pods, cinnamon sticks, and star anise in cheesecloth and secure with a string. Add to the pressure cooker along with the apricots, soaking water, and lemon juice. Lock the lid into place. Bring to pressure and cook on low pressure for 10 minutes. Remove from the heat and allow pressure to release naturally.
3. Uncover the pressure cooker. Remove and discard the cheesecloth spice bag, and stir in the sugar.
4. Return the pressure cooker to the heat and bring to a rapid boil over medium-high heat. Boil covered for 2 minutes and uncovered for 2 minutes or until the apricot mixture reaches the gel point.
5. Skim off and discard any foam. Ladle into hot, sterilized glass containers or jars, leaving ½" of head space. Seal the containers or jars. Cool and refrigerate for a week or freeze. (If you prefer, you can follow the instructions that came with your canning jars and process the preserves for shelf storage.)

What's Your Gel Point?

Basically, the gel point is the point at which your preserves are as thick as you would like. Spoon a small amount onto a chilled plate to check the thickness. Thinner preserves make good spreads but if you prefer thicker preserves, cook the mixture an additional 20 minutes or so.

Jalapeño Mango Chutney

 Makes 2 cups

2 almost-ripe mangoes

2 small serrano or jalapeño peppers

1 large clove garlic

2 teaspoons fresh ginger, grated

6 unsweetened dried plums, coarsely chopped

¾ cup dark brown sugar

¾ cup raw cane sugar or turbinado sugar

1 cup white wine vinegar

2 teaspoons mustard powder

Pinch sea salt

Chutneys are a delicious and easy way to add flavor, depth, and color to simple foods such as grilled chicken or baked pork chops, or mix in with a little steamed rice for a complete recipe makeover.

1. Peel mangoes. Remove the pit and cut the fruit into small pieces. Seed and mince the peppers. Peel and mince the garlic. Add the mangoes, peppers, and garlic to the pressure cooker along with the remaining ingredients. Stir to combine.
2. Lock the lid into place. Bring to high pressure and cook for 5 minutes. Remove from the heat and let sit for at least 7 minutes.
3. Quick-release any remaining pressure. Remove the lid, return the pan to the heat, and bring to a boil; boil briskly for 10 minutes or until the mixture is thick. Cover and refrigerate overnight before using. Can be stored covered in the refrigerator for up to 6 weeks.

Turbinado Sugar

Turbinado sugar is also known as turbinated sugar. It is a crystallized sugar that is made from sugar cane extract and tastes similar to light brown sugar.

Wild Berry Black Currant Jam

Makes 3 cups

3 cups cranberries

3 cups strawberries, hulled and diced

1 cup blueberries

¼ cup diced rhubarb stalk

¼ cup dried black currants or raisins

½ lemon

3 cups granulated cane sugar

2 tablespoons water

Pinch sea salt

This richly flavored jam is delightful in holiday stuffings or used as a filling in pies, cobblers, or dolloped over vanilla bean ice cream.

1. Add the cranberries, strawberries, blueberries, rhubarb, currants or raisins, and lemon zest and juice to the pressure cooker. Stir in the sugar. Set aside for 1 hour, until the fruit is juicy.
2. Stir in the water and sea salt. Put the cooker over medium-high heat and bring the mixture to a boil. Lock the lid into place and bring the cooker to high pressure. Lower the heat to medium-low or sufficient heat to maintain the pressure for 10 minutes.
3. Remove from the heat and allow pressure to release naturally.
4. Remove the lid and return the pressure cooker to the heat. Bring to a boil. Boil rapidly for 3 minutes or until the gel point is reached. Skim off and discard any foam. Ladle into hot, sterilized glass containers or jars, leaving ½" of head space. Seal the containers or jars. Cool and refrigerate for a week or freeze. (If you prefer, you can follow the instructions that came with your canning jars and process the jam for shelf storage.)

Rhubarb

Rhubarb is an herbaceous, perennial plant of which the leaves are actually toxic. When cooking, only use the stalks. They are great for not only jams, as here, but other culinary delights such as pies, cobblers, and sauces.

Traditional Louisiana Corn Maque Choux

 Serves 4

Total cost: $6.98
Serving size: ½ cup
Calories per serving: 158
Fat: 3g
Carbohydrates: 9g
Protein: 2g
Sodium: 158mg

3 tablespoons butter

2 small onions, peeled and diced

1 small green bell pepper, seeded and diced

½ cup celery, diced

2 cloves garlic, peeled and minced

4 cups whole-kernel corn

2 Roma tomatoes, peeled, seeded, and diced

½ cup cilantro leaves, chopped, plus additional for garnish

⅛ teaspoon cayenne pepper

½ cup tomato juice

Sea salt to taste

Freshly ground black pepper, to taste

You can use drained canned corn, fresh corn cut from the cob, or thawed frozen corn in this recipe.

1. Melt the butter in the pressure cooker over medium heat. Add the onion, bell pepper, and celery; sauté for 3 minutes or until the vegetables are soft. Add the minced garlic and sauté an additional 30 seconds.
2. Stir in the corn, tomatoes, chopped cilantro, cayenne pepper, tomato juice, salt, and pepper. Lock the lid into place and bring to low pressure; maintain pressure for 3 minutes.
3. Remove from heat and quick-release the pressure. Use a slotted spoon to immediately transfer the corn and vegetables to a serving bowl. Taste for seasoning and add additional salt and pepper if needed. Garnish with cilantro and serve.

Maque Choux

Maque Choux is traditional to Louisiana and is a combination of both French Cajun and Native American cultures and cuisines. Originally made with bacon fat, this leaner version uses real butter in place of bacon fat as well as less of it.

Medley of Citrus Marmalade

Makes 4 cups

$ Total cost: $5.21

Serving size: ½ cup

Calories per serving: 302

Fat: 2g

Carbohydrates: 38g

Protein: 2g

Sodium: 9mg

1 large orange

1 lime

2 lemons

2 kumquats

1 pink grapefruit

3 cups water

4 pounds jam sugar

Jam sugar contains pectin, the soluble dietary fiber extracted from citrus fruits used as a gelling agent for jams, jellies, and marmalades.

1. Wash the fruit. Remove the zest from the orange, lime, and lemons; add to the pressure cooker. Quarter all fruit and place in a large (doubled) piece of cheesecloth; twist the cheesecloth to squeeze out the juice into the pressure cooker. Tie the cheesecloth over the fruit and seeds and add it to the pressure cooker along with half of the water. Lock the lid in place and bring the cooker to high pressure; cook on high for 10 minutes. Remove from the heat and allow pressure to release naturally.

2. Remove the lid from the pressure cooker. Place the cooker over medium heat and add the remaining water and sugar. Bring to a boil, stirring continuously until all the sugar has dissolved.

3. While the mixture continues to boil, place the lid back on the cooker (but do not lock it into place). Leave the lid in place for 2 minutes, remove it, and then continue to let the mixture boil for 8 minutes or until the desired gel point is reached.

4. Skim off and discard any foam. Ladle into hot, sterilized glass containers or jars, leaving ½" of head space. Seal the containers or jars. Cool and refrigerate for a week or freeze until needed.

Marmalades and Jams

Most marmalades feature the zest, or rind, of the fruit, as here, giving it layers of texture that is pleasing to your palate. When zesting fruit, be sure to only get the very top layer of the rind and none of the white pith. The white pith has a bitter taste that will ruin your creation.

Peach Apricot Preserves with Toasted Almonds

Makes 4 cups

6 fresh ripe peaches

1 cup water

1 (8-ounce) package dried apricots, diced

½ cup toasted almonds

1¼ cups orange juice

¼ cup lemon juice

4½ cups granulated cane sugar

2 whole cloves

1 (3") cinnamon stick

Pinch sea salt

1 (1.75-ounce) package pectin powder

Toasting the almonds is an important step that enhances the rich flavor of these preserves.

1. Use a toothpick to poke holes in the peaches. Place peaches in the pressure cooker and pour the water over them. Lock on the lid. Bring to high pressure and maintain for 3 minutes.
2. Quick-release the pressure and remove the lid. Use a slotted spoon to move the peaches to a large bowl of ice water or to a bowl under cold running water. Peel the peaches and then cut them into small pieces, discarding the pits.
3. Add the peaches, apricots, almonds, orange juice, lemon juice, sugar, cloves, cinnamon stick, and salt to the water remaining in the pressure cooker. Stir to combine. Lock on the lid and bring to high pressure; maintain pressure for 2 minutes.
4. Remove the pressure cooker from the heat. Quick-release the pressure and remove the lid. Remove and discard the cloves and cinnamon stick. Stir the pectin into the fruit mixture. Return to the heat and bring to a rolling boil over medium-high heat, stirring constantly.
5. Skim off and discard any foam. Ladle into hot, sterilized glass containers or jars, leaving 1" of head space. Seal the containers or jars. Cool and then refrigerate for up to 5 weeks or freeze for up to 8 months.

Toasting Nuts

Toasting nuts brings out the natural oils of the nut and gives the outside of the nut a richer, deeper flavor that blends into your recipes. Toasting nuts is easy. To toast on a stovetop, place nuts in a heavy skillet over low to medium-low heat. Shake the pan occasionally to toss the nuts and toast until fragrant and lightly browned. To toast in an oven, heat oven to 250°F. Distribute nuts evenly on a parchment paper–lined baking sheet. Place in oven for about 15 minutes or until fragrant.

Traditional Hummus

 Makes about 2 cups

 Total cost: $2.89

Serving size: ¼ cup

Calories per serving: 210

Fat: 10g

Carbohydrates: 19g

Protein: 7g

Sodium: 229mg

1 cup chickpeas

2 teaspoons vegetable oil

4 cups water

1 tablespoon freshly chopped basil leaves

1 clove garlic, peeled and minced

2 tablespoons tahini

Sea salt to taste

2 tablespoons lemon juice

1 tablespoon sesame oil

1 tablespoon extra-virgin olive oil

6 tablespoons water

Serve hummus with toasted pita chips or as a vegetable dip. Punch up the flavor with some dried spearmint and freshly ground black pepper if desired.

1. Add the chickpeas, vegetable oil, and 4 cups of water to the pressure cooker. Lock the lid into place; bring to high pressure and maintain for 40 minutes. Remove from the heat and allow pressure to release naturally. Remove the lid and check that the beans are soft and cooked through. Drain the beans if they're cooked through; if not, lock the lid back into place and cook the beans on high pressure for another 5 to 10 minutes.

2. Add the drained, cooked beans, basil, garlic, tahini, salt, and lemon juice to a food processor or blender. Pulse to combine. Remove the lid and scrape down the sides of the food processor or blender bowl.

3. Reattach the lid to the food processor or blender, and add the sesame and olive oils with the machine running. Process until smooth, adding water or reserved cooking liquid 1 tablespoon at a time if necessary.

What Is Tahini?

Tahini is sesame seed butter and is sometimes referred to as tahini paste. You can substitute peanut butter for tahini if it's not available, as they are similar in flavor as well as low in saturated fat.

The $7 a Meal Pressure Cooker Cookbook

Simple Stuffed Grape Leaves

Serves 16

⅓ cup olive oil

4 scallions, minced

⅓ cup fresh mint, minced

⅓ cup fresh parsley, minced

3 cloves garlic, peeled and minced

1 cup uncooked long-grain white rice

2 cups chicken broth

1 teaspoon sea salt

¼ teaspoon freshly ground black pepper

½ teaspoon fine grate lemon zest

1 (16-ounce) jar grape leaves

2 cups water

½ cup fresh lemon juice

Grape leaves are usually sold in jars marinating in a brine (a salt-based liquid) to keep them fresh and tender.

1. Bring the oil to temperature in the pressure cooker over medium-high heat. Add the scallions, mint, and parsley; sauté for 2 minutes or until the onions are soft. Add the garlic and sauté for an additional 30 seconds. Add the rice and stir-fry in the sautéed vegetables and herbs for 1 minute. Add the broth, salt, pepper, and lemon zest; stir to mix. Lock the lid into place. Bring to high pressure; maintain pressure for 8 minutes.

2. Quick-release the pressure. Remove lid and transfer the rice mixture to a bowl.

3. Drain the grape leaves. Rinse them thoroughly in warm water and then arrange them rib-side up on a work surface. Trim away any thick ribs. Spoon about 2 teaspoons of the rice mixture on each grape leaf; fold the sides of each leaf over the filling and then roll it from the bottom to the top. Repeat with each leaf. Pour the water into the pressure cooker. Place a steamer basket in the pressure cooker and arrange the stuffed grape leaves seam side down in the basket. Pour the lemon juice over the stuffed grape leaves and then press heavy plastic wrap down around them.

4. Lock the lid into place. Bring to high pressure; maintain pressure for 10 minutes.

5. Quick-release the pressure. Remove the lid. Lift the steamer basket out of the pressure cooker and, leaving the plastic in place, let the stuffed grape leaves rest for 5 minutes. Serve hot or cold with Lemon Dijon Sauce (Chapter 1) if desired.

Pineapple Cilantro Pesto on Crostini

 Serves 12

1½ cups red or white kidney beans

7 cups water, divided

2 teaspoons vegetable oil

Sea salt to taste

2 tablespoons tahini paste

¾ cup crushed pineapple, drained

4 cloves garlic, peeled and minced

¼ teaspoon dried cumin

¼ teaspoon ground ginger

¼ teaspoon freshly ground white pepper

½ cup fresh cilantro, minced

2 sourdough baguettes, sliced into ½" slices and lightly toasted

Fresh Tomato Salsa

Toss 2 large, diced hot-house or similar tomatoes in a large mixing bowl with thawed frozen kernel corn, diced green onion, a little olive oil, sea salt, and pepper. Squeeze in a little fresh lime juice, and voilà! Serve as a finishing touch to these already delicious crostini or on their own with pita crisps or with cooked proteins such as boneless, skinless chicken breasts.

Think of this relish as hummus with a Caribbean flair. Serve with tomato relish as a condiment for grilled chicken or pork, or as a dip for corn chips.

1. Add the beans to the pressure cooker and pour 3 cups of the water over them, or enough to cover the beans completely. Cover and let soak overnight. Drain and return to the pressure cooker. Pour 4 cups of water over the beans. Add the oil. Lock the lid into place. Bring to high pressure; maintain pressure for 10 minutes. Remove from the heat and allow pressure to release naturally for 10 minutes.

2. Quick-release any remaining pressure. Remove the lid and, if the beans are cooked through, drain them. If additional cooking time is needed, lock the lid into place, return to high pressure, and cook for an additional 2–5 minutes.

3. Add the cooked beans, salt, tahini, pineapple, garlic, cumin, ginger, pepper, and cilantro to a blender or food processor. Pulse until mixed but still chunky. Transfer to a covered container and chill. Serve with toasted sourdough slices, crostini.

Eggplant Purée in Endive Cups

 Makes about 1½ cups

$ Total cost: $6.34

Serving size: ¼ cup

Calories per serving: 168

Fat: 4g

Carbohydrates: 23g

Protein: 5g

Sodium: 131mg

1 tablespoon olive or sesame oil

1 large eggplant

4 cloves garlic, peeled and minced

½ cup water

3 tablespoons fresh parsley

½ teaspoon sea salt

2 tablespoons fresh lemon juice

2 tablespoons tahini

1 tablespoon extra-virgin olive oil

4 Roma tomatoes, seeded and diced

3 to 4 endives, root trimmed, leaves separated

You can also skip the endive cups and instead serve this purée with toasted pita chips or as a vegetable dip.

1. Add the olive or sesame oil to the pressure cooker and bring to temperature over medium heat. Peel and dice the eggplant and add it to the pressure cooker. Sauté the eggplant in the oil until it begins to get soft. Add the garlic and sauté for 30 seconds. Add the water.
2. Lock on the lid. Bring to high pressure; maintain pressure for 4 minutes. Remove the pan from the heat, quick-release the pressure, and remove the lid.
3. Strain the cooked eggplant and garlic and add to a food processor or blender along with the parsley, salt, lemon juice, and tahini. Pulse to process. Scrape down the side of the food processor or blender container if necessary. Add the extra-virgin olive oil and process until smooth. Serve in endive cups topped with diced tomatoes as desired.

Spiced Split Pea Purée on Pita Crisps

 Makes 2 cups

1 tablespoon olive oil

1 teaspoon unsalted butter

1 small onion, peeled and diced

2 teaspoons fresh ginger, grated

1 serrano chili pepper, seeded and finely diced

1 clove garlic, peeled and minced

½ teaspoon garam masala

¼ teaspoon ground turmeric

½ teaspoon dry mustard

1 cup dried yellow split peas

2 cups water

¼ cup plain yogurt or sour cream

2 tablespoons fresh cilantro, minced

This recipe is also tasty served spread on toasted flatbread or as a vegetable dip.

1. Add the oil and butter to the pressure cooker and bring to temperature over medium heat. Add the onion, ginger, and chili; sauté for 3 minutes or until soft. Add the garlic, garam masala, turmeric, and dry mustard; sauté for an additional minute. Stir in the split peas. Pour in the water.
2. Lock on the lid. Bring the pressure cooker to high pressure; maintain for 8 minutes. Remove from the heat and allow pressure to release naturally. Transfer the cooked split pea mixture to a bowl; stir until cooled.
3. Add the yogurt or sour cream; whisk until smooth. Stir in the cilantro.

Sandwiches and Wraps

This flavorful purée is great as a base to any sandwich or wrap. Spread on a whole-wheat tortilla, pita pocket, or sandwich bread and top with grilled vegetables or proteins such as grilled chicken or even whitefish.

Purple Cabbage Rolls with Beef, Mint, and Tarragon

 Makes about 30 rolls

1 medium head cabbage

3 cups water, divided

1 pound lean ground beef

1½ cups cooked, long-grain white rice

1 red bell pepper, seeded and minced

1 medium sweet onion, peeled and diced

1 cup beef broth

⅓ cup extra-virgin olive oil

2 tablespoons freshly chopped mint leaves

2 teaspoons freshly chopped tarragon

Sea salt and freshly ground black pepper, to taste

2 tablespoons lemon juice

You can substitute ground turkey for an even lighter dish.

1. Wash the cabbage. Remove the outer leaves and set aside. Remove the remaining leaves and place them in the cooker. Pour in 1 cup of water. Lock on the lid. Bring to low pressure; maintain for 1 minute. Quick-release the pressure. Drain the inner cabbage leaves and then move them to a cotton towel.

2. Add the ground beef, rice, bell pepper, onion, broth, oil, mint, tarragon, salt, and pepper to a bowl. Stir to combine.

3. Add the reserved cabbage leaves to the bottom of the cooker.

4. Remove the stem running down the center of each steamed cabbage leaf and tear each leaf in half lengthwise. Place 1 tablespoon of the ground beef mixture in the center of each cabbage piece. Loosely fold the sides of the leaf over the filling and then fold the top and bottom of the leaf over the folded sides. As you complete them, place each stuffed cabbage leaf in the pressure cooker.

5. Pour the remaining 2 cups of water and lemon juice over the stuffed cabbage rolls. Lock the lid into place and bring to high pressure; maintain pressure for 15 minutes. Remove from the heat and allow pressure to release naturally. Carefully move the stuffed cabbage rolls to a serving platter.

Lemon Dijon Sauce

Lemon Dijon Sauce is made by simply whisking 2 beaten eggs, 1 tablespoon olive oil, 2 tablespoons lemon juice, 2 teaspoons Dijon mustard, and 1 teaspoon granulated cane sugar in a heavy saucepan over low heat until the sauce is thick. It's a great sauce for chicken, pork, and, when cooled, could even be used as a dressing for salads.

Spicy Black Bean Purée with Monterey Jack

Serves 12

1 cup dried black beans

2 cups water

4 slices bacon, finely diced

1 tablespoon olive oil

1 small onion, peeled and diced

3 cloves garlic, peeled and minced

1 (14.5-ounce) can diced tomatoes

2 (4-ounce) cans mild green chilies, finely chopped

1 teaspoon chili powder

1 teaspoon freshly chopped oregano leaves

¼ cup freshly chopped cilantro

Sea salt to taste

1 cup Monterey jack cheese, grated

Serve with corn chips or baked tortilla chips.

1. Add the beans and water to a container; cover and let the beans soak overnight at room temperature.
2. Add the bacon and oil to the pressure cooker. Fry over medium-high heat until the bacon is almost done. Add the onion; sauté for 3 minutes or until the onion is soft. Add the garlic and sauté for 30 seconds.
3. Drain the beans and add them to the pressure cooker along with the tomatoes, chilies, chili powder, and oregano. Stir well, scraping up any bacon bits clinging to the bottom of the cooker. Lock the lid into place. Bring to high pressure; maintain pressure for 12 minutes. Remove from heat and allow pressure to release naturally for 10 minutes.
4. Quick-release any remaining pressure. Remove the lid. Transfer the cooked beans mixture to a food processor or blender. Add the cilantro and process until smooth. Taste for seasoning; add salt if desired.
5. Transfer the dip to a bowl or fondue pot. Stir in the cheese. Serve warm.

Torta of Sun-Dried Tomato

Makes 1 (7") torta

Total cost: $6.99
Serving size: ½ cup
Calories per serving: 185
Fat: 12g
Carbohydrates: 24g
Protein: 4g
Sodium: 221mg

3 tablespoons butter, melted

⅓ cup bread crumbs or savory cracker crumbs

½ cup sun-dried tomatoes in oil

6 cloves garlic, peeled and minced

1 teaspoon freshly chopped oregano leaves

3 large eggs

3 tablespoons all-purpose flour

2 (8-ounce) packages low-fat cream cheese

¾ cup low-fat sour cream

½ cup scallion, diced

2 cups hot water

Freeze this savory torta for a perfect make-ahead appetizer. Thaw overnight in the refrigerator and serve at room temperature with crudités, crackers, or breadsticks.

1. Coat the sides and bottom of a 7" Springform pan with melted butter. Evenly distribute the crumbs over the bottom and sides. Place a 16" × 16" piece of plastic wrap on top of an equal-sized piece of aluminum foil. Put the Springform pan in the center of the plastic wrap–topped foil; form and crimp the foil around the pan to seal the bottom.

2. Drain the tomatoes, leaving about 1 tablespoon oil on them, and add to a food processor along with the garlic, oregano, eggs, flour, cream cheese, and ¼ cup of the sour cream. Purée until smooth. Stir in the scallion. Pour into the Springform pan. Cover the top of the pan with foil; crimp to seal.

3. Place a trivet or rack on the bottom of the pressure cooker. Pour in the hot water. Use two 24" lengths of foil folded in half lengthwise twice to create 24" × 2"

strips of foil. Crisscross the strips on the counter and place the Springform pan in the center. Bring the ends of the strips up over the pan; hold on to the strips and use to lower the pan into the pressure cooker until it rests on the rack or trivet.

4. Lock the lid and bring to high pressure; maintain for 20 minutes. Remove from the heat and let rest for 7 minutes before quick-releasing any remaining pressure. Remove the lid and let the torta continue to cool in the cooker until all the steam has dissipated.

5. Use the foil strips to lift the Springform pan from the cooker. Remove the foil lid. If there is any moisture on top of the torta, sop up with a paper towel. Once the torta has cooled completely and just prior to serving, evenly spread the remaining ½ cup of sour cream over the top.

Mexicali Dip of Chicken and Bacon

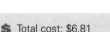

Serves 24

3 slices bacon, diced

2 tablespoons olive oil

1 medium white onion, peeled and diced

3 cloves garlic, peeled and minced

½ cup fresh cilantro, minced

⅓ cup mild or medium salsa

¼ cup ketchup

½ cup chicken broth

1 teaspoon chili powder

1 pound chicken breast tenders, diced

¼ cup plain flour, as needed to thicken

1 cup Monterey jack cheese, grated

½ cup low-fat sour cream

Sea salt and freshly ground black pepper, to taste

You can adjust the heat of this dip depending on what type of salsa or chili powder you use. To add more heat, you can also add some crushed red pepper flakes and use jalapeño jack cheese.

1. Add the bacon and oil to the pressure cooker; bring to temperature and add the onion, garlic, and cilantro. Sauté for 3 minutes or until the onion is soft. Stir in the salsa, ketchup, broth, chili powder, and diced chicken. Lock the lid into place and bring to low pressure; maintain pressure for 6 minutes.

2. Use natural-release method to release pressure. Safely remove the lid and simmer over medium heat to thicken the sauce. If needed, whisk the flour into the dip, bring to a boil, and then simmer for 2 minutes or until the flour taste is cooked out. Lower the heat and add the cheese, stirring constantly until it is melted into the dip. Fold in the sour cream. Taste for seasoning and add salt and pepper if desired. Serve warm with baked corn or flour tortilla chips.

Turkey Bacon

You can use turkey bacon instead of full-fat bacon in this recipe. However, quality and flavor varies by brand, so shop around and try them out before deciding on the one that works for you.

The $7 a Meal Pressure Cooker Cookbook

Fresh Herb Marinara

 Makes 4 cups

2 tablespoons olive oil

2 cloves garlic, peeled and minced

2½ pounds fresh, vine-ripened tomatoes

2 teaspoons fresh Italian flat-leaf parsley

2 teaspoons freshly chopped basil

1 tablespoon balsamic vinegar

½ teaspoon granulated cane sugar

Sea salt, to taste

Freshly ground black pepper, to taste

Nothing tastes better than homemade marinara. This recipe is so easy you'll find you make some ahead of time and keep in your freezer for quick meals on a busy day.

1. Add the oil to the pressure cooker and bring to temperature over medium heat. Add the garlic; sauté for 30 seconds.
2. Peel and dice the tomatoes. Add them to the pressure cooker along with the tomato juice and the remaining ingredients.
3. Lock the lid in place and bring to low pressure; maintain for 10 minutes. Remove from the heat and allow pressure to release naturally.
4. Remove the lid and stir the sauce. If you prefer a thicker sauce, return to the heat and simmer uncovered for 10 minutes or until it reaches the desired thickness.

Marinara Is Versatile!
Use fresh marinara sauce on pizzas, as a dipping sauce for breadsticks and bread, or toss with cooked, diced chicken for a refreshing twist on the usual family spaghetti dinner.

Plum Tomato Sauce with Spicy Italian Sausage and Mushrooms

Makes about 5 cups

 Total cost: $6.85

Serving size: ½ cup

Calories per serving: 391

Fat: 29g

Carbohydrates: 8g

Protein: 18g

Sodium: 1257mg

1 tablespoon olive oil

2 medium sweet onions, peeled and diced

8 ounces ground beef

1 pound Italian sausage

1 red bell pepper, seeded and diced

4 cloves garlic, peeled and minced

1 cup cremini mushrooms, sliced

1 medium carrot, peeled and grated

2½ teaspoons freshly chopped oregano

1 teaspoon freshly chopped basil

½ teaspoon fennel seed

1 teaspoon granulated cane sugar

1 bay leaf

1 (15-ounce) can plum tomatoes

2 cups tomato juice

½ cup dry red wine such as Cabernet or Zinfandel

¼ cup tomato paste

Sea salt and freshly ground black pepper, to taste

Italian sausage comes in mild, medium, or spicy-hot levels of heat and you can buy it with a variety of herbs and spices, such as garlic. Any type will work in this recipe.

Plum Tomato Sauce (continued)

1. Bring the oil to temperature in the pressure cooker over medium-high heat. Add the onion and sauté for 2 minutes. Add the ground beef; fry for 5 minutes or until it renders its fat and loses its pink color. Drain and discard any fat.

2. Remove the casing from the Italian sausage; break the meat apart and add to the pressure cooker along with the bell pepper, garlic, mushrooms, and carrots. Sauté and stir for 3 minutes. Stir in the oregano, basil, fennel seed, and sugar. Add the bay leaf.

3. Dice or purée the plum tomatoes and juices in the blender. Stir into the meat mixture in the pressure cooker along with the tomato juice, wine, and tomato paste.

4. Lock the lid into place. Bring to high pressure; maintain for 20 minutes. Remove from the heat and quick-release the pressure.

5. Return to the heat; stir and simmer the sauce uncovered for a few minutes to thicken it. Taste for seasoning and add salt and pepper if needed. Serve over pasta such as penne or farfalle.

Quick and Easy Gumbo

Throw together a simply delicious gumbo by simmering 1 cup of this Plum Tomato Sauce with 2 cups of beef or chicken broth and a 12-ounce bag of frozen mixed vegetables over medium heat in a large saucepan until everything is heated through. Add in a cup of cooked white rice or macaroni pasta for extra bulk, flavor, and texture.

Fresh Marinara with Beef and Herbs

 Serves 6

1 pound lean ground beef

1 large sweet onion, peeled and diced

1 stalk celery, diced

1 medium green bell pepper, seeded and diced

1 clove garlic, peeled and minced

Sea salt, to taste

Freshly ground black pepper, to taste

1 cup water

1 (8-ounce) can tomato sauce

1 (32-ounce) can whole peeled Italian tomatoes

⅛ teaspoon dried red pepper flakes

1 teaspoon freshly chopped Italian flat-leaf parsley

½ teaspoon freshly chopped oregano

½ teaspoon freshly chopped basil

¼ teaspoon freshly chopped thyme

2 teaspoons sugar

1 (6-ounce) can tomato paste

Fresh herbs make all the difference in a simple marinara sauce.

1. Add the ground beef, onion, celery, and green bell pepper to the pressure cooker. Fry for 5 minutes over medium-high heat or until the fat is rendered from the meat. Drain and discard the fat. Stir in the remaining ingredients, except for the tomato paste.
2. Lock the lid into place. Bring the pressure cooker to low pressure; maintain pressure for 10 minutes.
3. Quick-release the pressure. Remove the lid and stir in the tomato paste. Simmer the sauce uncovered for 5 minutes or until desired thickness is reached. Serve hot over spaghetti or penne pasta.

Barbecue Sauce with Smoked Paprika and Molasses

 Makes 4 cups

$ Total cost: $4.71

Serving size: ¼ cup

Calories per serving: 98

Fat: 2g

Carbohydrates: 11g

Protein: 2g

Sodium: 34mg

2 tablespoons smoked paprika

3½ cups ketchup

½ cup light brown sugar

¼ cup molasses

¼ cup white distilled or white wine vinegar

¼ teaspoon cayenne pepper

1 tablespoon onion powder

1½ teaspoons celery seed

1 teaspoon celery salt

1½ teaspoons garlic powder

1 teaspoon ground cumin

2 teaspoons mustard powder

1½ teaspoons chili powder

1 teaspoon fresh lemon juice

1 teaspoon freshly ground black pepper

¼ teaspoon ground ginger

¼ teaspoon ground allspice

¼ teaspoon dried thyme

Not everyone knows that molasses is a commonly used ingredient in barbecue sauces. Its thick consistency and bold, sweet flavor give a nice balance to traditional barbecue spices.

Add the smoked paprika to the pressure cooker. Lightly toast it over medium heat until it begins to release its smoked fragrance. Stir in the remaining ingredients. Lock on the lid and bring to low pressure; maintain pressure for 20 minutes. Quick-release the pressure. Allow sauce to cool and then refrigerate in a covered container for up to a week, or freeze until needed.

True Southern-Style Barbecue Sauce

 Makes 4 cups

$ Total cost: $2.74

Serving size: ¼ cup

Calories per serving: 52

Fat: 2g

Carbohydrates: 5g

Protein: 1g

Sodium: 102mg

2 cups ketchup

1½ cups distilled white vinegar

¼ cup light brown sugar

2 tablespoons onion powder

¼ cup Worcestershire sauce

¼ cup prepared mustard

1 teaspoon freshly ground black pepper

Sea salt, to taste

Cayenne pepper, to taste

Worcestershire sauce and ketchup are frequently used in Southern barbecue dishes. Worcestershire contains a variety of ingredients and spices, one of which is anchovies, which makes it perfect for Caesar salads.

Add all ingredients except the salt and cayenne pepper or hot sauce to the pressure cooker. Lock on the lid and bring to low pressure; maintain pressure for 5 minutes. Quick-release the pressure. Stir the sauce and taste for seasoning; add salt and cayenne pepper or hot sauce if desired. Allow sauce to cool and then refrigerate in a covered container for up to a week or freeze until needed.

Hearty Bolognese Sauce

 Makes 4 cups

💲 Total cost: $7.00

🥄 Serving size: ½ cup
Calories per serving: 398
Fat: 12g
Carbohydrates: 28g
Protein: 17g
Sodium: 863mg

1 tablespoon unsalted butter

1 medium sweet onion, peeled and diced

1 medium carrot, peeled and diced

1 stalk celery with leaves, diced

1 clove garlic, peeled and minced

12 ounces ground round beef

8 ounces ground pork

4 ounces ground veal

2 tablespoons tomato paste

½ cup dry white wine

1 (15-ounce) can diced tomatoes

1 bay leaf

½ cup heavy cream

Sea salt and freshly ground black pepper, to taste

Beef Bolognese

Often mistaken for marinara sauce with meat, traditional Bolognese is a meat-based sauce that originated in Bologna, Italy. As in this recipe, various combinations of meat are used to give the sauce a rich flavor. It is also defined by the minimal use of tomato and the addition of cream or milk.

This rich meat sauce is the perfect topping for fettuccine. Serve with a tossed salad and crusty, warm garlic bread.

1. Melt the butter in the pressure cooker over medium-high heat. Add the onion, carrot, and celery; sauté for 3 minutes or until the vegetables begin to soften. Add the garlic and ground meat. Fry for about 5 minutes or until the meat loses its pink color, breaking the meat apart as you do so. Drain and discard any rendered fat. Stir in the tomato paste and sauté for 1 minute. Stir in the white wine and boil for about 2 minutes.

2. Stir in the undrained tomatoes. Add the bay leaf. Lock the lid into place and bring to high pressure; maintain pressure for 15 minutes.

3. Remove from heat and quick-release the pressure. Remove the lid. Return the pan to medium-high heat and bring to a boil. Stir in the cream, continuing to cook for about 5 minutes. Taste for seasoning and add salt and pepper as needed.

Fresh Cranberry Sauce with Apples

Serves 8

4 medium tart apples

4 medium sweet apples

1 cup cranberries

Zest and juice from 1 large orange

½ cup dark brown sugar

½ cup granulated cane sugar

1 tablespoon unsalted butter

2 teaspoons ground cinnamon

½ teaspoon ground cloves

¼ teaspoon freshly ground black pepper

⅛ teaspoon sea salt

1 tablespoon fresh lemon juice

Always use real butter in your recipes and remember, when using a pressure cooker, to try not to overstuff it. This will throw off the pressure and can result in an explosion in your kitchen.

1. Peel, core, and grate the apples. Wash the cranberries. Add the cranberries to the pressure cooker and top with grated apples. Add the remaining ingredients.
2. Lock the lid into place and bring to low pressure; maintain pressure for 5 minutes. Remove from heat and allow pressure to release naturally. Remove the lid; lightly mash the apples with a fork. Stir well. Serve warm or chilled.

Curried Spinach Sauce with Chicken

 Serves 6

½ cup chicken broth or water

1 pound boneless, skinless chicken, cut into 1" pieces

2 (10-ounce) packages frozen spinach, rinsed and lightly drained

1½ cups traditional marinara sauce

1 tablespoon mild curry powder

2 tablespoons applesauce

Sea salt and freshly ground black pepper to taste

6 cups cooked rice

Freshly chopped cilantro leaves for garnish

The chicken and spinach create a layer in the pressure cooker that keeps the pasta sauce from burning on the bottom of the pan.

1. Add the broth and chicken to the pressure cooker and place the frozen blocks of spinach on top. Mix the marinara sauce together with the curry powder and pour it over the spinach. Do not mix the sauce into the other ingredients.
2. Lock the lid in place. Bring to high pressure over medium heat; maintain the pressure for 5 minutes. Quick-release the pressure. Carefully remove the lid, add the applesauce, and stir well. If the moisture from the spinach thinned the sauce too much, simmer uncovered for 5 minutes or until the sauce is the desired consistency. Taste the sauce and add more curry powder, salt, and pepper if needed. Serve over cooked rice. Garnish with cilantro.

Rice Alternatives
You can also toss this sauce with higher-fiber brown rice or pasta, or simply serve as a separate sauce over chicken, pork, or meatballs.

CHAPTER 3

WHAT'S FOR BREAKFAST?

Hash Browns with Country Sausage and Eggs / 37

Toasted Oats with Dates / 38

Veggie Breakfast Burrito / 39

Smothered Sausage with Corn and Potatoes / 40

Smoked Sausage Hash Browns with Apples and
    Walnuts / 41

Southern Sausage Gravy over Buttermilk Biscuits / 42

Sweet Ham with Red-Eye Au Jus / 43

Sweet Cream Breakfast Polenta / 44

Breakfast Sausage with Tri-Color Bell Peppers and Hash
    Browns / 45

Oatmeal with Dried Fruits / 46

Creamy Gravy with Pork Sausage and Bell Peppers over Fried
    Eggs / 47

Breakfast Bread Pudding with Apples and Raisins / 48

Bread Pudding "Parfait" / 49

Hash Browns of Sweet Potato with Bacon and Pecans / 50

Breakfast Rolls of Sausage and Pear Chutney / 51

Four-Cheese Breakfast Casserole / 52

Ham and Swiss "Panini" / 53

Frittata with Potato, Herbs, and Dried Apricots / 54

Breakfast Pita Pockets with Egg Scramble / 55

Egg Casserole with Spinach and Cheese / 56

Hash Browns with Country Sausage and Eggs

Serves 4

$ Total cost: $6.45

Serving size: 1 cup

Calories per serving: 360

Fat: 21g

Carbohydrates: 32g

Protein: 14g

Sodium: 761mg

8 ounces ground sausage

⅓ cup water

1 (1-pound) bag frozen, country-style hash browns, thawed

4 large eggs

1 cup Cheddar cheese, grated

Mild or medium salsa, as desired

Freshly chopped cilantro leaves, as desired

A breakfast favorite, hash browns go with practically everything, including eggs, sausage, and salsa—so why not serve them with all three?

1. Add the sausage to the pressure cooker; fry it over medium heat until it's browned and cooked through, breaking it apart as you do so.
2. Drain and discard any rendered fat. Pour in the water, stirring it into the meat and scraping up any meat stuck to the bottom of the pan.
3. Stir in the hash browns. Lightly beat the eggs and evenly pour them over the sausage and hash browns mixture.
4. Lock the lid into place and bring to low pressure; maintain pressure for 4 minutes.
5. Remove from the heat and quick-release the pressure. Remove the lid, evenly sprinkle the cheese over the top of the hash browns, and cover the pressure cooker.
6. Let sit for 5 minutes to allow the cheese to melt. Serve warm. Top each serving with salsa and fresh cilantro if desired.

Hash Browns

Frozen hash browns are much more convenient than making them from scratch, but if you have a little time, making fresh hash browns is a great way to use up those last few potatoes. Thickly grate the potato with a traditional grater and cook in a little butter or olive oil with some diced yellow onion and red bell pepper.

Toasted Oats with Dates

 Serves 2

$ Total cost: $3.47

Serving size: 1 cup

Calories per serving: 195

Fat: 4g

Carbohydrates: 15g

Protein: 5g

Sodium: 98mg

4 cups water, divided

1 cup steel-cut oats, toasted

¼ cup diced, pitted dates

1 tablespoon butter

Pinch sea salt

Steel-cut oats are whole-grain oats that have been cut into only two or three pieces. They are sometimes referred to as Irish oatmeal and are high in B vitamins, calcium, protein, and fiber.

1. Place the rack in the pressure cooker; pour ½ cup of the water over the rack.
2. In a metal bowl that will fit inside the pressure cooker and rest on the rack, add the oats, dates, butter, salt, and 3½ cups of the water. Lock the lid into place.
3. Bring to low pressure. For chewy oatmeal, maintain the pressure for 5 minutes. For creamy oatmeal, maintain pressure for 8 minutes.
4. Remove from the heat and allow pressure to release naturally. Use tongs to lift the metal bowl out of the pressure cooker.
5. Spoon the cooked oats into bowls; season and serve as you would regular oatmeal.

Toasting Oats

Toasting oats, or any nuts for that matter, helps bring out the natural flavors of the food as well as giving it a nutty flavor layer. Simply scatter oats on a parchment paper–lined baking sheet and place in a 275° oven for about 25 minutes. Toasting them on low heat helps to prevent burning, especially if you forget they are in the oven!

Veggie Breakfast Burrito

 Serves 4

Total cost: $6.72

Serving size: 1 burrito

Calories per serving: 295

Fat: 7g

Carbohydrates: 18g

Protein: 9g

Sodium: 267mg

1 tablespoon olive or vegetable oil

1 small sweet onion, peeled and diced

2 large carrots, peeled and diced

2 medium potatoes, peeled and diced

1 stalk celery, diced

1 large red bell pepper, seeded and diced

1 tablespoon low-sodium soy sauce

¼ cup water

1 cup zucchini or summer squash, peeled and diced

2 medium tomatoes, peeled and diced

Freshly ground black pepper, to taste

4 large whole-wheat tortillas

As a delicious breakfast alternative, skip the potatoes and add a nutrient-rich vegetable like asparagus tips and a few toasted chopped almonds or walnuts, which have the added benefit of containing good fats and protein.

1. Add the oil to the pressure cooker and bring to temperature over medium heat. Add the onion; sauté for 2 minutes.
2. Stir in the carrots, potatoes, celery, and bell pepper; sauté for 2 minutes. Add the soy sauce and water.
3. Lock on the lid and bring to high pressure; maintain pressure for 2 minutes. Remove from the heat and quick-release the pressure.
4. Return to the heat and add the squash and tomatoes. Bring to high pressure and maintain for 1 minute. Remove from the heat and quick-release the pressure.
5. Taste for seasoning and add pepper, to taste. Serve over rice or as a filling in sandwich wraps, topped with your choice of toasted nuts if desired.

Add-Ons

Diced firm tofu is a great addition to this recipe. Or, if you are not a vegan, add a scrambled egg.

Smothered Sausage with Corn and Potatoes

Serves 4

Total cost: $6.76

Serving size: 1 cup

Calories per serving: 345

Fat: 23g

Carbohydrates: 32g

Protein: 18g

Sodium: 763mg

¾ pound pork sausage links

4 large potatoes, peeled and sliced thin

1 medium sweet onion, peeled and diced

1 (16-ounce) can creamed corn

¼ teaspoon pepper

¾ cup tomato juice

Sea salt, to taste

Hearty family breakfasts are perfect for weekends, giving you plenty of energy for a busy day of activities. This breakfast has all the components you need, but if you still want an extra something, opt for a boiled or poached egg on the side.

1. Add the sausage links to the pressure cooker and brown them over medium heat. Remove the sausages to a plate.
2. Layer the potatoes, onion, and corn in the cooker. Sprinkle on the pepper. Place sausage links on top of the corn.
3. Pour the tomato juice over the top of the other ingredients in the cooker. Lock the lid, bring to high pressure, and maintain for 7 minutes.
4. Remove from the heat and let sit for 10 minutes or until the pot returns to normal pressure. Taste for seasoning and add salt and additional pepper if needed.

Savory Additions

This recipe is simple enough, but can be dressed up with added fiber and nutrients with a little chopped red bell pepper or a few fresh spinach leaves.

The $7 a Meal Pressure Cooker Cookbook

Smoked Sausage Hash Browns with Apples and Walnuts

 Serves 4

Total cost: $6.67

Serving size: 1 cup

Calories per serving: 338

Fat: 15g

Carbohydrates: 15g

Protein: 6g

Sodium: 533mg

2 tablespoons olive oil

2 tablespoons butter

1 (12-ounce) bag frozen hash brown potatoes

Sea salt and freshly ground pepper, to taste

4 ounces cooked smoked sausage, coarsely chopped

2 medium apples, such as Golden Delicious, cut into thin slices

1 teaspoon cinnamon

2 tablespoons chopped toasted walnuts

Maple syrup, as desired (optional)

Adding apples and walnuts to your meals gives you a sweet, nutty combination that is pleasing to your palate. Additionally, the apples add fiber while the walnuts provide good fats and protein.

1. Add the oil and butter to the pressure cooker and bring to temperature over medium heat.
2. Add the hash brown potatoes; sauté for 5 minutes, stirring occasionally, until they are thawed and just beginning to brown. Season with the salt and pepper.
3. Use a wide metal spatula to press the potatoes down firmly in the pan. Add the sausage and apple over the top of the potatoes.
4. Sprinkle the cinnamon over the apples, top with the toasted walnuts, and drizzle with the maple syrup if desired.
5. Lock the lid in place and bring to low pressure; maintain pressure for 6 minutes. Remove from the heat and quick-release the pressure. Serve.

Other Nuts to Try

Other delicious nuts that pair nicely with cinnamon apples are pecans, almonds, and cashews.

Southern Sausage Gravy over Buttermilk Biscuits

 Serves 6

1 pound ground pork sausage

1 tablespoon butter

¼ cup all-purpose flour

1¼ cups whole milk

6 frozen buttermilk biscuits

Sea salt and freshly ground
    black pepper, to taste

In the South, sausage gravy is a breakfast must-have—
but it's not just for breakfast. This gravy is tasty served
over mashed potatoes for dinner or even on a baked
potato for lunch.

1. Preheat oven as directed on package for baking the biscuits.
   Add the sausage to the pressure cooker. Breaking it apart as
   you do so, fry over medium-high heat for 5 minutes or until
   the sausage begins to brown.
2. Lock the lid into place and bring to low pressure; maintain
   for 8 minutes. Remove from the heat and quick-release the
   pressure. Drain and discard most of the fat.
3. Return the pressure cooker to medium-high heat. Add the
   butter and stir into the sausage until it's melted.
4. Sprinkle the flour over the meat and stir-fry it into the meat
   for 1 minute. Whisk in the milk a little at a time.
5. Bring to a boil and immediately reduce the heat; maintain a
   simmer for 3 minutes or until the gravy thickens. Taste for
   seasoning and add salt and pepper.
6. While gravy is cooking, bake biscuits as directed on package. To serve, spoon 2 tablespoons of gravy over biscuit
   halves.

Cut the Fat

If you're watching your fat
and calorie intake, it's easy
to find health-conscious
alternatives for this recipe.
Opt for leaner turkey sausage, low-fat milk, and use
only ½ the biscuit. You still
satisfy your craving but don't
sabotage your regimen.

Sweet Ham with Red-Eye Au Jus

Serves 4

1 tablespoon vegetable oil

4 (4-ounce) slices country ham

¾ cup coffee, prepared

1 teaspoon sugar

Red-eye gravy is akin to au jus (a dipping sauce) rather than a traditional thickened gravy. Serve over polenta or with biscuits for breakfast or over rice for dinner!

1. Heat the oil in a pressure cooker. Add ham and fry on both sides for 2 minutes. Add coffee. Lock the lid into place, bring to low pressure, and maintain for 8 minutes.
2. Remove from heat and quick-release the pressure. Remove ham to a serving platter. Add the sugar to the pan and stir until it dissolves, scrapping the bottom of the pan as you do so. Pour over the ham and serve immediately.

Cajun Red-Eye Au Jus

Spice can add a great kick to this recipe, and an added benefit is that hot spices have metabolism-boosting qualities. For Cajun Red-Eye Au Jus, substitute a pound of cooked roast beef for the country ham. When you add the coffee, add cayenne pepper or hot sauce, to taste. Serve over cooked rice and butter beans or peas.

Sweet Cream Breakfast Polenta

 Serves 6

 Total cost: $1.58

Serving size: ½ cup

Calories per serving: 211

Fat: 3g

Carbohydrates: 34g

Protein: 3g

Sodium: 47mg

1 cup yellow cornmeal

4 cups water, divided

½ teaspoon sea salt

1 tablespoon sweet cream butter

Pan-Fried Polenta Cakes

After you quick-release the pressure, you could try serving the polenta pan-fried instead. First, transfer the cooked polenta to a buttered 4" × 8" loaf pan. Cover with plastic wrap and chill until firm. Before frying, cut into 2" × 2" squares. Bring 1 tablespoon of butter to medium-high heat in a nonstick skillet. Without crowding the pan, add the slices of polenta and fry for 2 minutes on each side or until crisp. Serve with maple syrup or other pancake topping for breakfast, or as a dinner side dish, serve with a drizzle of olive oil.

Polenta is actually cornmeal as cooked here, it becomes thick and creamy. It's perfect for breakfast or even as a side dish for dinner entrées.

1. In a bowl, whisk the cornmeal together with 1 cup water and salt. Set aside.
2. Add the remaining 3 cups water to the pressure cooker. Bring to a boil over medium heat. Stir the cornmeal and water mixture into the boiling water. Add the butter and stir continuously until the mixture returns to a boil.
3. Lock the lid into place. Bring to low pressure; maintain for 10 minutes.
4. Remove from heat and quick-release the pressure. Spoon into bowls and serve with a sweetener and milk or cream, like oatmeal.

Breakfast Sausage with Tri-Color Bell Peppers and Hash Browns

 Serves 8

$ Total cost: $6.76

Serving size: ¾ cup

Calories per serving: 300

Fat: 20g

Carbohydrates: 32g

Protein: 21g

Sodium: 573mg

1 tablespoon olive oil or vegetable oil

1 large sweet onion, diced

1 green bell pepper, seeded and diced

1 red bell pepper, seeded and diced

1 yellow or orange bell pepper, seeded and diced

1 pound ground sausage

1 (1-pound) bag frozen hash browns, thawed

8 large eggs

¼ cup water or heavy cream

Hot sauce, as desired

Sea salt and freshly ground pepper, to taste

2 cups grated Cheddar cheese

This recipe gives you everything you need to get your day off to a healthy, high-protein, energy-filled start.

1. Add the oil to the pressure cooker and bring it to temperature over medium-high heat.
2. Add the onion and diced peppers; sauté until the onion is transparent, about 5 minutes. Stir in the sausage and hash browns.
3. Bring to low pressure; maintain for 10 minutes. Remove from the heat and quick-release the pressure. Remove the lid. Drain and discard any excess fat.
4. Return the pan to medium heat. Whisk together the eggs, water or heavy cream, hot sauce, and salt and pepper.
5. Pour the egg mixture over the sausage-potato mixture. Stir to combine and scramble the eggs until they begin to set.
6. Add the cheese and continue to scramble until the eggs finish cooking and the cheese melts.
7. If you prefer, instead of stirring the cheese into the mixture, you can top it with the cheese, then cover the pressure cooker and continue to cook for 1–2 minutes or until the cheese is melted. Serve immediately.

Veggies for Breakfast
Don't be afraid to enjoy fresh vegetables for breakfast. Grilled bell peppers, as here, and other vegetables such as bok choy and leeks, are delicious with eggs and hash browns.

Oatmeal with Dried Fruits

Serves 2

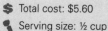
3 cups water, divided

1 cup toasted steel-cut oats

2 teaspoons butter

1 cup apple juice

1 tablespoon dried cranberries

1 tablespoon golden raisins

1 tablespoon snipped dried apricots

1 tablespoon maple syrup

¼ teaspoon ground cinnamon

Pinch sea salt

1 tablespoon brown sugar or maple syrup

1 tablespoon coarsely chopped toasted walnuts or pecans

You can substitute other dried fruit according to your tastes. Try prunes, dates, and cherries for different flavors. Adding butter to this recipe gives it additional flavor and helps prevent the oatmeal from foaming, which can clog the pressure release valve on the pressure cooker.

1. Place the rack in the pressure cooker; pour ½ cup of the water over the rack.
2. In a metal bowl that will fit inside the pressure cooker and rest on the rack, add the oats, butter, 2½ cups of the water, apple juice, cranberries, raisins, apricots, maple syrup, cinnamon, and salt; stir to combine.
3. Lock the lid into place. Bring to low pressure. For chewy oatmeal, maintain the pressure for 5 minutes. For creamy oatmeal, maintain pressure for 8 minutes.
4. Remove from the heat and allow pressure to release naturally. Use tongs to lift the metal bowl out of the pressure cooker.
5. Spoon the cooked oats into bowls. Serve warm with brown sugar or additional maple syrup, and chopped nuts.

To Cream or Not to Cream
Many people like to enjoy their oatmeal with milk. If you do, keep it lean by using nonfat or low-fat milk. Or, opt for equally delicious nondairy rice or soy milk.

The $7 a Meal Pressure Cooker Cookbook

Creamy Gravy with Pork Sausage and Bell Peppers over Fried Eggs

 Serves 8

¾ pound ground pork sausage

1 small sweet onion, peeled and diced

1 green bell pepper, seeded and diced

1 red bell pepper, seeded and diced

4 tablespoons butter, divided

¼ cup all-purpose flour

2 cups whole milk

Sea salt and freshly ground black pepper, to taste

8 eggs

Cut down on fat and calories by adding fresh vegetables and cutting out some of the high-fat sausage.

1. Add the sausage, onion, and diced bell peppers to the pressure cooker. Fry over medium-high heat and break sausage apart for 5 minutes or until it begins to brown.
2. Lock the lid into place and bring to low pressure; maintain for 10 minutes. Remove from the heat and quick-release the pressure. Remove the lid. Drain and discard any excess fat.
3. Return the pressure cooker to medium-high heat. Add 2 tablespoons of butter and stir into the sausage mixture until it's melted.
4. Add the flour and stir-fry it into the meat for 1 minute, stirring continuously. Whisk in the milk a little at a time.
5. Bring to a boil and then immediately reduce the heat; maintain a simmer for 3 minutes or until the gravy thickens. Taste for seasoning and add salt and pepper if needed.
6. Meanwhile, to fry eggs, working two at a time in a large skillet, heat ½ tablespoon butter over medium-high heat. Crack egg into skillet, being careful not to break the yolks. Cook until whites have set. Gently flip egg over and continue to fry until desired doneness. Place one egg on a plate and spoon gravy over top. Repeat with remaining butter.

Breakfast Bread Pudding with Apples and Raisins

Serves 6

2 Granny Smith apples, cored and diced

¼ cup unsweetened apple juice

⅓ cup light brown sugar, packed

¼ cup honey

2 tablespoons unsalted butter, melted

4 eggs, beaten

⅓ cup whole milk

1 teaspoon vanilla extract

Finely grated lemon zest of ½ lemon

½ teaspoon ground cinnamon

8 slices raisin bread, torn into cubed pieces

½ cup golden raisins

Bread pudding is delicious for both breakfast and dessert. Serve this simple recipe with fresh berries such as sliced strawberries and raspberries.

1. Combine apples and apple juice in pressure cooker and simmer over medium heat for about 5 minutes, stirring frequently. Remove from cooker and set aside.
2. Separately, combine sugar, honey, and butter. Mix well. Then, in another mixing bowl, combine eggs, milk, vanilla, lemon zest, and cinnamon.
3. In pressure cooker, layer in bread cubes, raisins, apple mixture, and sugar mixture, then pour in egg mixture, coating all.
4. Latch lid securely and bring to low pressure for about 10 minutes. Remove from heat and let rest until pressure has been released naturally. Serve warm with fresh berries, if desired.

Bread Pudding

Bread puddings can be made in endless variations. Other delicious breads to try include sweet Hawaiian rolls, brioche, and challah loaves.

Bread Pudding "Parfait"

 Serves 4

 Total cost: $5.52

Serving size: ¾ cup

Calories per serving: 360

Fat: 17g

Carbohydrates: 19g

Protein: 12g

Sodium: 241mg

¼ cup heavy cream

¼ cup fresh orange juice

Fine zest of ½ orange

3 eggs, beaten

1 egg white, beaten

2 tablespoons sugar

1 tablespoon honey

½ teaspoon ground cinnamon

Pinch ground nutmeg

1 teaspoon vanilla extract

4 cups cubed French bread

1 cup granola

½ cup chopped toasted walnuts

2 Granny Smith apples, peeled, cored, and cubed

While walnuts are deliciously good for you, they can sometimes be expensive. Other, less-expensive nuts that complement this dish are pistachios, almonds, and pecans.

1. Spray pressure cooker with nonstick spray. In a medium bowl, combine cream, orange juice, zest, eggs, egg white, sugar, honey, cinnamon, nutmeg, and vanilla. Mix well using a wire whisk. Set aside.
2. Place ⅓ of the bread in bottom of pressure cooker. Sprinkle with ⅓ of the granola, nuts, and apples. Repeat layers and finish by pouring egg mixture over all.
3. Latch lid securely and bring to low pressure for 10 minutes. Remove from heat and allow pressure to release naturally. When released, serve warm.

Healthy Substitutes

In most recipes, switching out honey for some of the sugar is an easy way to add natural sweeteners to your foods that are more easy for your body to digest and break down. As well, using the combination of both whole eggs and egg whites is a simple way to cut calories and cholesterol without sacrificing the flavor or texture of the dish.

Hash Browns of Sweet Potato with Bacon and Pecans

Serves 4

Total cost: $5.72

Serving size: ½ cup

Calories per serving: 340

Fat: 15g

Carbohydrates: 21g

Protein: 6g

Sodium: 720mg

4 slices lean bacon

1 yellow onion, diced

3 medium sweet potatoes, peeled and cut into 1" cubes

⅓ cup packed brown sugar

¼ cup fresh orange juice

¼ cup unsweetened applesauce

½ tablespoon minced fresh mint leaves

3 tablespoons butter, melted

Pinch sea salt

Pinch black pepper

¼ cup chopped pecans

Sweet potatoes are often overlooked as a breakfast food. They are a healthy way to start your day, as they are filled with vitamins and minerals, and they complement the flavors of both the bacon and the pecans.

1. Cook bacon over medium heat in a pressure cooker pot until crisp. Remove and drain on paper towels, then roughly chop. Remove all but 2 tablespoons of grease from cooker. Add onion and cook about 5 minutes, until tender. Add potatoes and stir to coat.

2. Separately, in mixing bowl, combine remaining ingredients except pecans. Pour over potato mixture. Latch lid securely and heat at low for 10 minutes. Use quick-release pressure method. Add bacon and pecans to sweet potatoes and stir to combine. Latch lid securely and return cooker to heat. Heat to low pressure for an additional 8 minutes. Serve warm.

Fresh Herbs

An easy way to give a refreshing taste to almost any food is to add freshly chopped herbs. Some versatile ones are cilantro, Italian flat-leaf parsley, and basil.

The $7 a Meal Pressure Cooker Cookbook

Breakfast Rolls of Sausage and Pear Chutney

Serves 8

$ Total cost: $6.49

Serving size: 1 roll

Calories per serving: 362

Fat: 21g

Carbohydrates: 16g

Protein: 15g

Sodium: 762mg

¾ cup soft bread crumbs

1 egg, beaten

¼ cup packed light brown sugar

¼ cup pear chutney

Pinch sea salt

Pinch black pepper

1 tablespoon freshly chopped Italian flat-leaf parsley

1½ pounds mild or hot ground pork sausage

2 tablespoons butter

¼ cup honey

¼ cup fat-free chicken broth

Chutneys and preserves are perfect complements to many dishes, including pork and chicken entrées, mixed green salads, or just alone as a dipping sauce. Here, pear chutney blends the flavors of the sausage while adding moisture to the recipe overall.

1. In a large bowl, combine crumbs, egg, brown sugar, pear chutney, salt, pepper, and parsley. Mix well and stir in sausage.
2. Shape into rolls 3" × 1". In a large skillet, melt butter over medium heat. Add sausage rolls, about 8 at a time, and cook until browned on all sides, about 5 to 6 minutes. As the rolls cook, drain on paper towels, then place in the pressure cooker.
3. In a mixing bowl, combine honey and chicken broth. Mix well. Pour over sausage rolls in pressure cooker. Latch lid securely and heat to low pressure. Maintain pressure for 8 minutes. Quick-release pressure. Remove rolls using slotted spoon.

Prefer Meatballs?

If you prefer to use meatballs instead, go right ahead! If using meatballs, slice in half when cooked and layer into a small whole-wheat or flour tortilla for a mini-burrito, adding scrambled eggs or grilled veggies.

Four-Cheese Breakfast Casserole

 Serves 5

 Total cost: $7.00

Serving size: ½ cup

Calories per serving: 388

Fat: 21g

Carbohydrates: 30g

Protein: 25g

Sodium: 806mg

½ pound breakfast link sausage

5 slices cracked wheat bread, cubed

1 red bell pepper, seeded and diced

¼ cup freshly chopped chives

½ cup shredded Swiss cheese

½ cup shredded provolone cheese

4 eggs

½ cup whole milk

½ cup small curd low-fat cottage cheese

1 tablespoon prepared mustard

Pinch sea salt

Pinch white pepper

Small pinch cayenne pepper

¼ cup shredded Romano or pecorino cheese

Don't like the four-cheese combination here? Use any combination of cheeses that you like!

1. Cook the link sausage in a large skillet over medium heat until done. Drain on paper towels and cut into 1" pieces.
2. Layer sausage pieces in bottom of pressure cooker pot, then layer with bread, bell pepper, chives, and Swiss and provolone cheeses.
3. In a food processor or blender, combine eggs, milk, cottage cheese, mustard, salt, white pepper, and cayenne pepper. Process until smooth and pour over sausage and bread mixture in pressure cooker pot. Add in Romano (or pecorino, if using) cheese and let stand for 20 minutes.
4. Latch lid securely and bring to low pressure. Maintain pressure for 9 minutes. Use quick-release method to remove pressure. Casserole should be set. If more cooking time is needed, secure lid, bring back to pressure for about 5 minutes. Serve warm.

Lighten Up!

You can get away with fewer calories and less fat by using reduced-fat milk and substituting ¼ cup of the provolone cheese with ¼ cup of part-skim ricotta cheese. You won't sacrifice any flavor!

Ham and Swiss "Panini"

 Serves 6

8 slices sourdough bread, cubed

1 (12-ounce) can chicken, drained

1 cup shredded Swiss cheese

½ cup chopped cooked ham

6 eggs

½ cup heavy cream

Pinch sea salt

Pinch black pepper

1 teaspoon chopped fresh oregano

2 teaspoons chopped fresh Italian flat-leaf parsley

3 tablespoons apple cider vinegar

¼ cup blackberry jelly or jam

3 tablespoons water

2 tablespoons honey

Pinch paprika

2 tablespoons butter

2 tablespoons powdered sugar

½ cup crispy rice cereal

Patterned after the Monte Cristo sandwich, this breakfast casserole gives layer upon layer of flavor. If ham is not your favorite protein, substitute deli turkey or diced cooked chicken breasts.

1. Layer cubed bread, chicken, cheese, and ham in pressure cooker.
2. In a large bowl, combine eggs, cream, salt, pepper, oregano, and parsley and beat well. Pour into pressure cooker. Let mixture stand for 20 minutes. Push bread back down into egg mixture as needed. Latch lid securely and bring to low pressure. Maintain pressure for 12 minutes or until egg mixture is set (to check, use quick-pressure release method and remove lid, resecuring if needed).
3. In a small saucepan, combine vinegar, jelly, water, honey, paprika, and butter. Bring to a simmer and stir frequently about 8 minutes, until sauce is blended and slightly thickened. When serving, place "Panini" on plate and drizzle with sauce. Finish with dusting of powdered sugar and crispy rice.

Crispy Versus Fried

True Monte Cristo sandwiches are fried. Using crispy rice cereal, as here, helps satisfy your palate's desire for crunch yet doesn't carry the heavy fat and calories that come with consuming fried foods—and, as a bonus, it's less messy!

Frittata with Potato, Herbs, and Dried Apricots

● Serves 5

$ Total cost: $5.75

Serving size: ½ cup

Calories per serving: 331

Fat: 9g

Carbohydrates: 21g

Protein: 19g

Sodium: 289mg

¼ cup diced pancetta

1 (16-ounce) package frozen hash brown potatoes

1 yellow onion, diced

2 cloves garlic, minced

¾ cup shredded Cheddar cheese

¼ cup shredded Muenster cheese

6 eggs

½ cup nonfat sour cream

2 tablespoons water

Pinch sea salt

Pinch black pepper

1 cup chopped dried apricots

2 tablespoons honey

1 tablespoon freshly chopped thyme

Frittatas are open-faced omelets made even more simple here by combining everything into one pressure cooker.

1. Cook pancetta in pressure cooker pot until crispy. Remove from cooker and set aside. Layer potatoes, onions, garlic, cheeses, and pancetta in cooker.
2. In large mixing bowl, combine eggs with sour cream and water. Beat until blended. Stir in salt and pepper and mix well. Pour into pressure cooker over other ingredients.
3. Secure pressure cooker lid. Bring to low pressure. Maintain pressure for 8 to 9 minutes, or until eggs are set. (To check, use quick-release pressure method; resecure if needed.)
4. In separate bowl, combine apricots, honey, and thyme. Mix well. Serve over top of cooked frittata.

Customize Your Frittata
Use your favorite ingredients in your frittata—try freshly diced red bell peppers, fresh basil, sliced mushrooms, and your favorite cheeses.

Breakfast Pita Pockets with Egg Scramble

 Serves 4

 Total cost: $4.75

Serving size: 2 pita pockets

Calories per serving: 381

Fat: 23g

Carbohydrates: 22g

Protein: 21g

Sodium: 745mg

2 tablespoons butter

1 yellow onion, diced

2 cloves garlic, diced

8 eggs, beaten

Pinch sea salt

Pinch black pepper

½ mild, medium, hot salsa

1 cup shredded Monterey jack cheese

2 tablespoons freshly chopped cilantro

4 pita breads

Pita bread is a healthy way to enjoy breakfast, lunch, dinner, and even snacks. Whole-wheat pita is optimal because of its high fiber content, but regular pita pockets are flavorful and lean. Stuff them with your favorite ingredients for a quick start to your day or a light midafternoon snack.

1. In a small skillet over medium heat, melt the butter. Add onion and garlic and cook until tender, stirring occasionally, about 5 minutes.
2. In a large bowl, combine eggs, salt, and pepper and beat well. Stir in onion mixture, salsa, cheese, and cilantro.
3. Pour into pressure cooker. Secure lid and bring to low pressure. Cook for 10 minutes or until done.
4. To serve, spoon one to two heaping tablespoons of egg mixture into split pita pocket. Serve warm.

Breakfast Sandwiches

A good way to start your day is with healthy carbs, protein, and fiber, which give you needed energy and strength, and help you digest foods and break down protein.

Egg Casserole with Spinach and Cheese

Serves 6

 Total cost: $6.85

Serving size: ½ cup

Calories per serving: 288

Fat: 15g

Carbohydrates: 10g

Protein: 20g

Sodium: 842mg

1 (16-ounce) bag frozen cut leaf spinach

2 cups nonfat cottage cheese

1 (3-ounce) package low-fat cream cheese

½ cup shredded Cheddar cheese, divided

½ cup shredded Monterey jack cheese, divided

4 eggs, beaten

¼ cup plain flour

Pinch sea salt

1 tablespoon freshly chopped basil

Pinch black pepper

4 tablespoons butter, melted

1 tablespoon freshly chopped Italian flat-leaf parsley

2 teaspoons water

Spinach is full of antioxidants, vitamins, minerals, and fiber, making it a nutritious food for you and your family any time of day.

1. Thaw spinach and drain. Place in a large bowl. In a food processor, combine cottage cheese with cream cheese and blend until well combined and smooth. Fold into spinach along with ¼ cup of the Cheddar cheese and ¼ cup of the Monterey jack cheese.
2. In a small bowl, beat eggs with flour, salt, basil, pepper, and butter and mix well. Stir into spinach mixture. Place all in pressure cooker and top with remaining cheese, parsley, and water. Latch pressure cooker lid and bring to low pressure. Maintain pressure for 10 minutes. Release pressure using quick-release method. Serve warm.

Delicious Additions

Easy and flavorful additions to this simple casserole are lean turkey bacon, full-fat bacon, turkey sausage, pork sausage, or diced ham.

CHAPTER 4

CHICKEN AND TURKEY MADE SIMPLE

Indian Chicken Masala / 58

Penne Chicken Cacciatore / 59

Basil Pesto Chicken / 60

Chicken with Mushrooms in White Wine / 61

Curried Chicken Salad / 62

Chili Pepper Chicken with Fresh Ginger / 63

Grand Marnier Chicken with Sweet Potatoes / 64

Citrus Spice Chicken / 65

Paprika Chicken with Bell Peppers / 66

Cayenne Chicken with a Hint of Cinnamon / 67

Lemon Herbed Chicken / 68

Mushroom Chicken with Potatoes / 69

No-Fuss Chicken Piccata / 70

Curry Yogurt Chicken / 71

Satay-Flavored Chicken / 72

Five-Spice Turkey Chili / 73

Turkey "Pot Pie" / 74

Turkey Thighs with Balsamic Fig Glaze / 76

Turkey Breast with Herbs and Port Wine Sauce / 77

Turkey Breast with Citrus Cranberry Chutney / 78

Spiced Mustard-Glazed Turkey Breast / 79

Turkey with Fresh Herb Blend and Romano Cheese / 80

Louisiana Gumbo with Turkey and Sausage / 81

Turkey à la King / 82

Turkey Breast with White Wine Tarragon Sauce / 83

Petit Turkey Meatloaf / 84

Turkey with Zucchini and Eggplant / 85

Chicken with Carrots and Herbs / 86

Ginger Honey Chicken with Olives / 87

Indian Chicken Masala

Serves 4

$ Total cost: $6.85

Serving size: ½ cup

Calories per serving: 288

Fat: 15g

Carbohydrates: 10g

Protein: 20g

Sodium: 842mg

2 tablespoons canola oil

1 stalk celery, finely diced

1 medium sweet onion, peeled and diced

1 large carrot, peeled and grated

1½ tablespoons garam masala

1 clove garlic, peeled and minced

⅓ cup flour

½ cup chicken broth

1 (14.5-ounce) can diced tomatoes, drained

1 cup coconut milk

1 pound boneless, skinless chicken breasts, diced

1 cup frozen peas, thawed

Sea salt and freshly ground black pepper, to taste

Garam masala, meaning "hot mixture," is a blend of ground spices commonly used in Indian and South Asian cuisines. It is easy to find in the spice section of most supermarkets.

1. Add the oil to the pressure cooker and bring to temperature over medium heat.
2. Add the celery; sauté for 1 minute. Add the onion; sauté for 3 minutes or until the onion is transparent. Stir in the carrot, garam masala, and garlic; sauté for 1 minute.
3. Stir in the flour, then whisk in the chicken broth. Stir in the tomatoes, coconut milk, and chicken.
4. Lock the lid into place and bring to low pressure. Maintain pressure for 10 minutes. Remove from heat and allow pressure to release naturally.
5. Remove the lid and stir. If the sauce is too thick, loosen it by stirring in chicken broth or coconut milk a tablespoon at a time.
6. Return pan to medium heat, stir in the peas, and cook until the peas are heated through. Taste for seasoning and add salt and pepper if needed.

Coconut Milk

Coconut milk comes from the meat of a fresh coconut. Although high in fat, it has zero saturated fat and is high in vitamins and minerals such as iron. Its rich, creamy flavor and texture make it ideal for cooking as well as for smoothies and cocktails.

Penne Chicken Cacciatore

 Serves 4

1 (3-pound) chicken, cut up

3 tablespoons all-purpose flour

½ teaspoon sea salt

⅛ teaspoon freshly ground pepper

2 tablespoons olive oil

¼ cup diced salt pork

1 large onion, peeled and sliced

2 cloves garlic, peeled and minced

1 tablespoon chopped fresh Italian flat-leaf parsley

2 teaspoons Italian seasoning

2 large carrots, peeled and diced

1 stalk celery, diced

1 (15-ounce) can diced tomatoes

Sea salt and freshly ground pepper, to taste

½ cup white wine

1 (6-ounce) can tomato paste

1 (1-pound) package penne pasta, cooked according to directions on package

Cacciatore means a meal that is prepared with tomatoes, onions, mushrooms, bell peppers, and fresh herbs.

1. Add the flour, salt, and pepper to a large zip-closure bag. Add the chicken, seal the bag, and shake to coat the chicken.

2. Bring the oil to temperature in the pressure cooker over medium-high heat. Add the salt pork and sauté until it begins to render its fat.

3. Add the meatier pieces of chicken, skin side down, and brown until crisp. Add the remaining ingredients except for the tomato paste and pasta.

4. Lock the lid into place. Bring to low pressure; maintain pressure for 20 minutes.

5. Remove the pan from the heat and quick-release the pressure. Using a slotted spoon, transfer the chicken to a serving platter and keep warm, leaving in remaining ingredients.

6. Return the pan to the heat, stir the tomato paste into the sauce in pressure cooker, and simmer for 5 minutes or until thickened. Place chicken on top of pasta and pour sauce over the chicken to serve.

Basil Pesto Chicken

 Serves 4

3 pounds bone-in chicken thighs

⅓ cup basil pesto

½ cup chicken broth

1 large sweet onion, peeled and sliced

8 small red potatoes, peeled

1 (1-pound) bag baby carrots

Most of the salt in pesto comes from the Parmesan cheese. To avoid oversalting the dish, serve a little extra salt on the side so each guest can add to their liking.

1. Remove the skin and trim the chicken thighs of any fat; add to a large zip-closure bag along with the pesto. Seal and shake to coat the chicken in the pesto.
2. Add the broth and onions to the pressure cooker. Place the trivet or cooking rack on top of the onions. Arrange the chicken on the rack and then add the potatoes and carrots to the top of the chicken.
3. Lock the lid into place. Bring to high pressure; maintain pressure for 11 minutes.
4. Remove the pressure cooker from the heat. Quick-release the pressure. Transfer the chicken, potatoes, and carrots to a serving platter. Use tongs to remove the trivet or cooking rack.
5. Remove any fat from the juices remaining in the pan, then strain the juices over the chicken and vegetables. Serve hot.

Traditional Pesto

Traditional pesto is made with fresh basil, pine nuts, Parmesan cheese, and olive oil. Make your own variation, however, using a combination of herbs such as fresh basil and a little fresh rosemary or cilantro leaves. Fresh dill makes a delicious dill pesto that is perfect with chicken, turkey, or pork.

Chicken with Mushrooms in White Wine

 Serves 4

 Total cost: $4.89
Serving size: 1 cup
Calories per serving: 326
Fat: 6g
Carbohydrates: 24g
Protein: 30g
Sodium: 425mg

3 tablespoons vegetable oil

1 clove garlic, peeled and crushed

3 pounds chicken pieces

1 teaspoon cracked black pepper

1 cup dry white wine

1 (15-ounce) can diced tomatoes

4 ounces mushrooms, sliced

Often called Chicken Bordeaux, this simple and delicious chicken dish is perfect with egg noodles or cooked rice. Opt for whole-grain rice for extra fiber and nutrients.

1. Bring the oil to temperature in the pressure cooker over medium-high heat. Add garlic; sauté to infuse the garlic flavor into the oil. Remove garlic and discard.
2. Rub chicken with pepper. Arrange the chicken pieces skin-side down in the pressure cooker. Pour in the wine and tomatoes. Add the mushrooms.
3. Lock the lid into place and bring to low pressure; maintain for 10 minutes. Remove from the heat and quick-release the pressure.
4. Remove chicken to a serving platter and keep warm. Return the pressure cooker to the heat and simmer the sauce until it thickens. Pour over the chicken.

Other Uses for Pressure-Cooker Chicken

Cook a whole chicken in your pressure cooker and then place it in the refrigerator overnight. Debone the chicken the next day and use it for homemade chicken salad by combining it with a little mayonnaise, a few sliced green seedless grapes, diced celery, diced red onion, and perhaps a few chopped, toasted pecans.

Curried Chicken Salad

 Serves 6

 Total cost: $6.76

Serving size: 1 cup

Calories per serving: 145

Fat: 8g

Carbohydrates: 9g

Protein: 15g

Sodium: 275mg

1 medium sweet onion, peeled and quartered

1 large carrot, peeled and diced

1 stalk celery, diced

8 peppercorns

1 cup water

3 pounds chicken breast halves, bone-in and with skin

¼ cup mayonnaise

½ cup sour cream

2–3 tablespoons curry powder

Sea salt, to taste

½ teaspoon freshly ground black pepper

1½ cups apples, diced

½ cup seedless green grapes, halved

1 cup celery, sliced

1 cup slivered almonds, toasted

2 tablespoons red onion or shallot, diced

For a healthy alternative, leave out the regular mayo and add in reduced-fat mayo, soynnaise, or even nonfat vanilla yogurt.

1. Add the onion, carrot, celery, peppercorns, water, and chicken to the pressure cooker.
2. Lock the lid into place and bring to high pressure; maintain pressure for 10 minutes.
3. Remove from heat; allow pressure to release naturally for 10 minutes and then quick-release any remaining pressure.
4. Use a slotted spoon to transfer chicken to a bowl. Strain the broth in the pressure cooker and then pour it over the chicken. Allow chicken to cool in the broth.
5. To make the salad, add the mayonnaise, sour cream, curry powder, salt, and pepper to a bowl. Stir to mix. Stir in the apples, grapes, celery, almonds, and red onion or shallot.
6. Remove the chicken from the bones. Discard the bones and skin. Dice the chicken and fold into the salad mixture. Chill until ready to serve.

The $7 a Meal Pressure Cooker Cookbook

Chili Pepper Chicken with Fresh Ginger

Serves 6

 Total cost: $6.43

Serving size: 1 cup

Calories per serving: 346

Fat: 6g

Carbohydrates: 25g

Protein: 32g

Sodium: 451mg

1 cup plain yogurt

1 clove garlic, peeled and minced

2 teaspoons fresh ginger, grated

¼ teaspoon cayenne pepper

3 pounds boneless, skinless chicken thighs

1 (15-ounce) can diced tomatoes

8 teaspoons ketchup

½ teaspoon chili powder

4 tablespoons butter

1 teaspoon sugar

½ cup cashews, crushed

Sea salt and freshly ground black pepper, to taste

Add more or less spice as you like, or really kick up the fresh flavor and color of the dish with freshly chopped cilantro or Italian flat-leaf parsley leaves. Add when serving.

1. Mix together the yogurt, garlic, ginger, and cayenne pepper in a bowl or zip-closure bag; add the chicken thighs and marinate for 4 hours.
2. Remove the chicken thighs from the marinade and add them to the pressure cooker along with the undrained diced tomatoes, ketchup, and chili powder.
3. Lock the lid into place and bring to low pressure; maintain pressure for 8 minutes. Quick-release the pressure.
4. Use a slotted spoon to move cooked chicken thighs to a serving platter and keep warm.
5. Use an immersion blender to purée the tomatoes. Whisk in the butter and sugar. Stir in the cashews. Taste for seasoning and add salt and pepper to taste.
6. If the sauce is spicier than you'd like, stir in some plain yogurt or sour cream, 1 tablespoon at a time, until you're pleased with the taste. Add red food coloring if desired. Pour over the chicken thighs and serve.

Grand Marnier Chicken with Sweet Potatoes

Serves 4

12 pitted dried plums, chopped

8 dried apricots, chopped

½ small lemon, cut into 6 thin slices

1 (3-pound) chicken, cleaned and rinsed

1 tablespoon canola oil

¼ cup finely minced shallots

2 stalks celery, finely minced

1 tablespoon finely minced fresh ginger

1 cup chicken stock

¼ teaspoon sea salt or to taste

2 medium sweet potatoes, peeled and halved

1 tablespoon grated orange zest

¼ cup Grand Marnier liqueur or orange juice

Orange liqueur blends the flavors of the dried fruits with the chicken and is rounded out with naturally sweet sweet potatoes.

1. Mix together with the prunes, apricots, and lemon slices. Add the mixture to the chicken cavity.
2. Bring the oil to temperature in the pressure cooker. Add the shallots and celery; sauté for 2 minutes. Stir in the ginger.
3. Place the chicken, breast-side down, in the pressure cooker. Pour in the broth and add the salt. Place the sweet potatoes around the chicken.
4. Lock the lid into place and bring to low pressure; maintain pressure for 25 minutes. Remove the pan from the heat and quick-release the pressure. Carefully move the sweet potatoes and chicken to a serving platter; keep warm.
5. Stir the orange zest and liqueur or orange juice into the pan juices. Return pressure cooker to the heat; bring to boil over medium-high heat. Cook until alcohol burns off or sauce thickens slightly. Either pour the sauce over the chicken and potatoes or transfer to a gravy boat to serve the sauce on the side.

Citrus Spice Chicken

Serves 8

$ Total cost: $6.97

Serving size: 1 cup

Calories per serving: 227

Fat: 7g

Carbohydrates: 13g

Protein: 22g

Sodium: 180mg

2 tablespoons butter

3 pounds boneless, skinless chicken thighs

1 teaspoon paprika

½ teaspoon sea salt

⅛ teaspoon cinnamon

⅛ teaspoon ginger

Pinch ground cloves

½ cup white raisins

½ cup slivered almonds

¾ cup orange juice

¼ cup lemon juice

½ cup apple juice

1 (1-pound) bag baby carrots, quartered

1 tablespoon cornstarch

¼ cup cold water

Hints of spice round out the overall flavors of this dish, which are enhanced by the natural citric acid in the juices.

1. Bring the butter to temperature in the pressure cooker over medium heat. Add the chicken thighs and fry for 2 minutes on each side. Add the paprika, salt, cinnamon, ginger, cloves, raisins, almonds, orange juice, lemon juice, apple juice, and carrots.

2. Lock the lid into place. Bring to low pressure; maintain pressure for 10 minutes. Quick-release the pressure; remove the lid.

3. Combine cornstarch with the water and whisk into the sauce. Stir and cook for 3 minutes or until the sauce is thickened and the raw cornstarch taste is cooked out of the sauce.

Love Orange?

Enjoy this same recipe but with a focus on orange. Instead of using the combination of orange, lemon, and apple juices, use 1½ cups of orange juice for a dish that is equally flavorful and easy. Top with freshly chopped mint leaves for a refreshing finish.

Paprika Chicken with Bell Peppers

Serves 4

$ Total cost: $6.24

Serving size: 1 breast half

Calories per serving: 245

Fat: 5g

Carbohydrates: 6g

Protein: 26g

Sodium: 245mg

2 tablespoons canola oil

1 medium sweet onion, peeled and diced

1 green bell pepper, peeled and diced

5 cloves garlic, peeled and minced

4 chicken breast halves

¼ cup tomato sauce

2 tablespoons Hungarian paprika

1 cup chicken broth

1 tablespoon flour

¾ cup sour cream

Sea salt and freshly ground black pepper, to taste

Paprika is a spice that is made by grinding varieties of dried peppers. Paprika can be spicy, sweet, or mild.

1. Bring the oil to temperature in the pressure cooker over medium-high heat. Add the onion and green pepper; sauté for 3 minutes. Stir in the garlic. Add the chicken pieces, skin-side down. Brown chicken for a few minutes.
2. Mix together the tomato sauce, paprika, and chicken broth. Pour over the chicken.
3. Lock the lid into place. Bring to low pressure; maintain pressure for 10 minutes.
4. Remove the pan from the heat and quick-release the pressure. Transfer the chicken to a serving platter and keep warm. Return the pan to the heat.
5. Stir the flour into the sour cream, then stir into the pan juices. Cook and stir until mixture simmers; simmer for 5 minutes or until the broth is thickened. Stir in salt and pepper to taste. Pour sauce over chicken.

Spice It Up or Cool It Down

If you like your meals spicy, add cayenne pepper, but if you don't, sour cream is a great way to cool down spicy flavor. In fact, if you accidentally consume something super spicy, don't drink water (which can actually increase the heat)—drink milk!

The $7 a Meal Pressure Cooker Cookbook

Cayenne Chicken with a Hint of Cinnamon

 Serves 4

1½ tablespoons olive oil

4 chicken leg-thigh pieces

Sea salt and freshly ground pepper, to taste

2 cups water

1 tablespoon paprika

1 medium carrot, scrubbed and halved

1 stalk celery, halved

1 bay leaf

1 (1") cinnamon stick

Pinch cayenne pepper

4 whole cloves

2 small yellow onions, peeled and halved

½ cup dry sherry

1 tablespoon fresh lemon juice

¼ cup almonds, toasted

Sherry wine is a dry, lightly sweet wine. Although made from white grapes, it is reddish in color.

1. Bring the oil to temperature in the pressure cooker over medium-high heat. Remove and discard the skin from the chicken.
2. Add the chicken to the pressure cooker. Sprinkle the pieces with salt and pepper, to taste.
3. Add the water, paprika, carrot, celery, bay leaf, cinnamon, and cayenne pepper. Stick a whole clove into each onion half; add them to the pressure cooker.
4. Lock the lid in place and bring to low pressure; maintain for 12 minutes. Remove from the heat and let rest for 10 minutes. Quick-release any remaining pressure.
5. Transfer the chicken to a serving platter and keep warm. Remove and discard the carrot and celery pieces, bay leaf, cinnamon stick, and onion.
6. Return the pressure cooker to the heat. Add the sherry and bring to a boil over medium-high heat. Simmer for 3 minutes. Stir in the lemon juice. Pour the sauce over the chicken and top with the almonds.

Cooking with Wine

A lot of people don't want to cook with wine because of its alcohol content (even though most of the alcohol cooks off and is not present in the final dish). If that is the case, use nonalcoholic white or rose wine or apple juice.

Lemon Herbed Chicken

Serves 4

 Total cost: $5.26

Serving size: 1 cup

Calories per serving: 328

Fat: 4g

Carbohydrates: 24g

Protein: 18g

Sodium: 471mg

2 tablespoons olive oil

1 pound boneless, skinless chicken breast

½ cup white wine

2 tablespoons fresh lemon juice

2 cloves garlic, peeled and minced

½ teaspoon chicken base paste or chicken bouillon powder

1 teaspoon Dijon mustard

1 teaspoon fresh chopped Italian flat-leaf parsley

½ teaspoon fresh chopped basil

½ teaspoon fresh chopped rosemary

¼ teaspoon fresh chopped oregano

Everyone in the family will love this easy, flavorful chicken. Serve with long-grain white rice, basmati rice, linguini noodles, or even roasted new potatoes.

1. Bring the oil to temperature in the pressure cooker over medium heat. Cut the chicken into bite-sized pieces. Add to the pressure cooker; stir-fry for 5 minutes.
2. Add the remaining ingredients; mix well. Lock the lid into place and bring to low pressure; maintain for 10 minutes. Remove from heat and quick-release pressure.
3. If the sauce needs thickening, use a slotted spoon to transfer the chicken to a serving bowl and keep warm. Return the pan to the heat and simmer, uncovered, for 5 to 10 minutes. Pour the sauce over the chicken and serve.

Frozen Foods and the Pressure Cooker

One of the reasons this recipe is so easy is because I've assumed you're using fresh or already thawed chicken. Make sure foods are completely thawed before putting them in your pressure cooker, to ensure even cooking time and a more accurate result.

Mushroom Chicken with Potatoes

Serves 4

1 tablespoon olive oil

1 tablespoon butter

2 large sweet onions, peeled and diced

8 ounces fresh mushrooms, sliced

4 boneless, skinless chicken breasts

1 (10-ounce) can cream of mushroom soup

4 medium potatoes, peeled and sliced

1 (1-pound) bag baby carrots

2 tablespoons whole milk

This is a one-pot wonderful meal for the whole family. Serve with fresh grilled vegetables or a simple salad of sliced romaine with your favorite dressing.

1. Bring the oil and butter to temperature in the pressure cooker over medium heat. Add the onion; sauté for 2 minutes. Stir in the mushrooms; sauté for 3 minutes.
2. Add the chicken, mushroom soup, potatoes, and carrots to the pressure cooker. Lock the lid in place and bring to low pressure; maintain pressure for 8 minutes. Remove from the heat and let the pressure release naturally.
3. Remove the lid and transfer the carrots, potatoes, and chicken to a serving platter; keep warm.
4. Return the pan to the heat and stir in the milk. Simmer for several minutes and then pour sauce over the chicken and vegetables on the serving platter. Serve immediately.

No-Fuss Chicken Piccata

 Serves 6

 Total cost: $6.98

 Serving size: 1 cup

Calories per serving: 253

Fat: 10g

Carbohydrates: 9g

Protein: 24g

Sodium: 721mg

2 tablespoons olive

4 shallots, peeled and minced

3 cloves garlic, peeled and minced

6 chicken breast halves

¾ cup chicken broth

⅓ cup fresh lemon juice

1 tablespoon dry sherry

½ teaspoon sea salt

¼ teaspoon freshly ground white pepper

1 teaspoon fresh chopped basil

1 cup pimiento-stuffed green olives, minced

2 tablespoons extra-virgin olive oil

1 tablespoon butter

1 tablespoon all-purpose flour

¼ cup sour cream

¼ cup Asiago cheese, grated

If you prefer a more intense lemon flavor, add 1 or 2 teaspoons of grated lemon zest to the sauce just before you return the pan to the heat to bring it to a boil.

1. Bring oil to temperature in the pressure cooker over medium-high heat. Add shallots; sauté for 3 minutes. Stir in the garlic.

2. Arrange the chicken breast halves in the pressure cooker, skin-side down. Add the broth, lemon juice, sherry, salt, pepper, basil, and olives. Lock the lid into place. Bring to high pressure; maintain for 10 minutes.

3. Remove from the heat and quick-release the pressure. Use tongs to transfer the chicken to a broiling rack, arranging them skin-side up.

4. Brush the skin with the extra-virgin olive oil. Place under the broiler at least 6" from the heat and broil to crisp the skin while you finish the sauce.

5. In a small bowl, mix the butter and flour together to form a paste. Stir in 2 table-spoons of the pan juices.

6. Return the pressure cooker to the heat and bring to a boil over medium-high heat. Once it reaches a boil, stir in the flour mixture.

7. Reduce heat to maintain a simmer for 3 minutes or until the mixture is thickened and the raw flour taste is cooked out of the sauce. Stir in the sour cream.

8. Move the chicken from the broiling rack to a serving platter. Pour the sour cream sauce over the chicken. Sprinkle the cheese over the top. Garnish with lemon slices if desired.

Curry Yogurt Chicken

 Serves 6

$ Total cost: $7.00

Serving size: 1 breast
with sauce
Calories per serving: 250
Fat: 2g
Carbohydrates: 2g
Protein: 35g
Sodium: 240mg

1 cup water

½ cup plain yogurt

1 tablespoon lemon juice

2 cloves garlic, peeled and minced

2 teaspoons grated fresh ginger
or ½ teaspoon ground ginger

1 teaspoon turmeric

¼ teaspoon sea salt

1 teaspoon paprika

1 teaspoon curry powder

¼ teaspoon freshly ground
black pepper

6 boneless, skinless chicken
breasts

2 teaspoons cornstarch

2 teaspoons cold water

Serve this East Indian–style dish with basmati rice, cous-cous, or lentils.

1. Mix water, yogurt, lemon juice, garlic, ginger, turmeric, salt, paprika, curry powder, and pepper in a bowl; add the chicken and marinate in refrigerator for 1 hour.
2. Pour the chicken and marinade into the pressure cooker. Lock the lid into place and bring to low pressure; maintain pressure for 10 minutes.
3. Remove the pressure cooker from the heat and quick-release the pressure. Transfer the chicken to a serving platter and keep warm.
4. Mix the cornstarch with the cold water. Stir into the yogurt mixture in the pressure cooker.
5. Return the pressure cooker to heat and bring to a boil on medium-high heat. Boil for 3 minutes or until mixture thickens. Pour sauce over the chicken. Serve immediately.

Satay-Flavored Chicken

Serves 4

$ Total cost: $5.98

Serving size: 1 cup

Calories per serving: 250

Fat: 12g

Carbohydrates: 15g

Protein: 17g

Sodium: 338mg

½ cup coconut milk

1 tablespoon fish sauce

2 teaspoons red curry paste

1 teaspoon light brown sugar

½ teaspoon ground turmeric

¼ teaspoon freshly ground
black pepper

1 pound boneless, skinless
chicken breasts

Serve this chicken dish over cooked jasmine rice drizzled with the peanut sauce. Serve with Indian flatbread and a cucumber salad.

1. Add all ingredients to the pressure cooker. Stir to mix. Lock the lid into place and bring to low pressure; maintain pressure for 15 minutes. Remove from the heat and allow pressure to release naturally.

2. Remove the lid, return pan to the medium heat, and simmer until the sauce is thickened. Pour over cooked jasmine rice.

Chicken Satay

Use this chicken recipe to make Thai Chicken Skewers and serve with a peanut sauce. Simply slice the chicken breasts into "tenders" and place on wooden skewers that have been soaked in water for about 45 minutes. Purchase pre-made peanut sauce which is widely available at most supermarkets.

Five-Spice Turkey Chili

 Serves 8

 Total cost: $6.98

Serving size: 1 cup

Calories per serving: 430

Fat: 13g

Carbohydrates: 21g

Protein: 36g

Sodium: 805mg

2 tablespoons extra-virgin olive oil

1½ pounds lean ground turkey

2 large sweet onions, peeled and diced

1 large red bell pepper, seeded and diced

4 cloves garlic, peeled and minced

3 tablespoons chili powder

1½ teaspoons ground cumin

1 teaspoon ground allspice

1 teaspoon ground cinnamon

1 teaspoon ground coriander

1 teaspoon dried oregano

2 (15-ounce) cans diced tomatoes

¼ cup chicken broth

1 bay leaf

2 tablespoons cornmeal

Sea salt and freshly ground black pepper, to taste

Save money by purchasing ground turkey, ground beef, and chicken in bulk. Freeze in batches for ease of use.

1. Bring the oil to temperature in the pressure cooker over medium-high heat. Add the turkey and fry it for 5 minutes, occasionally breaking it apart with a spatula.

2. Stir in the onion and bell pepper; stir-fry with the meat for 3 minutes. Stir in the garlic, chili powder, cumin, allspice, cinnamon, coriander, and oregano.

3. Sauté the spices together with the meat for 2 minutes. Stir in the undrained tomatoes and broth, and add the bay leaf.

4. Lock the lid into place and bring to high pressure; maintain pressure for 10 minutes. Remove from the heat and allow pressure to release naturally. Remove the lid.

5. Return the pressure cooker to the heat. Stir in the cornmeal and simmer for 15 minutes or until the cornmeal thickens the chili. Remove and discard the bay leaf. Stir in salt and pepper to taste.

Cincinnati Turkey Chili

My husband is from the Cincinnati area and taught me the proper way to eat chili. Thicken the chili by cooking in a little cornmeal, then serve over cooked spaghetti with grated Cheddar cheese and freshly diced white onion.

Turkey "Pot Pie"

Serves 8

 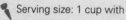

Total cost: $6.97

Serving size: 1 cup with ½ biscuit

Calories per serving: 441

Fat: 10g

Carbohydrates: 33g

Protein: 15g

Sodium: 289mg

1 tablespoon extra-virgin olive oil

1 clove garlic, peeled and minced

4 cups turkey or chicken broth

4 medium potatoes, peeled and diced

4 large carrots, peeled and sliced

1 large sweet onion, peeled and diced

2 stalks celery, finely diced

¼ cup dried mushrooms

¼ teaspoon freshly chopped oregano

¼ teaspoon freshly chopped rosemary

1 bay leaf

2 (1-pound) turkey drumsticks, skin removed

2 tablespoons butter

2 tablespoons all-purpose flour

1 (10-ounce) package frozen green beans, thawed

1 (10-ounce) package frozen whole kernel corn, thawed

1 (10-ounce) package frozen baby peas, thawed

Sea salt and freshly ground black pepper, to taste

4 large buttermilk biscuits

Biscuits make great substitutes for pastry crust, as here for pot pies, but also are great for strawberry shortcakes, or chicken or turkey à la king. You can also use crescent rolls for this pot pie recipe.

1. Add the oil to the pressure cooker and bring to temperature over medium heat. Add the garlic and sauté for 10 seconds.
2. Stir in the broth, potatoes, carrots, onions, celery, mushrooms, oregano, rosemary, and bay leaf. Stand the two drumsticks meaty-side down in the pan, arranging them so they don't block the pressure cooker vent when the lid is in place.

Turkey "Pot Pie" (continued)

3. Lock the lid and bring to high pressure; maintain pressure for 12 minutes. Remove from the heat and allow the pressure to drop naturally, and then use the quick-release method for your cooker to release the remaining pressure if needed. Remove the drumsticks; cut the meat from the bone and into bite-sized pieces and return the pieces to the pot.

4. Mix the flour together with the butter, and then stir in some of the broth from the pan to make a paste. Return the pan to the heat, and bring it to a boil over medium-high heat.

5. Stir in the flour mixture; reduce the heat to medium. Maintain a simmer and stir for 5 minutes or until the broth is thickened.

6. Stir in the green beans, corn, and peas; cook over medium heat for 5 minutes or until the vegetables are heated through. Remove and discard the bay leaf. Taste for seasoning and add salt and pepper if needed.

7. To serve, place buttermilk biscuit half in serving bowls. Spoon the turkey and vegetables over the biscuit half. Serve immediately.

Turkey Thighs with Balsamic Fig Glaze

Serves 4

Total cost: $7.00

Serving size: 1 cup

Calories per serving: 227

Fat: 5g

Carbohydrates: 2g

Protein: 22g

Sodium: 180mg

2¾-pound bone-in turkey thighs, skin removed

1 large onion, peeled and quartered

2 large carrots, peeled and sliced

½ stalk celery, finely diced

½ cup balsamic vinegar

2 tablespoons tomato paste

1 cup chicken, turkey, or veal broth

Sea salt and freshly ground black pepper, to taste

12 dried figs, cut in half

Finely grated zest 1 lemon

½ teaspoon freshly minced rosemary

Both balsamic vinegar and figs are tart and sweet with complementary flavors. This sauce tastes great with pork and chicken, too.

1. Add the turkey and onion to the pressure cooker. Cut the carrots and celery into several pieces; add them. Add the balsamic vinegar, tomato paste, and broth to a bowl or measuring cup; whisk to combine and then pour into the pressure cooker. Season with the salt and pepper. Add the figs. Lock the lid into place and bring to high pressure; maintain pressure for 14 minutes. Remove from the heat and allow pressure to release naturally.

2. Remove the lid. Transfer the thighs, carrots, and figs to a serving platter. Tent loosely with aluminum foil and keep warm while you finish the sauce. Strain the pan juices. Discard the onion and celery. Skim and discard any fat. Pour the resulting strained sauce over the thighs. Serve garnished with lemon zest and rosemary.

Fig Sauce

Once the turkey legs and vegetables are transferred to a serving platter, skim and discard the fat from the pan juices. Use an immersion blender to purée the sauce. Bring to a boil over medium-high heat and cook until the sauce is syrupy.

Turkey Breast with Herbs and Port Wine Sauce

 Serves 6

1 tablespoon canola oil

3 tablespoons butter, divided

1 large sweet onion, peeled and diced

1 pound fresh mushrooms, sliced

4 cloves garlic, peeled and minced

2 teaspoons Italian seasoning

1 (2-pound) boneless rolled turkey breast

1¾ cups chicken or turkey broth

½ cup sweet Madeira or port

1 bay leaf

¼ cup all-purpose flour

Sea salt and freshly ground black pepper, to taste

Other great wines for this dish are cabernet or merlot.

1. Bring the oil and 1 tablespoon of the butter to temperature in the pressure cooker over medium-high heat. Add the onion; sauté for 3 minutes or until transparent.

2. Add the mushrooms; sauté for 3 minutes. Stir in the garlic and herb blend. Push the sautéed vegetables to the sides of the pan and add the turkey breast.

3. Cook the turkey until it browns on the bottom; turn over and fry for another 3 minutes.

4. Use tongs to lift the turkey out of the pressure cooker. Spread the sautéed mixture over the bottom of the pot, and then insert the cooking rack.

5. Nestle the turkey on the rack. Add the broth, Madeira or port, and bay leaf.

6. Lock the lid into place. Bring to low pressure; maintain low pressure for 25 minutes. Remove from the heat and allow pressure to release naturally.

7. Remove the lid and transfer the turkey to a serving platter. Tent the turkey in aluminum foil and let it rest for at least 10 minutes before you carve it.

8. To make the gravy, remove the rack. Remove and discard the bay leaf. Skim off any excess fat from the top of the broth.

9. In a small bowl, mix the remaining butter together with the flour. Stir in some of the broth to form a paste free of any lumps.

10. Bring the pan juices in the pressure cooker to a boil over medium-high heat. Stir in the flour mixture; lower the temperature to maintain a simmer and stir and cook for 3 minutes or until the gravy is thickened.

11. Taste for seasoning and add salt and pepper if needed. Pour into a gravy boat.

Turkey Breast with Citrus Cranberry Chutney

Serves 6

Total cost: $6.88

Serving size: 1 cup

Calories per serving: 297

Fat: 5g

Carbohydrates: 17g

Protein: 32g

Sodium: 96mg

2 cups cranberry juice

1 cup whole cranberries

1 large sweet onion, peeled and diced

1 (2-pound) whole turkey breast

1 teaspoon dried thyme

Sea salt and freshly ground black pepper, to taste

2 tablespoons butter, melted

1 teaspoon finely grated orange zest

1 tablespoon lemon juice

¼ cup light brown sugar

If you are not a huge fan of cranberries, try dried cherries with cherry pie filling.

1. Place the rack in the pressure cooker. Add the cranberry juice, cranberries, and onion.
2. Rinse the turkey breast and pat dry with paper towels. Sprinkle the thyme, salt, and pepper over the breast. Place the turkey on the rack.
3. Lock the lid into place and bring to low pressure; maintain pressure for 25 minutes. Remove from the heat and allow pressure to release naturally.
4. Transfer the turkey breast to a broiling rack. Brush the skin with the melted butter. Place under the broiler; broil until the skin is browned and crisp.
5. Transfer the turkey to a serving platter and tent with aluminum foil; let rest for 10 minutes before carving.
6. Drain all but about ¼ cup of the juice from the cranberries and onions. Stir in the orange zest and lemon juice.
7. Return the pressure cooker to the heat and bring contents to a boil. Taste and stir in brown sugar as needed. Maintain a low boil until the mixture is thickened. Transfer to a serving bowl and serve with the turkey.

Chutneys and Proteins
As with many recipes in this book, you can substitute the turkey for chicken, pork, or a roast.

The $7 a Meal Pressure Cooker Cookbook

Spiced Mustard-Glazed Turkey Breast

 Serves 6

Total cost: $6.24

Serving size: 1 cup

Calories per serving: 198

Fat: 4g

Carbohydrates: 21g

Protein: 25g

Sodium: 247mg

1 cup plain yogurt

1 teaspoon ground turmeric

1 teaspoon ground cumin

1 teaspoon yellow mustard seeds

¼ teaspoon sea salt

½ teaspoon freshly ground black pepper

1 pound boneless turkey breast

1 tablespoon butter

1 (1-pound) bag baby peas and pearl onions

Serve this dish with herb-roasted new potatoes, brown or white rice, or couscous.

1. In a bowl large enough to hold the turkey, mix together the yogurt, turmeric, cumin, mustard seeds, salt, and pepper.
2. Cut the turkey into bite-sized pieces. Stir into the yogurt mixture. Cover and marinate in the refrigerator for 4 hours.
3. Melt the butter in the pressure cooker. Add the turkey and yogurt mixture.
4. Lock the lid into place and bring to low pressure; maintain pressure for 8 minutes. Remove from the heat and let pressure release naturally for 5 minutes. Quick-release any remaining pressure.
5. Remove the lid and stir in the peas and pearl onions. Return pan to medium heat.
6. Simmer and stir until the vegetables are cooked through and the sauce is thickened. Serve immediately.

Great Rice Additions

Liven up basic white rice with freshly chopped herbs such as cilantro, a little lemon zest, and some toasted chopped pecans. All those options go perfect with this Spiced Mustard-Glazed Turkey Breast.

Turkey with Fresh Herb Blend and Romano Cheese

 Serves 8

 Total cost: $6.78

Serving size: 1 cup

Calories per serving: 229

Fat: 4g

Carbohydrates: 8g

Protein: 28g

Sodium: 130mg

½ cup all-purpose flour

½ teaspoon sea salt

½ teaspoon freshly ground black pepper

2 pounds boneless, skinless turkey breast

2 tablespoons olive oil

1 large sweet onion, peeled and diced

4 cloves garlic, peeled and minced

1 tablespoon fresh chopped oregano

1 teaspoon fresh chopped basil

2 tablespoons tomato paste

½ cup turkey or chicken broth

1 (10-ounce) can tomato sauce

1 teaspoon balsamic vinegar

2 (4-ounce) cans sliced mushrooms, drained

1 tablespoon sugar

1 cup grated Romano cheese

Chicken and pork work well with this recipe. Also, if you prefer, substitute Parmesan cheese for the Romano.

1. Add the flour, salt, and pepper to a large zip-closure bag; seal and shake to mix. Cut the turkey into bite-sized pieces. Add to the bag, seal, and shake to coat the turkey in the flour.
2. Bring the oil to temperature in the pressure cooker over medium-high heat. Add the turkey and onion; fry for 5 minutes or until the turkey begins to brown and the onion is transparent.
3. Stir in the garlic, oregano, basil, and tomato paste; sauté for 2 minutes. Stir in the broth, tomato sauce, vinegar, mushrooms, and sugar.
4. Lock the lid into place and bring to low pressure; maintain low pressure for 12 minutes. Remove from heat and allow pressure to release naturally for 10 minutes.
5. Quick-release any remaining pressure. Stir the cooked turkey and sauce; ladle it over cooked pasta and top with grated Romano cheese.

Fresh Frozen Vegetables

To make this even more of a meal, add 1 cup of fresh frozen mixed vegetables that have been thawed and drained.

The $7 a Meal Pressure Cooker Cookbook

Louisiana Gumbo with Turkey and Sausage

 Serves 4

Total cost: $6.91
Serving size: 1 cup
Calories per serving: 388
Fat: 6g
Carbohydrates: 37g
Protein: 34g
Sodium: 785mg

2 tablespoons olive oil

½ pound smoked andouille sausage or kielbasa

¾ pound boneless, skinless turkey breast

1 large sweet onion, peeled and diced

4 cloves garlic, peeled and minced

1½ teaspoons freshly chopped thyme leaves

1 teaspoon filé powder

¼ teaspoon dried red pepper flakes

½ teaspoon freshly ground black pepper

1 teaspoon freshly chopped sage leaves

½ cup white wine

2 stalks celery, sliced

1 large green bell pepper, seeded and diced

1 (10-ounce) package frozen sliced okra, thawed

½ cup fresh cilantro, minced

1 (15-ounce) can diced tomatoes

1 (14-ounce) can chicken broth

For more spice, add a little cayenne pepper.

1. Bring the oil to temperature in the pressure cooker over medium heat. Add the sausage slices.
2. Cut the turkey into bite-sized pieces and add to the pressure cooker along with the onion.
3. Stir-fry for 5 minutes.
4. Stir in the garlic, thyme, filé powder, red pepper flakes, black pepper, and sage.
5. Sauté for 1 minute and then deglaze the pan with the wine, scraping the bottom of the pressure cooker to loosen anything stuck to the bottom. Stir in the remaining ingredients.
6. Lock the lid into place and bring to low pressure; maintain pressure for 8 minutes. Remove from the heat and allow pressure to release naturally.
7. Remove the lid. Taste for seasoning and adjust if necessary.

Okra

Okra can often be hard to find, even frozen. If you are having trouble locating okra, use green beans or fresh frozen mixed vegetables, but be sure to thaw them before use.

Turkey à la King

 Serves 4

Total cost: $6.68

Serving size: 1 cup

Calories per serving: 382

Fat: 12g

Carbohydrates: 53g

Protein: 12g

Sodium: 266mg

3 tablespoons butter

1 pound skinless, boneless turkey breastt

1 small sweet onion, peeled and diced

1 cup frozen peas

1 (4-ounce) can sliced mushrooms, drained

1 (2-ounce) jar pimientos, drained and diced

1 (14-ounce) can chicken broth

¼ cup all-purpose flour

½ cup sour cream

½ cup whole milk

Sea salt and freshly ground black pepper, to taste

Cut down on the fat and calories by using low-fat sour cream and milk in this recipe.

1. Bring the butter to temperature in the pressure cooker over medium heat.
2. Cut the turkey into bite-sized pieces and add to the pressure cooker along with the onions.
3. Stir-fry for 5 minutes or until the turkey begins to brown and the onions are transparent. Stir in the peas, mushrooms, pimientos, and broth.
4. Lock the lid and bring to low pressure; maintain for 6 minutes. Remove from the heat and allow pressure to release naturally.
5. Remove the lid and return the pressure cooker to medium heat. Whisk the flour into the sour cream and add the milk.
6. Once the pan juices in the pressure cooker reach a low boil, whisk in the flour-cream-milk mixture.
7. Stir and cook for 3 minutes or until the mixture thickens and the flour taste is cooked out.
8. If the dish gets too thick, whisk in additional milk a tablespoon or so at a time to get it to the desired consistency. Taste for seasoning and add salt and pepper if needed.

The $7 a Meal Pressure Cooker Cookbook

Turkey Breast with White Wine Tarragon Sauce

 Serves 4

 Total cost: $6.82

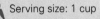 Serving size: 1 cup

Calories per serving: 319

Fat: 6g

Carbohydrates: 37g

Protein: 17g

Sodium: 339mg

2 slices bacon, cut in half

1 pound skinless, boneless turkey breast

1 medium sweet onion, peeled and diced

2 cloves garlic, peeled and minced

½ cup dry white wine

2 tablespoons fresh tarragon, minced

1 cup heavy cream

Sea salt and freshly ground black pepper, to taste

The perfect side for this dish is linguini and sautéed asparagus.

1. Cook the bacon in the pressure cooker over medium heat until crisp. Move the cooked bacon to paper towels and set aside.
2. Cut the turkey into bite-sized pieces and add to the pressure cooker along with the onion.
3. Stir-fry for 5 minutes or until the turkey is lightly browned and the onion is transparent. Stir in the garlic and sauté for 30 seconds. Deglaze the pan with the wine.
4. Lock the lid into place and bring to low pressure; maintain low pressure for 8 minutes. Remove from the heat and allow pressure to release naturally.
5. Remove the lid. Use a slotted spoon to transfer the cooked turkey to a serving bowl; keep warm.
6. Return the pressure cooker to medium heat. Stir the fresh tarragon into the pan juices. Bring the pan juices to a simmer. Whisk in the heavy cream; simmer until the cream is heated through.
7. Taste for seasoning and add salt and pepper if desired. Pour the sauce over the cooked turkey. Crumble the bacon over the top of the dish. Serve.

Fresh Tarragon

Tarragon is a leafy herb that has a licorice flavor. Because of its strong flavor, it pairs nicely with other strong-flavored ingredients such as heavy cream. Other great herbs to use in this recipe are Italian flat-leaf parsley or dill.

Petit Turkey Meatloaf

 Serves 4

Total cost: $6.72
Serving size: ½ loaf
Calories per serving: 392
Fat: 9g
Carbohydrates: 21g
Protein: 28g
Sodium: 786mg

1 pound lean ground turkey

1 small onion, peeled and diced

1 small stalk celery, minced

1 medium carrot, peeled and grated

½ cup butter cracker crumbs such as Ritz

1 clove garlic, peeled and minced

1 teaspoon fresh chopped basil

1 tablespoon mayonnaise

¼ teaspoon sea salt

¼ teaspoon freshly ground black pepper

1 large egg

3 tablespoons ketchup

1 tablespoon light brown sugar

Other great seasonings for meatloaf are freshly chopped Italian flat-leaf parsley, chives, Worcestershire sauce, and a little lemon zest.

1. Add all ingredients to a large bowl and mix well. Divide the mixture between 2 mini loaf pans. Pack down into the pans.
2. Add the rack to the pressure cooker. Pour enough hot water into the pressure cooker to come up to the level of the top of the rack. Place the pans on the rack.
3. Lock the lid into place and bring to low pressure; maintain pressure for 20 minutes. Remove from the heat and allow pressure to release naturally.
4. Remove the lid. Use oven mitts to protect your hands while you lift the pans from the pressure cooker. Serve directly from the pans or transfer to a serving platter.

Individual Loaves
Making individual loaves is a great idea no matter how many people you're cooking for. Serve ½ to 1 loaf per person then freeze the remaining individual loaves for a quick meal anytime.

Turkey with Zucchini and Eggplant

 Serves 4

 Total cost: $6.92

Serving size: 1 cup

Calories per serving: 346

Fat: 6g

Carbohydrates: 17g

Protein: 32g

Sodium: 452mg

¾ pound skinless, boneless turkey breast

2 tablespoons olive or vegetable oil

2 medium zucchini, sliced thick

1 medium eggplant, peeled and diced

1 medium sweet onion, peeled and diced

1 medium green bell pepper, seeded and diced

1 can sliced mushrooms, drained

1 (28-ounce) can diced tomatoes

3 tablespoons tomato paste

2 cloves garlic, peeled and minced

2 teaspoons fresh chopped basil

¼ teaspoon dried red pepper flakes

Sea salt and freshly ground black pepper, to taste

Parmigiano-Reggiano cheese, grated (optional)

Serve over cooked pasta or potatoes, or with thick slices of buttered French bread.

1. Cut the turkey into bite-sized pieces. Bring the oil to temperature over medium heat. Add the turkey and fry for several minutes until it begins to brown.
2. Stir in the zucchini, eggplant, onion, bell pepper, mushrooms, undrained diced tomatoes, tomato paste, garlic, basil, and red pepper flakes.
3. Lock the lid into place. Bring to low pressure; maintain the pressure for 5 minutes. Remove from the heat and quick-release the pressure.
4. Taste for seasoning and add salt and pepper, to taste. Serve topped with grated Parmigiano-Reggiano cheese.

Pricey Cheeses

Cheese can get pretty pricey. The Parmigiano-Reggiano cheese is used here for garnish. Don't worry if the Parmigiano-Reggiano at your market doesn't fit into your budget; just use pre-grated Parmesan instead.

Chicken with Carrots and Herbs

 Serves 4

3 stalks celery, cut into thirds

1 medium sweet onion, peeled and quartered

¾ teaspoon dried thyme

1 (3-pound) chicken

Sea salt, to taste

8 small carrots, peeled

½ cup chicken broth or water

¼ cup dry white wine

3 tablespoons butter

2 cups coarse dried bread crumbs

Chicken tastes great with all kinds of vegetables and herbs.

1. Place the celery pieces in the bottom of the pressure cooker and top with the onion wedges. Sprinkle with the thyme.
2. Rinse the chicken and pat dry. Season the chicken with salt to taste and place it on top of the onions and celery.
3. Place the carrots around and on top of the chicken. Pour in the broth or water and wine.
4. Lock the lid into place and bring to low pressure; maintain pressure for 25 minutes. Remove from the heat and allow pressure to release naturally for 5 minutes. Quick-release any remaining pressure.
5. Melt the butter in a nonstick skillet over medium heat. Add the bread crumbs and cook uncovered, stirring until toasted to a golden brown. Remove from the heat.
6. Transfer the chicken to a serving platter and cut into sections. Use a slotted spoon to move and arrange the vegetables around the chicken.
7. Skim and discard any fat from the pan juices and then pour the juices over the chicken and vegetables.
8. Sprinkle the toasted bread crumbs over the chicken and vegetables. Garnish with fresh parsley if desired. Serve.

Ginger Honey Chicken with Olives

Serves 6

$ Total cost: $6.43

Serving size: about 5 ounces

Calories per serving: 370

Fat: 9g

Carbohydrates: 24g

Protein: 20g

Sodium: 460mg

2 tablespoons butter

1 tablespoon extra-virgin olive oil

2 large onions, peeled and diced

2 cloves garlic, peeled and minced

2 teaspoons fresh ginger, grated

½ teaspoon ground cumin

2 pounds boneless, skinless chicken breast

2 cups chicken broth

1 lemon

2 tablespoons honey

8 large green olives, pitted

2 tablespoons cornstarch

2 tablespoons cold water

2 tablespoons chopped fresh flat-leaf parsley

Sea salt and freshly ground black pepper, to taste

Honey adds a sweet flavor that complements the spices in this easy chicken recipe your family will love.

1. Bring the butter and oil to temperature in the pressure cooker over medium heat. Add the onion; sauté for 5 minutes.
2. Stir in the garlic, ginger, and cumin. Sauté for 30 seconds. Cut the chicken into bite-sized pieces; add to the pressure cooker and stir-fry for 3 minutes. Stir in the broth, zest from half of the lemon, fresh lemon juice, and honey.
3. Lock the lid into place and bring to high pressure; maintain pressure for 8 minutes. Remove from the heat and quick-release the pressure.
4. Remove the lid; stir in the olives and the zest from the other half of the lemon.
5. In a bowl, mix together the cornstarch and water, and then whisk this mixture into the chicken mixture in the pressure cooker.
6. Simmer and stir until the mixture is thickened and the raw taste is cooked out of the cornstarch. Stir in the parsley. Taste for seasoning.

Other Ways to Use This Sauce

Delicious with pork chops, pork loin, and turkey, you could also drizzle this sauce over poached fish such as tilapia.

CHAPTER 5

EASY PORK DISHES

Melt-in-Your-Mouth Barbecue Ribs / 89

Pork Chops with Figs and Balsamic / 90

Pork Roast with Fresh Rosemary and Granny Smith Apples / 91

Boneless Pork Chops with Plums / 92

Beer BBQ Pork Sliders with Apple / 93

Sauerkraut Pork Chops with Red New Potatoes / 94

Pork Sausage with Bell Peppers and Onions / 95

Sweet Potato Pork with Cranberry / 96

Root Beer Pork / 97

Sesame Pork with Pineapple / 98

Maple-Glazed Ham with Raisins / 100

Pork Roast with Potatoes and Leeks / 101

Casserole of Eggplant with Pork / 102

Ginger Soy Pork Chops with Broccoli / 103

Shredded Barbecue Pork on Whole-Wheat Buns / 104

Quick-Cooking Pork and Beans / 105

Dijon Pork Chops with Pear / 106

Pork Chop Cabbage / 107

Pork Chop with Apricots Three Ways / 108

Quick and Easy Pork Fajitas / 109

Cabbage with Bratwurst and Beer / 110

Casserole of Pork with Black Beans and Jalapeño Taco Sauce / 111

Pork and Beans with Cayenne / 112

Jalapeño Pork over Long-Grain Rice / 113

Double Dijon Pork Chops with Horse-radish / 114

Three-Cheese Pork Chops with Potatoes / 115

Melt-in-Your-Mouth Barbecue Ribs

 Serves 4

1 cup barbecue sauce

½ cup apple jelly

1 (3") cinnamon stick

6 whole cloves

1 large sweet onion, peeled and diced

½ cup water

3 pounds pork Western ribs

By the time this pressure finishes, the meat on these ribs will be falling off the bone. Just the way we like it! Use this as a standalone dish or for pork sandwiches.

1. Add the barbecue sauce, jelly, cinnamon stick, cloves, onion, and water to the pressure cooker. Stir to mix.
2. Add the ribs, ladling some of the sauce over them. Lock the lid into place and bring to low pressure; maintain pressure for 55 minutes. Remove from heat and allow pressure to release naturally.
3. Use a slotted spoon to remove the meat and bones; cover and keep warm. Skim any fat from the sauce in the cooker.
4. Remove and discard the cinnamon stick and cloves. Return the pressure cooker to medium-high heat.
5. Cook uncovered for 15 minutes or until the sauce is reduced and coats the back of a spoon. Either remove the meat from the bones and stir back into the sauce or pour the sauce into a gravy boat and pass at the table.

Fig Sauce

Figs make great sauces for barbecue. Use the Fig Sauce in Chapter 4 (from Turkey Thighs with Balsamic Fig Glaze) as a variation on these barbecue pork ribs.

Pork Chops with Figs and Balsamic

 Serves 4

Total cost: $6.99

Serving size: 1 chop

Calories per serving: 356

Fat: 12g

Carbohydrates: 16g

Protein: 31g

Sodium: 412mg

4 (1"-thick) bone-in pork loin chops

Sea salt and freshly ground black pepper, to taste

2 teaspoons butter

2 teaspoons extra-virgin olive oil

2 medium sweet onions, peeled and sliced

4 cloves garlic, peeled and minced

1 teaspoon fresh chopped thyme

3 tablespoons balsamic vinegar

2 tablespoons dry white wine

½ cup chicken broth

1½ cups dried figs

Add a few diced apples and chopped toasted walnuts when serving for a delightful crisp, crunchy finish to this dish.

1. Lightly season the pork chops on both sides by sprinkling them with salt and pepper. Add the butter and oil to the pressure cooker and bring to temperature over medium-high heat. Add 2 pork chops; brown for 3 minutes on each side. Move chops to a plate and repeat with the other 2 chops. Remove those chops to the plate.

2. Add the onions; sauté for 4 minutes or until the onions are transparent. Stir in the garlic; sauté for 30 seconds. Stir in the thyme and balsamic vinegar. Cook uncovered until the vinegar is reduced by half. Stir in the wine and broth. Add the pork chops, spooning some of the onions over the chops. Place the figs on top.

3. Lock the lid into place and bring to high pressure; maintain pressure for 9 minutes. Remove from the heat and quick-release the pressure. Serve immediately.

Other Fruits to Use

Other delicious fruits for this recipe are dried apricots, dried cherries, dried cranberries, or dried apples.

Pork Roast with Fresh Rosemary and Granny Smith Apples

 Serves 4

1 (2-pound) pork shoulder roast

3 tablespoons Dijon mustard

1 tablespoon olive oil

½ cup dry white wine, apple juice, or water

2 Granny Smith apples, peeled and quartered

3 cloves garlic, peeled and minced

Sea salt and freshly ground black pepper, to taste

1 tablespoon chopped fresh rosemary

Rosemary and apples are one of my favorite combinations for pork recipes. Another tasty combo is sage and pear.

1. Coat all sides of the roast with the mustard. Bring the oil to temperature in the pressure cooker over medium-high heat. Add the pork roast; brown the roast on all sides, reducing the heat if necessary to avoid burning the mustard

2. Pour the wine, apple juice, or water around the roast. Working around the roast, use the liquid to deglaze the pan, scraping up any browned bits sticking to the bottom of the pan. Add the apples, garlic, salt, pepper, and rosemary.

3. Lock the lid into place and bring to low pressure; maintain pressure for 45 minutes. Remove from heat and allow pressure to release naturally.

4. Remove the lid. Use a meat thermometer to measure whether the roast has reached an internal temperature of 160°F.

5. Remove the roast to a serving platter. Tent and keep warm while you use an immersion blender to purée the pan contents. Slice the roast and pour the puréed juices over the slices. Serve.

Mustard

Prepared Dijon mustard is a versatile ingredient that works well with a variety of recipes, including protein dishes like this one and vinaigrettes for salads. Use spicy Dijon, spicy brown mustard, ground mustard, or traditional prepared mustard, depending upon your taste preferences.

Boneless Pork Chops with Plums

 Serves 6

8 pitted dried plums

4 (6-ounce) boneless pork chops, trimmed of fat

2 small Granny Smith apples, peeled, cored, and sliced

½ cup dry white wine or apple juice

½ cup sour cream

¼ cup nonfat milk

Sea salt and freshly ground pepper, to taste

1 tablespoon red currant jelly

When using pressure cookers, dried fruits tend to work better than fresh fruits for high-protein dishes like this one because fresh fruits will essentially turn to mush when cooked under high pressure for long periods of time. When making jams or jellies, however, fresh fruit can often be used as they create the desired consistency in the finished product.

1. Add the dried plums, pork chops, apple slices, wine or apple juice, sour cream, and milk to the pressure cooker. Add salt and pepper to taste.
2. Lock the lid into place and bring to high pressure; maintain pressure for 9 minutes. Quick-release the pressure.
3. Remove the meat and fruit to a serving platter. Either leave the pan juices as they are and keep them warm or skim the fat from the liquid in the pressure cooker and use an immersion blender to blend the fruit into the creamy broth.
4. Leave the pressure cooker on the heat and simmer uncovered for 10 minutes or until the mixture is reduced by half and thickened. Whisk in the red currant jelly. Taste for seasoning and add more salt and pepper if needed. Whisk in the butter 1 teaspoon at a time if you want a richer, glossier sauce. Ladle the sauce over the meat or pour it into a heated gravy boat.

Beer BBQ Pork Sliders with Apple

 Serves 6

1½ pounds pork Western ribs

6 ounces beer

½ cup unsweetened applesauce

⅓ cup diced peeled golden delicious apple

½ large sweet onion, diced

1 tablespoon brown sugar

½ teaspoon freshly ground black pepper

Sea salt, to taste

12 whole-wheat slider buns or 6 whole-wheat hamburger buns

Beer and applesauce provide a tangy sweetness to these already delicious sandwiches. Serve with a salad or traditional coleslaw.

1. Add the pork to the pressure cooker. Do not trim the fat from the ribs; it's what helps the meat cook up moist enough to shred for sandwiches. A lot of the fat will melt out of the meat as it cooks.

2. Pour the beer over the pork. Add the applesauce, apples, onion, brown sugar, black pepper, and salt. Lock the lid into place and bring to low pressure; maintain pressure for 55 minutes. Remove from heat and allow pressure to release naturally.

3. Remove the lid and use a slotted spoon to move the pork to a cutting board. Remove and discard any fat still on the meat. Use two forks to shred the meat. Skim and discard any fat from the top of the pan juices. Stir the shredded pork back into the sauce. Place the pressure cooker over medium heat and bring to a simmer. Taste for seasoning; stir in orange marmalade or apple jelly a tablespoon at a time if you prefer a sweeter barbecue.

4. Spoon the meat onto hamburger buns. Top the meat with a heaping tablespoon of North Carolina–style coleslaw.

Sliders

Pork and beef sliders are delicious as an appetizer or an entrée. Make ahead and reheat for parties or dinner.

Sauerkraut Pork Chops with Red New Potatoes

Serves 4

1 stalk celery, finely chopped

1 (1-pound) bag baby carrots

1 large onion, peeled and sliced

1 clove garlic, peeled and minced

2 slices bacon, cut into small pieces

4 (1"-thick) bone-in pork loin chops

1 (1-pound) bag sauerkraut, rinsed and drained

4 medium red potatoes, peeled and quartered

1 (12-ounce) can beer

2 teaspoons Bavarian seasoning

Sea salt and freshly ground pepper, to taste

Bavarian seasoning is often found in German dishes and is a blend of crushed brown mustard seed, dried rosemary, garlic, sage, thyme, and bay leaves.

1. Add the ingredients to the pressure cooker in the order given. Lock the lid in place. Bring to high pressure; maintain pressure for 9 minutes.
2. Remove from the heat and allow pressure to release naturally. Taste for seasoning and adjust if necessary. Serve hot.

Pork Sausage with Bell Peppers and Onions

 Serves 6

 Total cost: $7.00

Serving size: 1 sausage

Calories per serving: 391

Fat: 31g

Carbohydrates: 5g

Protein: 21g

Sodium: 1371mg

6 pork sausages, any combination

1 tablespoon olive oil

1 large green bell pepper, seeded and sliced

1 large red bell pepper, seeded and sliced

1 large yellow bell pepper, seeded and sliced

1 large sweet onion, sliced

2 cloves garlic, minced

½ cup chicken broth

Use a combination of spicy Italian sausage, bratwurst, or mild sausage links, if desired.

1. Add half of the sausages to the pressure cooker and brown them over medium-high heat. Remove them to a plate and brown the remaining sausages.
2. Drain and discard any rendered fat in the pressure cooker. Add the olive oil and bring it to temperature. Add the sliced peppers; sauté for 3 minutes or until they begin to get soft. Add the onion slices; sauté for 3 minutes or until transparent. Add the garlic; sauté for 30 seconds.
3. Return the sausages to the pressure cooker, pushing them down into the peppers and onions. Pour in the broth. Lock the lid into place and bring to high pressure; maintain pressure for 4 minutes. Quick-release the pressure. Serve.

Pork Sausage Hoagies
Serve this recipe on hoagie buns for a delicious pork sausage sandwich. Perfect for leftovers, if there are any!

Sweet Potato Pork with Cranberry

 Serves 6

1 (3-pound) pork butt roast

Sea salt and freshly ground pepper, to taste

1 (16-ounce) can sweetened whole cranberries

1 medium onion, peeled and diced

¼ cup orange marmalade

½ cup orange juice

¼ teaspoon ground cinnamon

⅛ teaspoon ground cloves

2 teaspoons cornstarch mixed with 2 teaspoons water

2 large sweet potatoes, peeled and quartered

New potatoes and fingerling potatoes also work well with this recipe.

1. Place the pork fat-side down in the pressure cooker. Season with salt and pepper to taste. Combine the cranberries, onion, marmalade, orange juice, cinnamon, and cloves in a large measuring cup; stir to mix and then pour over the pork roast.
2. Arrange the sweet potatoes around the meat. Lock the lid into place and bring to low pressure; maintain pressure for 45 minutes. Remove from heat and allow pressure to release naturally.
3. To serve with a thickened sauce, transfer the meat and sweet potatoes to a serving platter. Cover and keep warm. Skim any fat off of the pan juices, making sure you have 2 cups of juice remaining in the cooker.
4. Return the pressure cooker to medium heat. Whisk the cornstarch liquid into the pressure cooker; simmer and stir for 2 minutes or until the cornstarch flavor has cooked out of the sauce and it is thickened and bubbly.

The $7 a Meal Pressure Cooker Cookbook

Root Beer Pork

 Serves 6

1 (10-ounce) can golden cream
   of mushroom soup

1 (12-ounce) can root beer

1 (1-ounce) envelope dry onion
   soup mix

1 (3-pound) pork roast

Root beer has a distinct flavor that adds depth to this dish. Use regular root beer, however, not diet, for best results.

1. Add the soup, root beer, and onion soup mix to the pressure cooker. Stir to mix. Add the pork roast.
2. Lock the lid in place. Bring to low pressure; maintain pressure for 45 minutes. Remove from the heat and allow pressure to release naturally.
3. Transfer the roast to a serving platter; let rest for 5 minutes before slicing.
4. Skim any fat from the gravy in the pressure cooker. Stir to mix and then transfer to a gravy boat or pour over the sliced meat.

Sesame Pork with Pineapple

Serves 6

Total cost: $6.97

Serving size: 6 ounces

Calories per serving: 340

Fat: 7g

Carbohydrates: 18g

Protein: 32g

Sodium: 281mg

2 pounds pork shoulder

1 tablespoon all-purpose flour

2 tablespoons sesame oil

1 (14-ounce) can pineapple chunks

1 tablespoon light brown sugar

⅛ teaspoon mustard powder

½ teaspoon ground ginger

2 tablespoons apple cider vinegar

1 tablespoon low-sodium soy sauce

4 medium carrots, peeled and sliced

1 large red bell pepper, seeded and sliced

½ pound fresh sugar snap peas

1½ cups fresh broccoli florets

2 cloves garlic, peeled and thinly sliced

1 large sweet onions, peeled and diced, divided

2 tablespoons cornstarch

2 tablespoons cold water

¼ cup bean sprouts

Similar to Sweet-and-Sour Pork, serve this dish with Chinese noodles or steamed white rice. If it fits in your budget, pick up some fortune cookies at the supermarket just for fun.

1. Cut the pork into bite-sized pieces. Add to a zip-closure bag along with the flour; seal and shake to coat the pork in the flour.
2. Bring the oil to temperature in the pressure cooker over medium-high heat. Fry the pork for 3 minutes or until it begins to brown. Add the pineapple juice and reserve the pineapple chunks; stir and scrape up any bits stuck to the bottom of the pan.
3. Add the sugar, mustard powder, ginger, vinegar, soy sauce, carrots, pepper, and sugar snap peas. Cut the broccoli florets into bite-sized pieces and add them to the pressure cooker.

Vegetables

This vegetable combination keeps with the Asian sweet-and-sour pork style; however, feel free to use your favorite vegetables instead.

The $7 a Meal Pressure Cooker Cookbook

Sesame Pork with Pineapple (continued)

Add garlic and ¾ onion. Lock the lid into place and bring to low pressure; maintain pressure for 12 minutes.

4. Quick-release the pressure. Use a slotted spoon to transfer all solids from the pressure cooker to a serving bowl; keep warm.

5. To make the glaze, in a small bowl mix together the cornstarch and water. Stir in some of the pan juices. Put the pressure cooker over medium heat. Bring to a boil and then whisk in the cornstarch mixture.

6. Reduce the heat to maintain a simmer for 3 minutes or until the mixture is thickened and the raw cornstarch taste is cooked out of the glaze. Stir in the bean sprouts, reserved pineapple chunks, and onion. Pour over the cooked pork and vegetables in the serving bowl; stir to combine. Serve.

Maple-Glazed Ham with Raisins

Serves 6

$ Total cost: $6.98
Serving size: 6 ounces
Calories per serving: 342
Fat: 11g
Carbohydrates: 24g
Protein: 25g
Sodium: 695mg

1 (2-pound) ready-to-eat ham

1 large sweet onion, peeled and sliced

⅛ teaspoon ground cloves

¼ teaspoon ground ginger

½ teaspoon ground cinnamon

1 (14-ounce) can pineapple chunks

2 tablespoons brown sugar

½ cup raisins

½ cup apple butter

¼ cup maple syrup

1 tablespoon balsamic vinegar

Why buy expensive honey-baked ham when you can make your own in minutes? Make this for dinner, Sunday brunch, or just to have for ham sandwiches.

1. Add the ham and sliced onions to the pressure cooker. Stir together the cloves, ginger, cinnamon, pineapple juice (reserve the pineapple), brown sugar, and raisins. Pour over the ham.
2. Lock the lid into place. Bring to low pressure; maintain pressure for 20 minutes. Remove from the heat and allow pressure to release naturally.
3. Move the ham to a serving platter and keep warm while you finish the sauce.
4. Skim and remove any fat from the pan juices in the pressure cooker. Put the pan over medium heat; simmer to reduce the pan juices to about 1 cup. Stir in the pineapple chunks, apple butter, maple syrup, and vinegar. Taste for seasoning and adjust if necessary, adding additional maple syrup if you want a sweeter sauce or more vinegar if you need to cut the sweetness. Serve separately to spoon or pour over ham slices.

Pork Roast with Potatoes and Leeks

Serves 4

 Total cost: $7.00

Serving size: 4 ounces

Calories per serving: 325

Fat: 6g

Carbohydrates: 31g

Protein: 29g

Sodium: 301mg

1½-pound boneless pork loin

1 tablespoon canola oil

1 small onion, peeled and diced

Sea salt and freshly ground black pepper, to taste

½ cup white wine or apple juice

1 cup chicken broth

1 large turnip, peeled and diced

3 small Yukon Gold or red potatoes, scrubbed

4 carrots, peeled and diced

1 stalk celery, finely diced

1 leek, sliced, white part only

½ teaspoon mild curry powder

¼ teaspoon chopped fresh thyme

2 teaspoons chopped fresh Italian flat-leaf parsley

3 tablespoons fresh lemon juice

1 Granny Smith apple, peeled, cored, and diced

Pork is a versatile protein and holds up well under pressure.

1. Cut the pork into 1" cubes. Add the oil to the pressure cooker and bring to temperature over medium heat. Add the onion; sauté for 3 minutes. Add the pork and lightly season with salt and pepper. Stir-fry the pork for 5 minutes or until it just begins to brown. Add the wine or apple juice, broth, and turnip. Cut the potatoes into quarters and add them to the pot along with the carrots, celery, leeks, curry powder, thyme, parsley, and lemon juice.

2. Lock the lid into place and bring to high pressure; maintain pressure for 15 minutes. Turn off the heat and allow the pressure to drop naturally.

3. Carefully remove the lid and add the diced apples. Bring to a simmer over medium heat; reduce the heat and simmer, covered, for 5 minutes or until the apples are tender. Serve rustic-style in large bowls, garnished with fresh parsley or thyme if desired.

Tired of Apples?

Pressure cookers need ingredients that can hold up under pressure. If you prefer pears to apples, use Asian pears or any other firm, ripe pear—but stay away from softer Bartlett pears.

Casserole of Eggplant with Pork

Serves 6

Total cost: $6.84

Serving size: 5 ounces

Calories per serving: 302

Fat: 7g

Carbohydrates: 22g

Protein: 36g

Sodium: 179mg

2 pounds lean ground pork

1 large yellow onion, peeled and diced

1 stalk celery, diced

1 green pepper, seeded and diced

4 cloves garlic, peeled and minced

2 medium eggplants, cut into ½" dice

⅛ teaspoon dried thyme, crushed

1 tablespoon chopped fresh Italian flat-leaf parsley

3 tablespoons tomato paste

2 teaspoons Worcestershire sauce

Sea salt and freshly ground pepper, to taste

1 large egg, beaten

½ cup chicken broth

This simple casserole is delicious over rice or with a side of penne pasta. It's excellent for a midweek meal or as an appetizer over crostini.

1. Bring the pressure cooker to temperature over medium-high heat. Add the ground pork, onion, celery, and green pepper to the pressure cooker and stir-fry until the pork is no longer pink, breaking it apart as it cooks.
2. Drain and discard any fat rendered from the meat. Add the garlic, eggplant, thyme, parsley, tomato sauce, Worcestershire sauce, salt, pepper, and egg; stir to combine.
3. Pour in the chicken broth. Lock the lid into place and bring to low pressure; maintain pressure for 10 minutes. Remove from heat and allow pressure to release naturally.

Protein Substitutions

Ground beef works as well as pork in this recipe. Drain off some of the grease after browning or stir-frying for best results.

The $7 a Meal Pressure Cooker Cookbook

Ginger Soy Pork Chops with Broccoli

Serves 4

Total cost: $6.36

Serving size: 1 chop

Calories per serving: 340

Fat: 10g

Carbohydrates: 29g

Protein: 24g

Sodium: 812mg

4 boneless pork chops

2 tablespoons soy sauce

½ cup pineapple juice

3 tablespoons apple cider vinegar

2 tablespoons sugar

1 tablespoon fresh ginger root, minced

2 cups frozen broccoli florets

1 cup long-grain white rice

2 cups chicken broth

Use fresh green beans instead of broccoli, if you prefer, and try brown rice instead of long-grain white for added fiber.

1. Place pork chops in a zip-closure bag and add soy, pineapple juice, cider vinegar, sugar, and ginger. Seal bag and refrigerate for up to 2 hours.
2. Place entire contents of bag into the pressure cooker and discard bag. Latch lid securely and bring to high pressure for 8 minutes. Use quick-release method to release pressure.
3. Then add broccoli, rice, and broth. Resecure lid and bring to low pressure for 3 minutes. Allow pressure to naturally release for an additional 5 minutes. Serve immediately.

Other Juices to Try

Other juices that work well for this dish are apple juice, apple cider, and a combination of orange/pineapple or orange/papaya.

Shredded Barbecue Pork on Whole-Wheat Buns

 Serves 4

 Total cost: $7.00

 Serving size: ¼ cup on 1 bun

Calories per serving: 372

Fat: 12g

Carbohydrates: 26g

Protein: 34g

Sodium: 795mg

1 yellow onion, chopped

3 cloves garlic, minced

1 jalapeño pepper, seeded and minced

½ cup mild or medium taco sauce

⅓ cup sweet barbecue sauce

2 teaspoons chili powder

1 tablespoon dill pickle relish

¼ cup water or apple juice

¾ pound boneless pork loin roast

½ teaspoon sea salt

½ teaspoon black pepper, or to taste

4 whole-wheat buns

Shredded barbecue pork is one of the best appetizers or entrées for family dinners or for parties. Serve on full-sized whole-wheat buns or buy mini-buns for sliders.

1. Combine all ingredients except pork, salt, pepper, and buns in the pressure cooker. Season roast with salt and pepper and place in cooker.
2. Latch lid securely and bring to high pressure. Then, reduce pressure to low and maintain low pressure for about 45 minutes. Use quick-release method to release pressure. Remove pork.
3. Shred pork using two forks. Return to cooker and stir to incorporate flavors. Secure lid and bring to low pressure for an additional 5 minutes. Release pressure using natural-release method. Serve pork on whole-wheat bun.

Pickle Relish as a Secret Ingredient!

Believe it or not, pickle relish is a great ingredient to add sweet or sour flavors to foods. The dill relish used here helps to complement the sweetness of the barbecue sauce. For an even sweeter barbecue, use sweet pickle relish.

Quick-Cooking Pork and Beans

Serves 4

$ Total cost: $6.29

Serving size: ½ cup

Calories per serving: 344

Fat: 11g

Carbohydrates: 13g

Protein: 23g

Sodium: 836mg

¾ pound boneless pork loin, cubed

Sea salt, to taste

½ teaspoon Hungarian paprika

Black pepper, to taste

1 (16-ounce) can pork and beans

1 yellow onion, chopped

¼ cup ketchup

3 tablespoons spicy mustard

2 tablespoons honey

¼ cup apple juice

1 tablespoon brown sugar

Even though these cook quickly, they're on the dinner table even faster if you make them ahead of time and reheat just before serving.

1. Season pork with salt, paprika, and pepper and place in cooker. Pour pork and beans over top of pork.
2. Add onions, ketchup, mustard, honey, apple juice, and sugar. Stir to combine.
3. Latch lid and bring to high pressure. Once at high pressure, drop to low pressure and maintain pressure for 15 minutes. Release pressure using natural-release method.
4. Serve as a main dish with cornbread or as a side dish to the Melt-in-Your-Mouth Barbecue Ribs (Chapter 5).

Dijon Pork Chops with Pear

 Serves 4

2 tablespoons butter

1 yellow onion, chopped

1 clove garlic, minced

1 firm d'Anjou pear, cored and chopped

Sea salt and black pepper, to taste

¼ cup brown sugar

4 (6-ounce) boneless pork chops

¼ cup plain flour

¼ cup chicken broth

¼ cup apple juice

1 tablespoon Dijon mustard

Pork tastes great with all sorts of fruits such as cherries, apples, mangoes, and papaya. Use one or a combination of a couple for a variety of dishes.

1. Melt butter in cooker over medium heat. Add onion and garlic and sauté about 1 minute. Add pears, salt, pepper, and sugar and stir to combine. Turn off heat.
2. Cut a pocket in the side of each chop and stuff with about 1 tablespoon of onion mixture each. Dredge chops in the flour.
3. Add broth, juice, and mustard to cooker and stir to combine. Add chops. Latch lid securely and bring to high pressure.
4. Maintain pressure for 9 minutes. Release using natural-release method. Serve with rice.

Serve with Rice

These chops are delicious over a multitude of rice variations, such as popular long-grain white rice, wild rice, brown rice, or jasmine rice.

Pork Chop Cabbage

 Serves 4

1 yellow onion, chopped

2 cloves garlic, minced

4 cups chopped cabbage

1 apple, cored and diced

1 tablespoon olive oil

4 (4-ounce) boneless pork chops

Pinch white pepper

¼ cup brown sugar

¼ cup apple cider vinegar

1 tablespoon dry mustard

¼ cup chicken or vegetable broth

Cabbage is often overlooked as a family food but it tastes great, is easy to work with, and is filling. Many people complain about the smell of cooked cabbage. The apple cider vinegar in this recipe will help reduce the odor. If it's still a problem, add some fresh lemon slices as well, 2 or 3 maximum.

1. Combine onion, garlic, cabbage, and apple in cooker. Mix well. Add oil and heat over medium heat, stirring. Turn off heat.
2. Add pork chops to cooker. Add white pepper, brown sugar, vinegar, mustard, and broth to cooker and stir.
3. Latch lid securely and bring to high pressure. Maintain pressure for 7 minutes. Release pressure by using natural-release method. Serve warm with rice.

Apples That Work Well for This Recipe

For this recipe, use a firm apple such as Fuji or Honey-crisp, or green apples such as Granny Smith.

Pork Chops with Apricots Three Ways

Serves 4

4 (5-ounce) boneless pork chops

½ cup dried apricots, chopped

¼ cup apricot nectar

¼ cup apricot preserves

2 cloves garlic, minced

1 tablespoon Dijon mustard

3 tablespoons honey

Sea salt and pepper, to taste

2 carrots, sliced

3 green onions, diced

¼ cup white wine such as sauvignon blanc

This recipe calls for apricot preserves. If you like, use some of the Spiced Apricot Preserves (Chapter 2).

1. Place all ingredients in pressure cooker. Latch lid securely and bring to low pressure.
2. Maintain low pressure for 15 minutes. Use the quick-release method to relieve the pressure. Serve chops over rice or with pasta.

Quick and Easy Pork Fajitas

Serves 4

Total cost: $6.53

Serving size: 1 cup

Calories per serving: 448

Fat: 17g

Carbohydrates: 28g

Protein: 24g

Sodium: 940mg

2 (5-ounce) boneless pork chops, sliced into thin strips

1 tablespoon chili powder

Sea salt and black pepper, to taste

¼ teaspoon cayenne pepper

1 yellow onion, thinly sliced

2 cloves garlic, minced

½ cup chicken broth

1 red bell pepper, sliced into ½"-thick strips

¼ cup fresh frozen kernel corn, thawed

1 cup shredded Cheddar cheese

4 large (10") whole-wheat tortillas

¼ cup chopped fresh cilantro leaves, for garnish, if desired

No need to worry about the oil splatters that go along with pan frying. This pressure-cooked pork fajita is the perfect solution with one-pot easy cleanup.

1. Place pork chops in pressure cooker and sprinkle with chili powder, salt, and cayenne. Let stand for 10 to 15 minutes.
2. Add onion, garlic, and chicken broth to pressure cooker. Latch lid securely and bring to low pressure. Maintain pressure for 7 minutes. Release pressure using quick-release method.
3. Serve fajitas with red bell pepper strips, corn, cheese, tortillas, and cilantro. If desired, warm tortillas in microwave by wrapping individually in paper towel and microwaving on high for 15 seconds.

Fajitas for the Family

Fajitas are a fun family meal, especially when they are prepared as easily as they are in this recipe! For more servings in smaller portions, use the small flour or corn tortillas and serve two per person. Serve avocado slices, guacamole, sour cream, and hot sauce on the side, if desired.

Cabbage with Bratwurst and Beer

 Serves 6

1 pound bratwurst

1 yellow onion, chopped

4 cloves garlic, minced

1 head cabbage, shredded

3 tablespoons sugar

¼ cup red wine vinegar

Sea salt and black pepper, to taste

3 tablespoons spicy mustard

1 cup beer such as Samuel Adams

The yeast in beer aids in cooking foods and at the same time improves flavor. For heartier dishes, go for darker beers. For lighter dishes, go for a lighter beer.

1. Place bratwurst in pressure cooker and brown over medium heat until browned on all sides. Add onion and garlic and sauté 1 to 2 minutes.
2. Add cabbage, sugar, vinegar, salt (only a hint), pepper, mustard, and beer. Mix together.
3. Latch lid securely and heat to low pressure. Maintain low pressure for 12 minutes. Release pressure using natural-release method.
4. Serve alone, over rice, or as a sandwich filling.

Bratwurst Sandwiches
A delicious way to serve this recipe is on top of a toasted hoagie bun or toasted sourdough baguette. This sandwich will be so filling you may want to share!

The $7 a Meal Pressure Cooker Cookbook

Casserole of Pork with Black Beans and Jalapeño Taco Sauce

 Serves 4

 Total cost: $6.93

 Serving size: ½ cup pork with sauce

Calories per serving: 420

Fat: 15g

Carbohydrates: 9g

Protein: 41g

Sodium: 930mg

1 tablespoon chili powder

Pinch cumin

Sea salt and black pepper, to taste

Pinch cayenne pepper (or more as desired)

1 pound pork loin, cut into 1" cubes

1 tablespoon butter

1 yellow onion, chopped

2 cloves garlic, minced

1 jalapeño pepper, seeded and minced

½ cup chicken broth

½ cup medium taco sauce

1 (15-ounce) can black beans

½ red bell pepper, diced

Spice up your lunch or dinner with this easy dish. Serve with corn tortillas or over rice with guacamole and sour cream.

1. In pressure cooker, combine chili powder, cumin, salt, pepper, and cayenne and mix well. Add pork and toss to coat. Add butter and heat over medium heat, browning pork for about 4 minutes.
2. Add remaining ingredients to cooker. Stir to combine. Secure lid by latching properly. Bring pressure to low pressure. Maintain pressure for 15 minutes.
3. Release pressure using natural-release method. Serve with warm corn or flour tortillas (use whole-wheat tortillas for extra fiber), or serve over rice.

Tex-Mex

Tex-Mex indicates a combination of flavors commonly used in traditional Mexican or Spanish cooking infused with southwestern American cooking traditions. Make your dish more or less spicy by adding or using less cayenne pepper, jalapeño, and either mild, medium, or hot taco sauce.

Pork and Beans with Cayenne

 Serves 6

 Total cost: $3.81

Serving size: ½ cup

Calories per serving: 351

Fat: 9g

Carbohydrates: 12g

Protein: 21g

Sodium: 793mg

1 cup dried pinto beans

3 slices thick bacon

2 cups chicken broth

1 cup water

3 cloves garlic, minced

1 yellow onion, chopped

1 cup taco sauce

1 tablespoon chili powder

2 tablespoons brown sugar

½ teaspoon dried oregano

Sea salt and black pepper, to taste

Pinch cayenne pepper (or more as desired)

1 teaspoon ground mustard

¼ cup chopped fresh cilantro

Even pork and beans can have a southwestern flair. This recipe uses cilantro and cayenne pepper to give that added twist to a traditionally southern favorite.

1. Place dried pinto beans in cooker and cover with water. Bring to a boil and boil for 2 minutes. Remove from heat and let stand for 1 hour.
2. Drain beans and wipe excess water out of cooker. Add bacon to cooker and heat over medium heat, until done. Drain some of the grease but leave bacon in cooker.
3. Add beans to bacon as well as broth, water, garlic, and onion. Latch lid securely and bring to high pressure for 7 minutes. Use quick-release method to release pressure.
4. Open lid and add taco sauce, chili powder, sugar, oregano, salt, pepper, cayenne, mustard, and cilantro. Add additional ¼ cup of broth if needed.
5. Securely latch lid and bring to low pressure. Maintain pressure for 7 to 8 minutes. Release pressure using natural-release method. Serve with an entrée like grilled chicken with a simple side salad.

Bacon

Bacon is used often in recipes because it adds flavor both from the meat and the fat. If you're looking for a healthier meal, try your favorite turkey bacon.

The $7 a Meal Pressure Cooker Cookbook

Jalapeño Pork over Long-Grain Rice

 Serves 6

1 pound boneless pork shoulder roast, trimmed of fat and chopped into 1" cubes

3 tablespoons apple cider vinegar

3 tablespoons low-sodium soy sauce

½ cup apple juice

3 garlic cloves, minced

1 jalapeño pepper, seeded and minced

Pinch crushed red pepper flakes

¼ cup chopped fresh cilantro

1 cup long-grain rice

2 cups water

This recipe is served over rice but it also tastes great in pita pockets or rolled into small corn tortillas as a taco.

1. Place pork in large bowl with vinegar, soy sauce, apple juice, garlic, jalapeño, pepper flakes, and cilantro. Toss to coat, cover, and refrigerate overnight.
2. When ready to cook, place all contents of bowl in cooker. Latch lid securely and bring to high pressure. Maintain pressure for 9 minutes.
3. While that is cooking, make rice by using 1 cup rice with 2 cups water. Cook as directed on stove top or using rice cooker.
4. Release pressure using natural-release method. Serve over rice.

Marinating

When you can, preplan your meals so you not only stay on budget but are also on target for marinating foods overnight when possible, as with this recipe. Here, the pork gets most of its flavor by resting in the soy sauce and spices overnight.

Double Dijon Pork Chops with Horseradish

Serves 4

4 (4-ounce) boneless pork loin chops

Sea salt and black pepper, to taste

1 tablespoon olive oil

1 yellow onion, sliced

2 tablespoons grainy mustard

¾ cup chicken broth

1 tablespoon horseradish

2 tablespoons cornstarch

½ cup sour cream

2 tablespoons Dijon mustard

Horseradish makes this already mustard-spiced chop even spicier. If you prefer yours less spicy, skip the horseradish and stay with the Dijon.

1. Season pork chops with salt and pepper. Heat oil in pressure cooker over medium heat and add chops. Brown on each side, about 2 minutes per side. Remove chops.
2. Add onions to cooker. Spread grainy mustard over each side of each chop, lightly. Add to cooker along with broth. Latch lid securely and bring to high pressure. Maintain pressure for 3 minutes. Use quick-release method to release pressure.
3. In separate mixing bowl, whisk together horseradish, cornstarch, sour cream, and Dijon. Mix well. Pour into cooker over chops.
4. Latch lid securely and bring back to high pressure. Maintain pressure an additional 3 minutes. Release pressure using the natural-release method. Serve warm with a side of rice or a simple baked potato.

Cut the Mustard

Too much mustard for you? Instead of leaving out some of it, simply add 1 tablespoon of fresh lemon juice and a little lemon zest. It will naturally help balance the strong flavor.

Three-Cheese Pork Chops with Potatoes

 Serves 6

Total cost: $6.46

Serving size: 1 cup

Calories per serving: 369

Fat: 15g

Carbohydrates: 17g

Protein: 16g

Sodium: 890mg

16 ounces frozen, straight-cut French fry potatoes, thawed

1 yellow onion, chopped

2 cloves garlic, chopped

1¼ cups diced pork loin

1 cup shredded Swiss cheese

1 can cream of potato soup

½ cup ricotta cheese

Sea salt and black pepper, to taste

1½ cups frozen peas, thawed

¼ cup Parmesan cheese, grated

This recipe is great with ham, chicken, or even turkey and with other cheese combinations like provolone, goat cheese, white Cheddar, or traditional Cheddar.

1. Place potatoes, onions, garlic, pork, and Swiss in cooker and mix well. In medium bowl, combine soup, ricotta, and pepper. Pour over potato mixture in cooker.
2. Add in peas and Parmesan. Latch lid securely and bring to high pressure. Maintain pressure for 5 minutes.
3. Reduce pressure to low and maintain for 12 minutes. Use quick-release method to relieve pressure. Serve immediately.

Frozen Potatoes

Frozen potatoes are great in pressure cookers because the liquid helps to steam cook them as well as the other food products in the dish—plus, you save time cleaning, peeling, and grating them. Just be sure to thaw them first so the cooker comes to pressure effectively.

CHAPTER 6

BEEF AND SPECIALTY DISHES

Beer-Braised Ribs / 117

Old-Fashioned Pot Roast / 118

Spicy Beef BBQ / 119

Simple Swiss Steak / 120

Barbecue Chuck Roast / 121

Corned Beef and Cabbage / 122

Browned Beef with Onions / 123

Creamy Beef Enchiladas / 124

Shredded Beef Tacos / 125

Steak Fajitas / 126

Roast Beef with Yukon Potatoes / 127

"Corn" Corned Beef / 128

Meatloaf of Beef and Pork / 129

Traditional Sloppy Joes / 130

Sirloin Burger with Mushrooms / 131

Acorn Squash with Pork Vegetable Stuffing / 132

Jambalaya with Chicken, Sausage, and Shrimp / 133

Shredded Cabbage with Beef and Tomatoes / 134

Classic Open-Face Meatball Sandwich with Mozzarella / 135

Bell Peppers Stuffed with Beef, Rice, and Herbs / 136

Cabbage with Beef and Caraway / 137

Mexican Meatballs / 138

Onions Stuffed with Spicy Beef / 139

Spiced Black Beans and Rice / 140

Beef Stew with Apricots and Almonds / 141

Brandied Chicken Casserole / 142

Hungarian-Style Beef Stew / 144

Smoked Ham Sausage Soup / 145

Swedish Meatballs / 146

Root Vegetable Soup with Beef / 147

Soy Pepper Steak / 148

Pork Curry / 149

Asian Pork Ribs / 150

German Sauerbraten /151

Beer-Braised Ribs

Serves 4

 Total cost: $6.98

Serving size: 4 ounces

Calories per serving: 389

Fat: 12g

Carbohydrates: 10g

Protein: 36g

Sodium: 428mg

2 tablespoons Dijon mustard

Sea salt and freshly ground black pepper, to taste

1 teaspoon paprika

2 pounds flank steak, pounded to ¼" to ½" thick

1 tablespoon olive oil

6 ounces dark beer

2 tablespoons flour

1 tablespoon tomato paste

1 cup beef broth

1 medium yellow onion, peeled and diced

2 large carrots, peeled and diced

1 small stalk celery, finely diced

1 large leek, white part only

Generally, you should never cook with a wine or beer you wouldn't drink. You can find many good-quality, inexpensive options on the market these days.

1. Mix together the mustard, salt, pepper, and paprika. Spread both sides of the meat with the mustard mixture.
2. Bring the oil to temperature in the pressure cooker over medium-high heat. Fry the meat, 2 slices at a time, for 2 minutes on each side. Remove the meat and set aside.
3. Deglaze the pressure cooker with about ¼ cup of the beer, stirring and scraping to loosen any browned bits stuck to the bottom of the pan.
4. Whisk in the flour and the tomato paste. Whisk in the remaining beer. Add the beef back into the pan along with the broth, onion, carrots, and celery. Clean and slice the white part of the leek and add to the pressure cooker.
5. Lock the lid into place and bring to low pressure; maintain the pressure for 15 minutes. Remove from the heat and allow pressure to release naturally.
6. Remove the meat to a serving platter. If desired, use an immersion blender to purée the pan juices. Taste for seasoning and add additional salt and pepper if needed. Pour over the meat. Serve.

Old-Fashioned Pot Roast

 Serves 6

1 (3-pound) boneless chuck roast

1 (1-pound) bag baby carrots

2 stalks celery, diced

1 green bell pepper, seeded and diced

1 large yellow onion, peeled and sliced

1 envelope from package of onion soup mix

½ teaspoon black pepper

1 cup water

1 cup tomato juice

2 cloves garlic, peeled and minced

1 tablespoon Worcestershire sauce

1 tablespoon steak sauce

If you have leftovers, use them for roast beef sandwiches the next day, as this beef will be sandwich-tender. Be sure to keep the pan juices for dipping.

1. Cut the roast into serving-sized portions. Add the carrots, celery, green bell pepper, and onion to the pressure cooker. Place the roast pieces on top of the vegetables and sprinkle with soup mix and black pepper.
2. Add the water, tomato juice, garlic, Worcestershire sauce, and steak sauce to a bowl or measuring cup; mix well and then pour into the pressure cooker.
3. Lock the lid into place and bring to low pressure; maintain pressure for 45 minutes. Remove from the heat and allow pressure to release naturally.

Cuts of Beef

Bottom round roasts, top round, and other less-expensive cuts of meat work well in pressure cookers, as they become more tender through the cooking process. Those cuts are ideal for quick and affordable pressure-cooker family meals.

Spicy Beef BBQ

Serves 6

1 (2½-pound) beef shoulder roast

1 cup water

½ cup red wine

½ cup ketchup

1 tablespoon red wine vinegar

2 teaspoons Worcestershire sauce

2 teaspoons mustard powder

2 tablespoons dried minced onion

1 teaspoon dried minced garlic

1 teaspoon cracked black pepper

1 tablespoon brown sugar

1 teaspoon chili powder

½ teaspoon ground cinnamon

¼ teaspoon ground cloves

¼ teaspoon ground ginger

Pinch ground allspice

Pinch dried pepper flakes, crushed

This tender beef roast is perfect served over rice, or as an open-faced beef sandwich using only the bottom of the bun.

1. Halve the roast and stack the halves in the pressure cooker. Mix together all the remaining ingredients and pour over the beef.
2. Lock the lid into place and bring to low pressure; maintain pressure for 55 minutes. Remove from the heat and allow pressure to release naturally.
3. Use a slotted spoon to remove the beef from the slow cooker; pull it apart, discarding any fat or gristle. Taste the meat and sauce and adjust seasonings if necessary.
4. To thicken the sauce, return the pressure cooker to the heat. Skim any fat off the surface of the sauce and simmer uncovered while you pull apart the beef. Stir occasionally to prevent the sauce from burning.

Barbecue Seasonings

Sometimes it's more cost-effective to buy a premixed barbecue-style seasoning rather than make your own seasoning combination, as in this recipe. Experiment with a few over time to decide which seasoning you most prefer.

Simple Swiss Steak

Serves 6

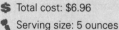
Total cost: $6.96
Serving size: 5 ounces
Calories per serving: 339
Fat: 5g
Carbohydrates: 35g
Protein: 29g
Sodium: 537mg

2½ pounds beef round steak, 1" thick

1 tablespoon vegetable oil

Sea salt and freshly ground pepper, to taste

1 medium yellow onion, peeled and diced

2 stalks celery, diced

1 large green pepper, seeded and diced

1 cup tomato juice

1 cup beef broth or water

6 large carrots, peeled, sliced into ¼" to ½" thick slices

6 small baking potatoes, scrubbed

2 tablespoons butter, softened

Remember that you should never fill a pressure cooker more than two-thirds full.

1. Cut the round steak into 6 serving-sized pieces. Add the oil and bring it to temperature over medium heat. Season the meat on both sides with salt and pepper.

2. Add 3 pieces of the meat and fry for 3 minutes on each side to brown them. Move to a platter and repeat with the other pieces.

3. Leave the last 3 pieces of browned meat in the cooker; add the onion, celery, and green pepper on top of them.

4. Lay in the other 3 pieces of meat and pour the tomato juice and broth or water over them. Place the carrots and potatoes on top of the meat.

5. Lock the lid into place; bring to high pressure and maintain the pressure for 17 minutes. Remove from the heat and allow pressure to release naturally.

6. Once pressure has dropped, open the cooker and move the potatoes, carrots, and meat to a serving platter. Cover and keep warm.

7. Skim any fat from the juices remaining in the pan. Set the uncovered cooker over medium heat and simmer the juices for 5 minutes.

8. Whisk in the butter, 1 teaspoon at a time, if desired. Taste for seasoning and add additional salt and pepper if needed.

9. Have the resulting gravy available at the table to pour over the meat. Serve immediately.

Barbecue Chuck Roast

 Serves 6

½ cup ketchup

½ cup apricot preserves

¼ cup dark brown sugar

¼ cup apple cider white vinegar

½ cup teriyaki or soy sauce

Dry red pepper flakes, crushed, to taste

1 teaspoon dry mustard

¼ teaspoon freshly ground black pepper

1 (3-pound) boneless chuck roast

1½ cups water for beef

1 large sweet onion, peeled and sliced

Enjoy this dish with crispy sweet potato fries or chips.

1. Add the ketchup, preserves, brown sugar, vinegar, teriyaki or soy sauce, red pepper flakes, mustard, and pepper to a gallon-sized plastic freezer bag; close and squeeze to mix. Trim the roast of any fat, cut the meat into 1″ cubes, and add to the bag. Refrigerate overnight.

2. Add the appropriate amount of water and the cooking rack or steamer basket to a 6-quart or larger pressure cooker. Place half of the sliced onions on the rack or basket. Use a slotted spoon to remove the roast pieces from the sauce and place them on the onions; reserve the sauce. Cover the roast pieces with the remaining onions.

3. Lock the lid in place on the pressure cooker. Place over medium heat and bring to high pressure; maintain for 50 minutes, or 15 minutes per pound (remember: you reduce the weight of the roast when you trim off the fat). Turn off the heat and allow 15 minutes for the pressure to release naturally. Use the quick-release method to release remaining pressure, and carefully remove the lid. Strain the meat, separate it from the onions, and return it to the pan. Purée the onions in a food processor.

4. Pour the reserved sauce into the cooker and use two forks to pull the meat apart and mix it into the sauce. Bring to a simmer over medium heat. Stir in the onion. Skim the sauce for fat. Add ½ cup of the pan juices to the cooker and stir into the meat and sauce. Reduce the heat to low and simmer for 15 minutes, or until the mixture is thick enough to serve on sandwiches.

Corned Beef and Cabbage

Serves 6

Total cost: $6.89

Serving size: 5 ounces

Calories per serving: 339

Fat: 5g

Carbohydrates: 26g

Protein: 29g

Sodium: 437mg

Nonstick spray

2 medium onions, peeled and sliced

1 (3-pound) corned beef brisket

1 cup apple juice

¼ cup brown sugar, packed

2 teaspoons orange zest, finely grated

2 teaspoons prepared mustard

6 whole cloves

6 cabbage wedges

For a heartier entrée, add quartered red potatoes with the cabbage wedges.

1. Treat the inside of the pressure cooker with nonstick spray. Arrange the onion slices across the bottom of the crock.
2. Trim and discard excess fat from the brisket and place it on top of the onions.
3. Add the apple juice, brown sugar, orange zest, mustard, and cloves to a bowl and stir to mix; pour over the brisket. Lock the lid into place and bring to low pressure; maintain for 45 minutes. Quick-release the pressure and remove the lid.
4. Place the cabbage on top of the brisket. Lock the lid into place and bring to low pressure; maintain pressure for 8 minutes. Quick-release the pressure and remove the lid.
5. Move the cabbage and meat to a serving platter, spooning some of the pan juices over the meat. Tent with aluminum foil and let rest for 15 minutes. Carve the brisket by slicing it against the grain. Remove and discard any fat from the additional pan juices and the cloves. Pour the pan juices into a gravy boat to pass at the table.

Working in Batches

If you find your pressure cooker becomes too full, increase the time you maintain the pressure in Step 3 to 55 minutes. Let the pressure release naturally. Wrap the brisket in aluminum foil; keep warm. Add the cabbage to the pressure cooker, lock the lid into place, bring to low pressure, maintain for 8 minutes, quick-release, and proceed with Step 5.

The $7 a Meal Pressure Cooker Cookbook

Browned Beef with Onions

Serves 4

1 tablespoon olive oil

3 large onions, sliced

1 pound round steak, cut into 4 pieces

3 cloves garlic, minced

1 tablespoon chopped fresh Italian flat-leaf parsley

1 cup beef stock or broth

1 teaspoon chopped fresh thyme

1 teaspoon chopped fresh rosemary

Pinch dried red pepper flakes

Sea salt and freshly ground black pepper, to taste

¼ cup milk

2 tablespoons all-purpose flour

This dish is perfect served over mashed potatoes for a true comfort family meal.

1. Use the oil to coat the bottom of the pressure cooker. In layers, add half of the onions, the meat, and the other half of the onions. Add the garlic, parsley, stock, thyme, rosemary, red pepper flakes, salt, and pepper. Lock the lid into place and bring to high pressure; maintain pressure for 14 minutes.

2. Quick-release the pressure and remove the lid. Move the meat to a serving platter; cover and keep warm. Whisk together the milk and flour, and then whisk the milk-flour paste into the onions and broth in the pan. Simmer and stir for 3 minutes or until the onion gravy is thickened and the flour taste is cooked out of the sauce. Pour over the meat or transfer to a gravy boat to pass at the table. Serve.

Vegetables

Feel free to add hearty carrots, sliced green beans, or zucchini to this dish. If you do, add ¼ cup additional broth.

Creamy Beef Enchiladas

 Serves 8

 Total cost: $6.78

Serving size: 1 cup

Calories per serving: 474

Fat: 17g

Carbohydrates: 24g

Protein: 21g

Sodium: 939mg

2 pounds lean ground beef

1 large onion, peeled and diced

1 (4.5-ounce) can chopped chilies

1 (12-ounce) jar mild enchilada sauce

1 (10.5-ounce) can golden mushroom soup

1 (10.5-ounce) can Cheddar cheese soup

1 (10.5 ounce) can cream of mushroom soup

1 (10.5-ounce) can cream of celery soup

2 cups refried beans

Baked tortilla chips, lightly crushed, as desired

The only thing you'll need to serve with this rich, creamy dish is shredded lettuce and guacamole. Enchiladas also taste great with chicken, turkey, shrimp, or served vegetarian-style.

1. Add the ground beef and diced onion to the pressure cooker. Bring to high pressure and maintain for 5 minutes. Quick-release the pressure and remove the lid. Remove and discard any rendered fat. Stir the ground beef into the onions, breaking the beef apart.

2. Stir in the chilies, enchilada sauce, soups, and refried beans. Lock the lid into place and bring to low pressure; maintain pressure for 5 minutes. If you'll be serving the dish immediately, you can quick-release the pressure. Otherwise, remove from the heat and allow the pressure to release naturally.

3. Stir 8 ounces or more of lightly crushed tortilla chips into the mixture in the pressure cooker. Cover and stir over medium-low heat for 15 minutes or until the tortilla chips are soft.

Shredded Beef Tacos

Serves 6

1 large sweet onion, peeled and diced

1 large green bell pepper, seeded and diced

1 (10-ounce) can enchilada sauce

¼ cup water

1 (3-pound) beef brisket

1 package small corn tortillas

If you like spice, use jalapeño, poblano, or Anaheim peppers instead of the green pepper and add hot enchilada sauce.

1. Add the onion, green pepper, and enchilada sauce to the pressure cooker. Stir in the water. Trim and discard any fat from the roast. Place the roast in the pressure cooker. Lock the lid into place and bring to low pressure; maintain pressure for 50 minutes. Remove from the heat and allow pressure to release naturally.
2. Remove the meat to a cutting board and shred it. Return the shredded beef into the sauce in the pressure cooker. Return the pan to medium heat; simmer uncovered for a few minutes to bring the meat back up to pressure and thicken the sauce.

Finishing Your Burrito
Top your burrito with shredded lettuce, diced tomatoes, grated Cheddar cheese, and sour cream, if desired.

Steak Fajitas

 Serves 4

$ Total cost: $6.84

Serving size: 1 cup

Calories per serving: 362

Fat: 13g

Carbohydrates: 10g

Protein: 25g

Sodium: 252mg

1 pound round steak

1 small onion, peeled and diced

1 small green bell pepper, seeded and diced

Sea salt and freshly ground black pepper, to taste

2 cups frozen whole kernel corn, thawed

1¼ cups tomato juice

½ teaspoon chili powder

2 teaspoons cornstarch mixed with 2 teaspoons water

Enjoy these fajitas with corn or flour tortillas with your favorite accompaniments, or on their own with a side of Mexican rice.

1. Trim and discard any fat from the meat. Cut the meat into ½" dice and add to the pressure cooker. Stir in the onion, bell pepper, salt, pepper, corn, tomato juice, and chili powder. Lock the lid into place and bring to low pressure; maintain pressure for 12 minutes. Remove from the heat and allow pressure to release naturally for 5 minutes. Quick-release any remaining pressure.

2. Optional: To thicken the sauce, in a small bowl or measuring cup whisk the cornstarch together with the cold water. Return the pressure cooker to medium heat and bring to a simmer; whisk in the cornstarch slurry and cook uncovered for 5 minutes or until the sauce is thickened and the raw cornstarch taste is cooked out of the sauce. Taste for seasoning and add additional salt and pepper if needed.

Roast Beef with Yukon Potatoes

 Serves 6

 Total cost: $6.99

Serving size: 5 ounces

Calories per serving: 339

Fat: 7g

Carbohydrates: 28g

Protein: 27g

Sodium: 298mg

1 tablespoon olive oil

1 stalk celery, finely diced

1 (1-pound) bag baby carrots, divided

1 large onion, peeled and diced

1 (3-pound) rump roast

Sea salt and freshly ground black pepper, to taste

1 tablespoon Dijon mustard

6 medium Yukon Gold potatoes, scrubbed

3 cups beef broth

Feel free to substitute red or fingerling potatoes instead.

1. Add the oil to the pressure cooker and bring it to temperature over medium-high heat. Add the celery. Grate 6 of the baby carrots and add to the pan. Sauté for 3 minutes.

2. Add the onion, stir it into the celery and carrots, and push to the edges of the pan. Put the meat in the pan, fat-side up. Season with salt and pepper.

3. Brown for 5 minutes and then turn the roast fat-side down. If desired, spread the mustard over the browned top of the roast. Season with salt and pepper.

4. Spoon some of the sautéed celery, carrots, and onion over the top of the roast. Quarter the potatoes; add potatoes and remaining carrots to the top of the meat.

5. Pour in the broth. Add water, if needed, to bring the liquid level with the ingredients in the pressure cooker; remember not to fill the pressure cooker more than ⅔ full.

6. Lock the lid. Bring the cooker to high pressure; lower the heat to maintain pressure for 1 hour.

7. Turn off the heat and let the pan set for 15 minutes to release the pressure; use the quick-release method to release any remaining pressure.

8. Move the roast, potatoes, and carrots to a serving platter; tent with foil and keep warm.

9. Skim the fat from the pan juices. Bring to a boil over medium-high heat; reduce the heat and simmer for 5 minutes, and then whisk in the butter 1 teaspoon at a time. Pour into a gravy boat to serve with the roast. Garnish the roast platter with fresh parsley if desired.

"Corn" Corned Beef

Makes 1 (3-pound) corned beef brisket

$ Total cost: $7.00

Serving size: 6 ounces

Calories per serving: 182

Fat: 7g

Carbohydrates: 0g

Protein: 29g

Sodium: 107mg

4 cups water

½ cup kosher salt

¼ cup brown sugar

1 tablespoon saltpeter

1 (3") cinnamon stick, broken in half

1 tablespoon pickling spice

6 black peppercorns

4 whole cloves

6 whole juniper berries

1 bay leaf, crumbled

1 pound ice

1 (3-pound) beef brisket, trimmed

1 small onion, peeled and quartered

1 large carrot, peeled and sliced

1 stalk celery, diced

Additional water

Corned beef got its name from the method of preserving the meat, referred to as corning (the size of the granulated salt was roughly the size of a corn kernel).

1. Add the water, salt, brown sugar, saltpeter, cinnamon stick, pickling spice, peppercorns, cloves, juniper berries, and bay leaf to a 4-quart or larger stockpot.

2. Stir and cook over high heat for 10 minutes or until the salt and sugar have dissolved. Remove from the heat and add the ice. Stir until the ice has melted.

3. When the brine has cooled to 45°F, place the brisket in a large covered container. Pour in the brine, making sure brisket is completely submerged in brine. Close the container and place in the refrigerator for 10 days. Turn the meat over in the brine daily, stirring the brine as you do so.

4. At the end of the 10 days, remove the meat from the brine and rinse it well under cool water.

5. Add the brisket to the pressure cooker along with the onion, carrot, and celery. Add enough water to cover the meat.

6. Lock the lid into place and bring to low pressure; maintain pressure for 55 minutes. Remove from the heat and allow pressure to release naturally.

7. Remove the lid and transfer the meat from the pressure cooker to a serving platter; cover and allow it to rest for 30 minutes. To serve, thinly slice the brisket across the grain.

Meatloaf of Beef and Pork

Serves 4

½ pound lean ground beef

½ pound lean ground pork

½ teaspoon sea salt

1½ teaspoons freshly ground black pepper

¾ cup oatmeal

1 tablespoon Worcestershire sauce

2 teaspoons dried parsley

1 medium yellow onion, peeled and finely diced

2 stalks celery, finely diced

2 cloves garlic, peeled and minced

1 small red or green bell pepper, seeded and finely diced

¼ cup ketchup

1 cup water

2 tablespoons tomato paste

Add more tomato flavor by substituting an 8-ounce can of tomato sauce for the water and tomato paste and use your favorite seasoning blends.

1. Add the ground beef, ground pork, salt, pepper, oatmeal, Worcestershire sauce, parsley, onion, celery, garlic, and bell pepper to a large bowl. Mix well.
2. Turn the mixture out onto a large piece of waxed paper or plastic wrap. Shape into a large, somewhat flat oval loaf.
3. Wrap and chill in the freezer for 30 minutes or in the refrigerator for at least 2 hours.
4. Bring a 2.5-quart pressure braiser or fry pan to temperature over medium-high heat. Add the meatloaf and brown for 5 minutes. Turn the loaf.
5. Top the meatloaf with the ketchup. Mix water and tomato paste and pour around the meatloaf.
6. Lock the lid into place and bring to high pressure; maintain pressure for 20 minutes. Remove from the heat and allow pressure to release naturally. Serve sliced, topped with some of the pan sauce if desired.

Size Matters

This meatloaf recipe has been adjusted for the meatloaf to be cooked in a 2.5-quart pressure fry pan or braiser. Allow an additional 15 minutes under pressure if you're shaping a shorter, taller loaf to fit into a 5-quart pressure cooker.

Traditional Sloppy Joes

 Serves 6

$ Total cost: $6.50

Serving size: 1 sloppy joe
Calories per serving: 428
Fat: 16g
Carbohydrates: 32g
Protein: 19g
Sodium: 567mg

1 tablespoon olive oil

1 large sweet onion, peeled and diced

2 cloves garlic, peeled and minced

1 pound lean ground beef or ground turkey

½ cup beef broth

¼ cup tomato paste

2 tablespoons light brown sugar

Sea salt and freshly ground black pepper, to taste

Pinch dried red pepper flakes

½ teaspoon chili powder

1 teaspoon prepared mustard

1 tablespoon Worcestershire sauce

⅛ teaspoon ground cinnamon

Pinch ground cloves

Serve this recipe as an appetizer on mini slider buns or as an entrée on hamburger buns.

1. Bring the oil to temperature in the pressure cooker over medium-high heat. Add the onion and sauté for 3 minutes. Add the garlic; sauté for 30 seconds.
2. Stir in the remaining ingredients. Lock the lid into place and bring to low pressure; maintain pressure for 10 minutes.
3. Quick-release the pressure and, leaving the pan over the heat, remove the lid. Remove and discard any fat floating on top of the meat mixture.
4. Stir and simmer, breaking apart the cooked ground meat to thicken the sauce. Serve by spooning onto hamburger buns.

Sloppy Joes

Sloppy Joes are an all-time American favorite. Enjoy with beef or ground turkey on white or whole-wheat buns.

The $7 a Meal Pressure Cooker Cookbook

Sirloin Burger with Mushrooms

 Serves 4

1 pound lean ground sirloin

1 tablespoon Italian herb
  seasoning

1 (10.5-ounce) can condensed
  cream of mushroom soup

8 ounces fresh cremini mushrooms, sliced

½ cup reduced-fat milk

For extra-fresh flavor, add a ½ tablespoon freshly
chopped cilantro leaves.

1. Mix the ground sirloin with the seasoning blend; shape the
   meat into 4 flattened patties.
2. Bring a 2.5-quart pressure braiser or fry pan to temperature
   over medium-high heat. Add the ground sirloin patties;
   brown for 3 minutes.
3. Turn the patties and top with the soup. Layer the mushrooms
   over the meat and soup. Pour the milk in around the meat.
4. Lock the lid into place and bring to low pressure; maintain
   pressure for 10 minutes.
5. Quick-release the pressure and remove the lid. Transfer
   the meat to a serving platter and keep warm. Remove and
   discard any fat. Simmer the pan sauce to thicken it and then
   pour over the meat.

Acorn Squash with Pork Vegetable Stuffing

 Serves 2

1 acorn squash

½ cup frozen country-style hash browns

¼ cup frozen peas

½ pound pork sausage

2 teaspoons extra-virgin olive oil

Sea salt and freshly ground black pepper, to taste

½ cup water

If you're looking to save some calories, try this dish without the hash browns.

1. Cut the squash in half lengthwise and scrape out the seeds. Use a fork to prick the inside of each squash half, being careful not to pierce the skin.
2. In a bowl, mix together the hash browns, peas, and sausage. Divide the mixture between the squash halves. Drizzle 1 teaspoon oil over each stuffed squash half. Season with salt and pepper to taste.
3. Place the rack in the pressure cooker. Pour the water into the pressure cooker and then carefully place the squash halves on the rack.
4. Lock the lid into place and bring to high temperature; maintain pressure for 12 minutes. Remove from the heat and allow pressure to release naturally.
5. Use tongs and a spatula to move each squash half to serving plates. Top each with a hardboiled, fried, or poached egg if desired. Serve.

This Stuffing Is Versatile!
Use this stuffing for other recipes, such as filling for puff pastry, baked apples, or stuffed bell peppers.

Jambalaya with Chicken, Sausage, and Shrimp

 Serves 6

$ Total cost: $7.00

Serving size: 5 ounces

Calories per serving: 279

Fat: 12g

Carbohydrates: 22g

Protein: 12g

Sodium: 760mg

2 tablespoons peanut oil

1 large carrot, peeled and grated

1 stalk celery, finely diced

1 large green bell pepper, seeded and chopped

1 medium yellow onion, peeled and diced

2 green onions, chopped

2 cloves garlic, minced

½ pound pork steak

½ pound boneless, skinless chicken thighs

¼ pound smoked sausage, thinly sliced

¼ pound cooked ham, diced

1 (15-ounce) can diced tomatoes, drained

2 cups chicken broth

½ tablespoon chopped fresh Italian flat-leaf parsley

½ teaspoon chopped fresh thyme

¼ teaspoon hot sauce

2 tablespoons Worcestershire sauce

½ pound shrimp, peeled and deveined

Sea salt and freshly ground pepper, to taste

6 servings cooked long-grain brown rice

Jambalaya was originally created as a flavorful way to enjoy leftovers.

1. Add the oil to the pressure cooker and bring it to temperature over medium heat.
2. Add the grated carrots, celery, and green bell pepper to the pan; sauté for 3 to 5 minutes or until soft. Add the yellow and green onions and sauté until transparent.
3. Add the garlic and sauté for an additional 30 seconds. Cut the pork and chicken into bite-sized pieces. Add to the pressure cooker and stir-fry for 3 minutes.
4. Stir in the sausage and stir-fry for 3 minutes; add the ham and stir-fry for 1 minute.
5. Stir in the tomatoes, broth, parsley, thyme, hot sauce, and Worcestershire sauce. Lock the lid into place and bring to low pressure; maintain pressure for 8 minutes.
6. Quick-release the pressure. If the shrimp are large, halve them; otherwise, add the shrimp to the pot, cover, and cook over medium heat for 3 to 5 minutes or until shrimp are cooked.
7. Taste for seasoning and add salt and pepper if needed. Serve over the rice or stir the rice into the Jambalaya.

Shredded Cabbage with Beef and Tomatoes

Serves 6

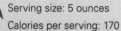

Total cost: $6.86

Serving size: 5 ounces

Calories per serving: 170

Fat: 6g

Carbohydrates: 21g

Protein: 8g

Sodium: 349mg

1½ pounds lean ground beef

1 large sweet onion, peeled and diced

1 (15-ounce) can diced tomatoes

1 cup tomato juice

1 tablespoon Italian seasoning

3 cups coleslaw mix or shredded cabbage

Sea salt and freshly ground black pepper, to taste

Serve this casserole-style dish over rice.

1. Add the ground beef and diced onion to the pressure cooker. Fry over medium-high heat, breaking apart the beef. Drain off any rendered fat and discard.
2. Stir in the undrained tomatoes, tomato juice, seasoning blend, and enough coleslaw mix to bring mixture to the fill line.
3. Lock the lid into place and bring to low pressure; maintain pressure for 8 minutes. Remove from heat and allow pressure to release naturally. Remove the lid. Stir. Check seasoning and add salt and pepper to taste.

Classic Open-Face Meatball Sandwich with Mozzarella

 Serves 6

1 pound lean ground beef

1 large egg

1 small onion, peeled and diced

½ cup bread crumbs

2 tablespoons Parmigiano-Reggiano cheese, freshly grated

1 tablespoon Italian seasoning

1 teaspoon garlic powder

Pinch dried red pepper flakes

Sea salt and freshly ground black pepper, to taste

1 teaspoon sugar

1 (28-ounce) jar pasta sauce

3 hoagie buns, halved

3 tablespoons extra-virgin olive oil

½ cup mozzarella cheese, grated

You can use traditional marinara pasta sauce or your favorite variation.

1. Add the ground beef, egg, onion, bread crumbs, grated Parmigiano-Reggiano cheese, Italian seasoning blend, garlic powder, red pepper flakes, salt, and pepper to a mixing bowl. Combine well. Shape into 12 golf ball–sized meatballs. Add to the pressure cooker.
2. Stir the sugar into the pasta sauce and pour over the meatballs. Lock the lid into place and bring to low pressure; maintain pressure for 8 minutes. Remove from heat and allow pressure to release naturally. Remove the lid. Skim and discard any fat.
3. Lay the buns flat on a broiling pan. Brush the insides of the buns with the olive oil. Place under the broiler until lightly toasted.
4. Spread 1 tablespoon sauce over the bottom portion of each bun. Halve the meatballs and add 2 meatballs to each bun, cut-side down on the bottom portion of the bun.
5. Top with the grated mozzarella cheese. Return to broiler; broil until cheese is melted and bubbly. Pour remaining sauce into a serving bowl.

Favorite Meatball Sandwich Add-Ons

Peel and slice a large sweet onion; add the slices to the pressure cooker after you pour in the pasta sauce. Add slices of green and red bell peppers. At the end of Step 2, move the cooked onions and peppers to a serving bowl. Serve at the table with the sandwiches.

Bell Peppers Stuffed with Beef, Rice, and Herbs

Serves 4

Total cost: $6.76

Serving size: 1 pepper

Calories per serving: 378

Fat: 8g

Carbohydrates: 23g

Protein: 36g

Sodium: 549mg

4 medium green bell peppers

1 pound lean ground beef

1 cup cooked rice

2 large eggs

3 cloves garlic, peeled and minced

1 small yellow onion, peeled and diced

Sea salt and freshly ground black pepper, to taste

Pinch of allspice, optional

Pinch of ground nutmeg, optional

½ cup chicken broth

½ cup tomato sauce

Bell peppers are delicious stuffed with many ingredients, including ground turkey, chicken, fresh herbs such as cilantro and parsley, rice, corn, and diced asparagus tips.

1. Cut the tops off the green peppers. Remove and discard the seeds and use a spoon to scrape out and discard some of the white pith inside the peppers. Set aside.
2. Dice any of the green pepper that you can salvage from around the stem and mix well with ground beef, rice, eggs, garlic, onion, salt, pepper, and allspice or nutmeg if using.
3. Evenly divide the meat mixture between the green peppers. Place the rack in the pressure cooker and pour the broth into the cooker.
4. Place the peppers on the rack and pour the tomato sauce over the peppers. Lock the lid into place and bring to low pressure; maintain pressure for 15 minutes.
5. Quick-release the pressure. Remove the peppers to serving plates. Remove the rack and pour the pan juices into a gravy boat to pass at the table.

Cabbage with Beef and Caraway

 Serves 6

2 tablespoons extra-virgin olive oil

2 stalks celery, diced

3 large carrots, peeled and diced

1 pound lean ground beef

1 medium yellow onion, peeled and diced

1 clove garlic, peeled and minced

½ teaspoon sea salt

¼ teaspoon freshly ground black pepper

Pinch caraway seeds

1 teaspoon sugar

1 (15-ounce) can diced tomatoes

1 cup cooked rice

2 cups coleslaw mix or rough-chopped cabbage

1½ cups chicken broth

¼ cup dry white wine such as sauvignon blanc

For a change, substitute canned seasoned Italian plum or Roma tomatoes and cooked orzo instead of the rice.

1. Bring the oil to temperature over medium heat in the pressure cooker. Add the celery and carrots; sauté for 5 minutes.
2. Add the ground beef and onion; stir-fry until beef is browned and onion is transparent. Drain off any excess fat.
3. Add the garlic, salt, pepper, caraway seeds, sugar, undrained tomatoes, rice, coleslaw mix or cabbage, and broth; stir into the beef mixture.
4. Use the back of a spoon to press the mixture down evenly in the pan. Add white wine if using, being careful not to exceed the fill line on your pressure cooker.
5. Lock the lid into place and bring to low pressure; maintain for 8 minutes. Remove from heat and allow pressure to release naturally.
6. Uncover and return the pressure cooker to medium heat. Simmer for 15 minutes or until most of the liquid has evaporated.

Mexican Meatballs

Serves 8

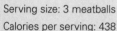
Total cost: $6.89

Serving size: 3 meatballs

Calories per serving: 438

Fat: 16g

Carbohydrates: 17g

Protein: 22g

Sodium: 394mg

1 tablespoon canola oil

1 large onion, thinly sliced

3 teaspoons garlic powder, divided

2 tablespoons chili powder, divided

¼ teaspoon dried Mexican oregano

2 canned chipotle chili peppers in adobo sauce

1 (15-ounce) can diced tomatoes

1 cup chicken broth

Sea salt and freshly ground black pepper, to taste

1 pound lean ground beef

½ pound ground pork

1 large egg

1 small white onion, peeled and diced

10 saltine crackers, crushed

Serve these over cooked white rice with additional sauce.

1. Add oil to the pressure cooker and bring to temperature over medium heat. Add the sliced onions; sauté for 3 minutes or until the onions are transparent.
2. Stir in 1½ teaspoons garlic powder, 1 tablespoon chili powder, oregano, chipotles in adobo sauce, undrained tomatoes, broth, salt, and pepper. Simmer uncovered while you prepare the meatballs.
3. Add the ground beef, ground pork, egg, diced onion, remaining chili powder, remaining garlic powder, and crumbled crackers to a large bowl; use hands to mix. Form into 16 meatballs.
4. Use an immersion blender to purée the sauce in the pressure cooker. Add the meatballs to the sauce.
5. Lock the lid into place and bring to low pressure; maintain pressure for 12 minutes. Remove from heat and allow pressure to release naturally.

All-Beef Meatballs

Make these meatballs with beef, pork, or ground turkey. For extra spice, add hot sauce or cayenne pepper to taste.

Onions Stuffed with Spicy Beef

Serves 4

4 medium onions, peeled

1 pound lean ground beef

¼ teaspoon ground allspice

¼ teaspoon dried dill

3 tablespoons fresh lemon juice, divided

2 teaspoons dried parsley

Sea salt and freshly ground black pepper, to taste

1 large egg

1–2 tablespoons all-purpose flour

2 tablespoons extra-virgin olive oil

1 cup chicken broth

So the onions hold their form, place onions beside each other in the bottom of the pressure cooker so they fit closely together.

1. Halve the onions, cutting through the middle (not from bottom to top). Scoop out the onion cores.
2. Chop cores and add to ground beef, allspice, dill, 2 tablespoons lemon juice, parsley, salt, pepper, and egg; mix well. Fill onion halves with meat mixture. Sprinkle the flour over the top of the meat.
3. Add oil to the pressure cooker and bring to temperature. Add onions to pan, meat-side down, and sauté until browned. Turn meat-side up. Pour remaining lemon juice and broth around the onions.
4. Lock the lid into place and bring to low pressure; maintain pressure for 8 minutes. Remove from heat and allow pressure to release naturally. Serve.

Other Ways to Stuff Onions

Onions are also delicious stuffed with other proteins such as lamb or turkey. Add flavor with chopped fresh cilantro or even mint leaves.

Spiced Black Beans and Rice

 Serves 6

 Total cost: $6.47

Serving size: 1 cup

Calories per serving: 240

Fat: 9g

Carbohydrates: 14g

Protein: 26g

Sodium: 157mg

1 cup dried black beans

4 cups water

3 tablespoons olive oil

1 medium green bell pepper, seeded and diced

½ stalk celery, finely diced

2 baby carrots, grated

1 medium onion, peeled and diced

2 cloves garlic, peeled and minced

¾ cup uncooked medium or long-grain white rice

2 cups chicken broth or water

2 teaspoons paprika

½ teaspoon cumin

¼ teaspoon chili powder

1 bay leaf

Sea salt and freshly ground black pepper, to taste

Hot sauce

In Step 2, you can substitute 4 diced slices of bacon for the oil. Fry the bacon until it begins to render its fat and then add and sauté the vegetables in the order given.

1. Rinse the beans and add them to a covered container. Pour in the water, cover, and let the beans soak overnight. Drain.
2. Bring the oil to temperature in the pressure cooker over medium-high heat. Add the green bell pepper, celery, and carrots; sauté for 2 minutes. Add the onion; sauté for 3 minutes or until soft. Stir in the garlic and sauté for 30 seconds.
3. Stir in the rice and stir-fry until the rice begins to brown. Add the drained beans, 2 cups of broth or water, paprika, cumin, chili powder, and bay leaf.
4. Lock the lid into place and bring to low pressure; maintain pressure for 18 minutes. Remove from the heat and allow pressure to release naturally. Stir, taste for seasoning, and add salt and pepper to taste. Top with hot sauce when serving, as desired.

Beef Stew with Apricots and Almonds

Serves 6

1 tablespoon olive oil

1½ pounds beef shoulder

1 large onion, peeled and diced

2 cloves garlic, peeled and minced

1 cup dried apricots

⅓ cup raisins

½ cup blanched whole almonds

1 tablespoon fresh ginger, minced

½ teaspoon ground cinnamon

¾ cup red wine

¼ cup freshly squeezed orange juice

½ cup fresh mint leaves, packed

Sea salt and freshly ground black pepper, to taste

You can make this stew in a 2.5-quart pressure fry pan or in a larger pressure cooker. Serve over cooked rice.

1. Bring the oil to temperature in the pressure cooker over medium-high heat. Cut the beef into bite-sized pieces.
2. Add the beef to the pressure cooker in batches and brown each batch for 5 minutes or until well browned. Use a slotted spoon to remove beef; set aside and keep warm.
3. Add the onion to the pressure cooker; sauté for 3 minutes; Stir in the garlic and sauté for 30 seconds.
4. Halve the apricots and add them to the pressure cooker along with the raisins, almonds, ginger, cinnamon, wine, orange juice, and mint leaves.
5. Lock the lid into place and bring to high pressure; maintain pressure for 20 minutes. Remove from the heat and allow pressure to release naturally.
6. Remove the lid, stir, and taste for seasoning. Add salt and pepper to taste.

Try It with Lamb

Lamb is a great substitute for the beef in this recipe, but it can be a little pricey. Buy when on sale and freeze for when you are ready to use.

Brandied Chicken Casserole

 Serves 4

$ Total cost: 6.80

Serving size: 6 ounces

Calories per serving: 319

Fat: 13g

Carbohydrates: 26g

Protein: 21g

Sodium: 398mg

1 medium onion, divided

2 stalks celery, diced

2 medium carrots, peeled and diced

5 cloves garlic, peeled, divided

½ teaspoon extra-virgin olive oil

1 (3-pound) chicken

1 lemon, washed and quartered

Sea salt and freshly ground black pepper, to taste

1 tablespoon olive or vegetable oil

½ cup dry red wine

¼ cup water

Several sprigs fresh rosemary

1 (1-pound) bag baby carrots

4 medium red potatoes, washed and quartered

4 shallots, peeled

1 tablespoon brandy

Cooking a whole chicken has never been easier. Serve with steamed rice or a side of pasta.

1. Peel the onion and cut in half. Set aside half of the onion and dice the other half.
2. Place the diced onion, celery, carrots, and 3 cloves garlic in a microwave-safe bowl. Stir in the extra-virgin olive oil. Cover and microwave on high for 2 minutes. Set aside, leaving the dish covered so the vegetables continue to cook.
3. Wash the chicken inside and out. Pat dry. Cut the reserved onion half in half and insert into the chicken cavity along with the lemon quarters and remaining 2 peeled cloves garlic. Salt and pepper the chicken inside and out. Truss the chicken.
4. Bring the olive or vegetable oil to temperature in the pressure cooker over medium-high heat. Add the chicken and brown on all sides, about 3 minutes per side. Remove and set aside the chicken.

Brandied Chicken Casserole (continued)

5. Remove and discard any excess oil in the pressure cooker. Stir in the red wine and use it to deglaze the pan, scraping up any browned bits sticking to the bottom of the pressure cooker.

6. Stir in the water, microwaved vegetables, and rosemary. Add the chicken, breast-side down.

7. Lock the lid into place and bring to high pressure; maintain pressure for 20 minutes. Remove from the heat and quick-release the pressure.

8. Remove the chicken to an oven-safe serving platter; tent with aluminum foil and put in a warm oven.

9. Remove and discard the rosemary and excess grease from the cooking liquid. Use an immersion blender to purée the cooking liquid.

10. Add the baby carrots, potatoes, and shallots to the puréed sauce. Return pressure cooker to heat and bring to high pressure; maintain pressure for 6 minutes. Remove from the heat and allow pressure to release naturally.

11. Remove the chicken from the oven; discard the aluminum foil tent. Use a slotted spoon to transfer the carrots, potatoes, and shallots to the serving platter.

12. Stir in the brandy and then return the pressure cooker to medium heat. Bring to a simmer; simmer for 3 minutes.

13. If desired, whisk the butter into the sauce 1 teaspoon at a time. Pour into a gravy boat to pass at the table.

Alternative to Whole Chicken

This recipe also works well if you buy a whole chicken cut-up. Prepare as you would for the whole chicken. Cut-up whole chickens are often available at great budget-friendly prices.

Hungarian-Style Beef Stew

 Serves 6

1 tablespoon olive oil

1 green bell pepper, seeded and diced

4 large potatoes, peeled and diced

3 strips bacon, cut into 1" pieces

1 large yellow onion, peeled and diced

2 tablespoons sweet paprika

1½ pounds round steak

1 clove garlic, peeled and minced

Pinch caraway seeds, chopped

2 cups beef broth

1 (15-ounce) can diced tomatoes

2 tablespoons sour cream, plus more for serving

Sea salt and freshly ground black pepper, to taste

This stew is also considered to be a goulash, which is essentially beef prepared in a soup-like fashion with onions and various vegetables.

1. Add the oil, bell pepper, potatoes, bacon, and onion to the pressure cooker over medium heat; sauté for 10 minutes or until the onion is transparent and the fat is rendering from the bacon.
2. Stir in paprika. Trim the beef of any fat and cut it into ½" cubes. Stir the beef into the vegetable mixture along with the garlic and caraway seeds.
3. Stir in the beef broth and tomatoes. Lock the lid into place and bring to low pressure; maintain pressure for 30 minutes.
4. Remove from heat and allow pressure to release naturally. Remove lid and stir 2 tablespoons sour cream into the goulash.
5. Taste for seasoning and add salt, pepper, and additional paprika if needed. Serve with additional sour cream on the side, and over prepared spaetzle or egg noodles if desired.

Beef Stews

Beef stews are often made with potatoes, as here, but you can also omit the potatoes in the recipe and serve over rice, toast, or even a baked potato.

Smoked Ham Sausage Soup

 Serves 8

Total cost: $6.91
Serving size: 1 cup
Calories per serving: 388
Fat: 10g
Carbohydrates: 27g
Protein: 34g
Sodium: 1225mg

1½ cups dried red kidney beans

5 cups water, divided

1 tablespoon canola oil

2 jalapeño peppers, seeded and diced

1 large onion, peeled and diced

8 ounces kielbasa or smoked ham sausage

4 cloves garlic, peeled and minced, if needed

1 bay leaf

1 tablespoon chili powder

1 teaspoon dried oregano

½ teaspoon freshly ground black pepper

¼ teaspoon cayenne pepper

3 cups beef broth

1 (15-ounce) can diced tomatoes

½ cup tomato sauce

2 tablespoons light brown sugar, packed

Sea salt, to taste

Smoked ham sausage is usually seasoned with lots of garlic. When substituting use andouille or Italian sausage, which tend to have more flavor.

1. Rinse the kidney beans. Put in a container and add enough water to cover them by an inch. Cover and let soak overnight.

2. Drain the beans and put in the pressure cooker. Add the remaining water and the oil. Lock the lid into place and bring to high pressure; maintain pressure for 12 minutes.

3. Remove from heat and allow pressure to release naturally. Drain the beans and set aside.

4. Add the jalapeño and onion to the pressure cooker. Dice the sausage and add to the cooker along with the garlic bay leaf, chili powder, oregano, black pepper, and cayenne pepper.

5. Lock the lid into place and bring to low pressure; maintain the pressure for 2 minutes. Quick-release the pressure.

6. Remove the lid and pour in the broth, tomatoes, tomato sauce, brown sugar, and drained beans.

7. Lock the lid into place and bring to high pressure; maintain the pressure for 20 minutes. Remove from the heat and allow pressure to release naturally.

8. Remove and discard the bay leaf. Taste for seasoning and add salt if desired. Serve.

Swedish Meatballs

 Serves 4

1 slice whole-wheat bread

½ cup reduced fat milk

1 pound lean ground beef

8 ounces lean ground pork

1 large egg

1 small onion, peeled and minced

1 teaspoon dried dill

Sea salt and freshly ground black pepper, to taste

4 tablespoons butter

¼ cup all-purpose flour

1½ cups beef broth

1 cup water

½ cup sour cream

Enjoy these traditional favorites by themselves or with egg noodles or rice.

1. Add the bread to a large bowl. Pour in the milk and soak the bread until the milk is absorbed.
2. Break up the bread and mix it into the beef, pork, egg, onion, dill, salt, and pepper. Form into 12 meatballs and set aside.
3. Add the butter to the pressure cooker and melt it over medium-high heat; whisk in the flour until it forms a paste. Whisk in the broth and water. Bring to a simmer and then add the meatballs.
4. Lock the lid into place and bring to high pressure; maintain pressure for 10 minutes. Remove from the heat and quick-release the pressure.
5. Carefully stir in the sour cream. Taste for seasoning and add additional salt and pepper if needed. Serve.

Added Crunch

For added texture, flavor, sweetness, and fiber, finely dice a Granny Smith apple and mix in with the meatball mixture. It's a new twist on a family favorite!

The $7 a Meal Pressure Cooker Cookbook

Root Vegetable Soup with Beef

 Serves 8

1½ tablespoons olive oil

1 clove garlic, minced

½ pound top sirloin, cut into
    ½" pieces

1 small yellow onion, diced

1 pound red beets

1 small head cabbage, cored
    and chopped

1 (15-ounce) can diced tomatoes

7 cups beef broth

¼ cup red wine vinegar

2 bay leaves

1 tablespoon lemon juice

Sea salt and freshly ground
    black pepper, to taste

Sour cream, as desired

Chopped fresh dill for garnish
    (optional)

If you prefer to use fresh tomatoes, substitute about a pound of diced, vine-ripened tomatoes for the canned tomatoes.

1. Add the oil, garlic, and beef to pressure cooker. Brown the beef over medium heat, stirring frequently to keep the garlic from burning. Add the onion and sauté until transparent.
2. Peel and dice the beets. Add the beets, cabbage, tomatoes, beef broth, vinegar, bay leaves, and lemon juice to the pressure cooker.
3. Lock the lid into place and bring to low pressure; maintain pressure for 10 minutes. Remove from the heat and allow pressure to release naturally.
4. Taste for seasoning and add salt and pepper to taste.
5. Ladle soup into bowls and garnish each bowl with a heaping tablespoon of sour cream and some fresh dill if using.

Root Vegetable Soup

If you prefer vegetarian soup, leave out the beef and substitute water or vegetable broth for the beef broth. Decrease the first pressure-cooking time to 5 minutes. If desired, add freshly grated orange or lemon zest to taste when you stir in the sour cream.

Soy Pepper Steak

Serves 6

$ Total cost: $7.00

Serving size: 1 cup

Calories per serving: 262

Fat: 13g

Carbohydrates: 1g

Protein: 31g

Sodium: 455mg

1 tablespoon sesame oil

2 tablespoons peanut or olive oil

1 large sweet onion, peeled and sliced

3 cloves garlic, peeled and minced

1 pound beef round steak

½ cup beef broth

1 tablespoon sherry

1 teaspoon light brown sugar

1 teaspoon fresh ginger, grated

Pinch dried red pepper flakes

2 tomatoes

1 large green bell pepper, seeded and sliced

4 green onions, sliced

¼ cup soy sauce

2 tablespoons cold water

2 tablespoons cornstarch

Serve over cooked rice, a baked potato, or noodles.

1. Bring the oil to temperature in the pressure cooker over medium-high heat. Add the onion; sauté for 3 minutes. Stir in the garlic; sauté for 30 seconds.
2. Cut the round steak into thin strips. Add to the pressure cooker; stir-fry for 3 minutes. Stir in the broth, sherry, brown sugar, ginger, and pepper flakes.
3. Lock the lid in place and bring to high pressure; maintain pressure for 10 minutes. Quick-release the pressure. Remove lid.
4. Peel the tomatoes and remove the seeds; cut them into eighths. Add to the pressure cooker along with the bell pepper and green onions.
5. Lock the lid into place and bring to low pressure; maintain pressure for 3 minutes. Quick-release the pressure and remove the lid.
6. In a small bowl, whisk together the soy sauce, water, and cornstarch. Stir the cornstarch mixture into the beef mixture in the pressure cooker.
7. Cook uncovered, stirring gently, for 3 minutes or until the mixture is thickened and bubbly.

Pork Curry

Serves 6

2 pounds boneless pork steaks

1 tablespoon peanut or canola oil

1 medium onion, peeled and diced

3 cloves garlic, peeled and minced

1 large eggplant, peeled and diced

1 jalapeño pepper, seeded and diced

3 carrots, peeled and sliced

2 medium waxy potatoes, peeled and diced

1 tablespoon sugar

1 tablespoon fresh ginger, grated

1 teaspoon curry powder

1 star anise

1 cup chicken broth or water

½ cup diced tomatoes

¼ cup fish sauce

1 tablespoon cold water

1 tablespoon cornstarch

6 green onions, roughly chopped

¼ cup chopped cilantro leaves

Serve this delicious dish over cooked rice.

1. Trim and discard the fat from the pork steaks; cut steaks into bite-sized pieces. Set aside.
2. Bring the oil to temperature in the pressure cooker over medium-high heat. Add the onion; sauté for 3 minutes. Add the garlic; sauté for 30 seconds.
3. Stir in the pork steak, eggplant, jalapeño pepper, carrot, potatoes, sugar, ginger, curry powder, star anise, broth or water, tomato, and fish sauce.
4. Lock the lid into place and bring to high pressure; maintain pressure for 20 minutes. Quick-release the pressure. Remove the lid. Remove and discard the star anise.
5. Stir together the water and cornstarch in a small bowl. Whisk into the pork mixture in the pressure cooker.
6. Cook, uncovered, for 5 minutes, stirring until mixture is thickened and bubbly. Stir in the green onion and cilantro. Serve.

Asian Pork Ribs

 Serves 6

¾ cup ketchup

½ cup water

¼ cup soy sauce

2 tablespoons balsamic or apple cider vinegar

⅓ cup light brown sugar

2 teaspoons ground ginger

1 teaspoon five-spice Chinese powder

1 teaspoon garlic powder

2 pounds baby back ribs

Five-spice Chinese powder is a blend of ground cinnamon, powdered cassia buds, powdered star anise or anise seed, ground ginger, and ground cloves. A little goes a long way, so measure with a measuring spoon dipped into the container to avoid spilling.

1. Add the ketchup, water, soy sauce, vinegar, brown sugar, ginger, five-spice powder, and garlic powder to the pressure cooker; stir to combine.
2. Cut ribs into single ribs and add to the pressure cooker, submerging in the sauce.
3. Lock the lid into place and bring to low pressure; maintain pressure for 30 minutes. Remove from the heat and allow pressure to release naturally.
4. Transfer the ribs to a serving platter. If desired, garnish with lime wedges.
5. Remove and discard any fat from the sauce in the pressure cooker. Add up to 1 tablespoon of liquid smoke, to taste, if desired. If necessary, thicken the sauce by simmering it for several minutes over medium heat. Pour sauce into a gravy boat to pass at the table.

Don't Have Five-Spice Powder?

Use a little more ground ginger, a pinch of ground cinnamon, and a pinch of ground cloves. If you have anise, add a little of that, too—if not, don't worry about it. Your dish will still have a nice flavor.

German Sauerbraten

 Serves 8

Total cost: $6.98
Serving size: about 5 ounces
Calories per serving: 341
Fat: 6g
Carbohydrates: 33g
Protein: 29g
Sodium: 537mg

2 tablespoons olive or vegetable oil

1 stalk celery, diced

1 carrot, peeled and grated

2 large onions, peeled and diced

2 cloves garlic, peeled and minced

2 cups beef broth

1 cup sweet red wine

1 teaspoon dried parsley

½ teaspoon dried thyme

½ teaspoon dried marjoram

4 whole cloves

2 bay leaves

1 teaspoon sea salt

½ teaspoon freshly ground black pepper

1 (3-pound) beef sirloin roast

4 medium potatoes, peeled and quartered

¼ cup butter, softened

¼ cup tomato sauce

¼ cup all-purpose flour

½ cup sour cream

This dish is often served with cooked cabbage, dumplings, or noodles.

1. Bring the oil to temperature in the pressure cooker over medium heat. Add the celery and carrot; sauté for 2 minutes.

2. Add the onion; sauté for 5 minutes or until the onion is softened. Stir in the garlic; sauté for 30 seconds.

3. Stir in the broth, wine, parsley, thyme, marjoram, cloves, bay leaves, salt, and pepper. Add the roast.

4. Lock the lid and bring to high pressure; maintain pressure for 1 hour. Remove from the heat and quick-release the pressure.

5. Remove the lid and transfer the roast to a serving platter; tent it with aluminum foil and keep warm.

6. Skim and discard the fat from the pan juices, and then strain the juices. Pour 2 cups of the strained juices into the pressure cooker.

7. Add the potatoes to the pressure cooker. Lock the lid in place and bring to high pressure; maintain pressure for 6 minutes.

8. Quick-release the pressure and remove the lid. Use a slotted spoon to transfer the potatoes to the serving platter.

9. In a small bowl, stir together the butter, tomato sauce, and flour. Bring the pan juices to a simmer and whisk in the flour mixture.

10. Cook and stir for 5 minutes or until the mixture is thickened. Stir in the sour cream. Pour the sauce into a gravy boat to serve with the beef and sauce.

CHAPTER 7

FISH AND SEAFOOD

Calamari with Marinara / 153
Fish Chowder / 154
Herb-Seasoned Whitefish with Tomatoes / 155
Whitefish Steamed in White Wine with Veggies / 156
Red Snapper in Rice Wine and Miso / 157
Paper-Poached Whitefish / 158
Creamy Crab "Dip" / 159
Paprika Catfish with Fresh Tarragon / 160
Parsleyed Trout / 161
Seafood Stew with Coconut Milk / 162
Tilapia with Black Olives / 163
Gulf Grouper with Peppers and Tomatoes / 164
Poached Salmon with Black Peppercorns and Red Wine / 165
Tuna with Swiss Cheese and Gemelli Pasta / 166
Hard Tacos with Shrimp and Potatoes / 167
Red Snapper Risotto / 168
Curried Tuna with Potatoes / 169
Whitefish with Corn, Celery, and Lima Bean Medley / 170
Fish Burritos with Black Beans and Green Chilies / 171
Southern Grits with Shrimp / 172
New Orleans–Style Shrimp with Black Beans and Rice / 173
Linguini with Clams / 174
Risotto with Crab and Spinach / 175

Calamari with Marinara

 Serves 4

2 tablespoons olive oil

1 small carrot, peeled and grated

1 small stalk celery, finely diced

1 small white onion, peeled and diced

3 cloves garlic, peeled and minced

2 pounds calamari

1 (28-ounce) can diced tomatoes

½ cup dry white wine

⅓ cup water

1 teaspoon chopped fresh Italian flat-leaf parsley

1 teaspoon chopped fresh basil

Sea salt and freshly ground black pepper, to taste

Sautéing or frying calamari can sometimes be tricky, as the result is often tough and chewy. Using the pressure cooker helps the calamari cook evenly with high steam, making them tender and delicious.

1. Bring the oil to temperature in the pressure cooker. Add the carrots and celery; sauté for 2 minutes.
2. Stir in the onions; sauté for 3 minutes or until the onions are transparent. Stir in the garlic; sauté for 30 seconds.
3. Clean and wash the calamari; pat dry. Add to the pressure cooker along with the remaining ingredients.
4. Lock the lid into place and bring to low pressure; maintain pressure for 10 minutes. Quick-release pressure. Serve.

Fish Chowder

Serves 4

2 tablespoons butter

1 large onion, peeled and diced

2 stalks celery, diced

2 large carrots, peeled and diced

2 medium potatoes, peeled and cut into ½" cubes

1 pound firm-fleshed white fish fillets, cut into ½" pieces

2 cups fish stock or clam juice

1 cup cold water

1 bay leaf

½ teaspoon dried thyme

1 cup whole milk

1 cup thawed frozen corn kernels

Sea salt and freshly ground white or black pepper, to taste

For fish chowders such as this one, use cod, tilapia, or another inexpensive white fish fillet, as the flavors of the soup blend with the fish. There's no need for more expensive fish such as halibut or swordfish.

1. Add the butter to the pressure cooker and bring it to temperature over medium heat. Add the onions; sauté for 3 minutes or until soft.
2. Stir in the celery, carrot, and potatoes; sauté for an additional minute. Add the fish, fish stock or clam juice, water, bay leaf, and thyme.
3. Lock the lid in place and bring the pressure cooker to high pressure; maintain pressure for 4 minutes. Quick-release the pressure.
4. Remove the lid, tilting it away from you to allow any excess steam to escape.
5. Remove and discard the bay leaf. Stir in the milk and corn. Taste for seasoning and add salt and pepper, to taste.
6. Simmer until the corn is cooked and the chowder is hot. Transfer to a serving tureen or individual bowls and top with additional butter if desired. Garnish with parsley if desired.

Herb-Seasoned Whitefish with Tomatoes

Serves 4

Total cost: $6.84
Serving size: about 5 ounces
Calories per serving: 150
Fat: 2g
Carbohydrates: 12g
Protein: 15g
Sodium: 610mg

4 (4-ounce) cod fillets

1 (15-ounce) can diced tomatoes

¼ onion, minced

¼ teaspoon onion powder

2 garlic cloves, minced

¼ teaspoon garlic powder

1 tablespoon chopped fresh
basil leaves

1 tablespoon chopped fresh
Italian flat-leaf parsley

1 teaspoon chopped fresh
oregano

¼ teaspoon sugar

Finely grated zest one lemon

Pinch chili powder

Pinch dried red pepper flakes

1 tablespoon grated Parmesan
cheese

Serve this dish over cooked polenta, rice, or over a medley of steamed mixed vegetables. You can also add or substitute raw, peeled, and deveined shrimp in Step 1.

1. Rinse the cod in cold water and pat dry between paper towels.
2. Add the tomatoes and all the remaining ingredients except the fish to the pressure cooker and stir to mix. Arrange the fillets over the tomatoes, folding thin tail ends under to give the fillets even thickness; spoon some of the tomato mixture over the fillets.
3. Lock the lid into place and bring the pressure cooker to low pressure; maintain pressure for 3–5 minutes (depending on the thickness of the fillets). Quick-release the pressure. Serve.

Whitefish Steamed in White Wine with Veggies

Serves 2

 Total cost: $6.97

Serving size: about 5 ounces

Calories per serving: 239

Fat: 13g

Carbohydrates: 8g

Protein: 17g

Sodium: 359mg

1 cup broccoli florets, cut into small pieces

1 large potato, peeled and diced

1 large carrot, peeled and grated

1 small zucchini, grated

4 ounces fresh mushrooms, sliced

1 teaspoon chopped fresh thyme leaves

Finely grated zest ½ lemon

½ pound sole or whitefish

½ cup white wine or chicken broth

½ cup fresh lemon juice

2 teaspoons chopped fresh Italian flat-leaf parsley

Sea salt and freshly ground black pepper, to taste

Pinch ground nutmeg

Other delicious fish for this recipe include salmon and grouper. The dish tastes great over a light pasta, such as linguini, or over rice. Also, keep in mind that nutmeg has a strong, distinct flavor. If you prefer, leave it out.

1. Place the steamer basket in the pressure cooker. Add the broccoli florets, potato, carrot, zucchini, and mushroom slices in layers to the basket. Sprinkle the thyme and lemon zest over the vegetables.
2. Place the fish fillets over the vegetables. Pour the broth or wine and lemon juice over the fish. Sprinkle the parsley, salt, and pepper over the fish and vegetables.
3. Lock the lid in place and bring the pressure cooker to low pressure; maintain the pressure for 5 minutes. Quick-release the pressure. Divide the fish and vegetables between two serving plates. Sprinkle freshly ground nutmeg to taste over each serving.

Red Snapper in Rice Wine and Miso

 Serves 4

Water, enough to fill the pan just below top of rack

1 tablespoon red miso paste

1 tablespoon rice wine

2 teaspoons fermented black beans

2 teaspoons sesame oil

1 teaspoon dark soy sauce

½ teaspoon Asian chili paste

Sea salt, to taste

2 pounds red snapper fillets

1 (2") piece fresh ginger

2 cloves garlic, peeled and minced

4 green onions

To prepare this dish, you'll need a glass pie pan that will fit on the rack inside the pressure cooker.

1. Insert the rack in the pressure cooker. Pour in enough water to fill the pan to just below the top of the rack.
2. In a small bowl, mix the miso, rice wine, black beans, sesame oil, soy sauce, and chili paste. Lightly sprinkle salt over the fish fillets and then rub them on both sides with the miso mixture.
3. Peel the ginger and cut into matchsticks 1" long. Place half of them on the bottom of a glass pie plate. Sprinkle half the minced garlic over the ginger.
4. Halve the green onions lengthwise and then cut them into 2"-long pieces; place half of them over the ginger and garlic. Place the fish fillets in the pie plate and sprinkle the remaining ginger, garlic, and onions over the top. Place the pie plate on the rack inside the pressure cooker.
5. Lock the lid into place and bring to high pressure; maintain pressure for 3 minutes. Remove from heat and quick-release the pressure. Serve.

Whole Fish

In some cultures, it's considered a delicacy to cook and serve the entire fish, including the head. If that is something you enjoy, feel free to use the whole fish in this recipe.

Paper-Poached Whitefish

 Serves 4

2 pounds whitefish fillets

3 tablespoons butter, softened

¼ cup fresh lemon juice

2 shallots, peeled and minced

2 cloves garlic, peeled and minced

1 tablespoon chopped fresh Italian flat-leaf parsley

¼ teaspoon freshly ground white pepper

2 medium potatoes, peeled and cut into matchsticks

3 large carrots, peeled and cut into matchsticks

2 small zucchini, thinly sliced

Sea salt, to taste

Water as needed to cover bottom of cooker

Parchment paper

Shallots are part of the onion family. If you can't find a shallot, use diced red onion.

1. Thoroughly rinse the fish. Cut away and discard any grayish bands of fat. Cut into 6 portions.
2. In a small bowl, mix together the butter, lemon juice, shallots, garlic, parsley, and white pepper.
3. Cut out 6 pieces of parchment paper to wrap around the fish fillets. Brush the parchment with some of the butter mixture. Lay a fish fillet on each piece of parchment. Equally divide the remaining butter mixture between the fish, brushing it over the tops of the fillets.
4. Layer the potatoes, carrots, and zucchini on top of the fish. Salt each fillet-vegetable packet to taste. Enclose the fish and vegetables in the parchment by wrapping the paper envelope-style over them. Crisscross the packets in the steamer basket for your pressure cooker.
5. Add enough water to the pressure cooker to come up to the bottom of the steamer basket. Lock the lid into place and bring to high pressure; maintain pressure for 5 minutes. Remove from the heat and quick-release the pressure.
6. Remove the steamer basket from the pressure cooker. Using a spatula and tongs, transfer the packets to 6 serving plates. Serve immediately.

Creamy Crab "Dip"

Serves 4

Total cost: $6.79

Serving size: 5 ounces

Calories per serving: 239

Fat: 9g

Carbohydrates: 10g

Protein: 15g

Sodium: 560mg

4 tablespoons butter

½ stalk celery, finely diced

1 small red onion, peeled and finely diced

1 pound uncooked lump crabmeat

¼ cup chicken broth

½ cup heavy cream

Sea salt and freshly ground black pepper, to taste

Serve this "dip" as a sauce over linguini or egg noodles. Or, serve as an appetizer dip.

1. Melt the butter in the pressure cooker over medium heat. Add the celery; sauté for 1 minute or until celery begins to soften. Stir in the onion; sauté for 3 minutes. Stir in the crabmeat and broth.

2. Lock the lid into place and bring to low pressure; maintain for 3 minutes. Quick-release the pressure and remove the lid. Carefully stir in the cream. Taste for seasoning and add salt and pepper to taste. Serve.

Seafood Seasonings

Enhance the flavor of this recipe by adding Old Bay Seasoning, which is common to many seafood dishes. Another great seasoning for fish is Crazy Jane Salt Blend, which is one of my favorites for both crab and shrimp dishes.

Paprika Catfish with Fresh Tarragon

 Serves 4

$ Total cost: $6.87

Serving size: 5 ounces

Calories per serving: 172

Fat: 4g

Carbohydrates: 3g

Protein: 17g

Sodium: 186mg

1 pound catfish fillets

1 (15-ounce) can diced tomatoes

2 teaspoons dried minced onion

¼ teaspoon onion powder

1 teaspoon dried minced garlic

¼ teaspoon garlic powder

1 teaspoon hot paprika

½ tablespoon chopped fresh tarragon

1 medium green bell pepper, seeded and diced

1 stalk celery, finely diced

¼ teaspoon sugar

½ cup chili sauce

Sea salt and freshly ground pepper, to taste

Catfish is terrific steamed or poached, as here, but it also is a great fish for frying. Serve with rice or if fried, with southern hush puppies. However, do NOT use your pressure cooker as a traditional deep fryer. The intense heat needed for frying can cause the pot to crack.

1. Rinse the catfish in cold water and pat dry between paper towels. Cut into bite-sized pieces.
2. Add all ingredients except fish to the pressure cooker and stir to mix. Gently stir the fillets into the tomato mixture.
3. Lock the lid into place and bring the pressure cooker to low pressure; maintain pressure for 5 minutes. Quick-release the pressure. Remove the lid. Gently stir and then taste for seasoning. Add salt and pepper to taste if needed. Serve.

To Avoid Bones

Catfish taste delicious; however, they do have lots of little bones. To avoid bones, use trout, cod, or whitefish fillets.

Parsleyed Trout

Serves 4

4 fresh (½-pound) river trout

Sea salt, to taste

4 cups torn red or green lettuce leaves

1 teaspoon distilled white or white wine vinegar

½ cup water

½ cup chopped fresh Italian flat-leaf parsley

1 shallot, peeled and minced

2 tablespoons mayonnaise

½ teaspoon fresh lemon juice

¼ teaspoon sugar

Pinch salt

2 tablespoons almonds, toasted

Lettuce leaves are a great way to steam fish and keep them firm, while adding extra overall flavor to the dish.

1. Rinse the trout inside and out; pat dry. Sprinkle with salt inside and out. Put 3 cups of the lettuce leaves in the bottom of the pressure cooker. Arrange the trout over the top of the lettuce and top the trout with the remaining lettuce. Stir the vinegar into the water and pour into the pressure cooker.

2. Lock the lid into place and bring to high pressure; maintain pressure for 3 minutes. Remove from the heat and allow pressure to release naturally for 3 minutes. Quick-release any remaining pressure.

3. Remove the lid and use a spatula to move the fish to a serving plate. Peel and discard the skin from the fish. Remove and discard the heads if desired.

4. To make the parsley sauce, mix together the parsley, shallot, mayonnaise, lemon juice, sugar, and salt. Evenly divide among the fish, spreading it over them. Sprinkle the toasted almonds over the top of the sauce. Serve.

Try These Herbs, Too

Other great herbs for this recipe are cilantro and dill. Use along with or in place of the parsley for an easy, delicious new recipe.

Seafood Stew with Coconut Milk

 Serves 4

$ Total cost: $7.00

Serving size: 8 ounces

Calories per serving: 335

Fat: 18g

Carbohydrates: 21g

Protein: 26g

Sodium: 280mg

2 cloves garlic, minced

1 small Granny Smith apple, seeded and diced

1 banana, peeled and sliced

½ cup raisins

2 tablespoons light brown sugar

¼ teaspoon ground cumin

2 tablespoons curry powder

2 cups chicken broth

1½ cups unsweetened coconut milk

2 tablespoons lemon or lime juice

1 teaspoon Worcestershire sauce

¼ cup heavy cream

½ cup sour cream

½ pound shrimp, peeled and deveined

½ pound cod, snapper, or other firm white fish

1 small red bell pepper, seeded and diced

½ cup canned white northern beans

¼ cup minced fresh cilantro leaves

The sweetness of the fruit and coconut milk in this dish mellows and enhances the spicy richness of the curry. Serve in bowls over cooked basmati or jasmine rice.

1. Add the garlic, apple, banana, raisins, brown sugar, cumin, curry powder, broth, coconut milk, lemon or lime juice, and Worcestershire sauce to the pressure cooker; stir to combine. Lock the lid into place and bring to high pressure; maintain pressure for 10 minutes.

2. Remove from the heat and quick-release the pressure. Use an immersion blender to purée. Stir in the cream and sour cream. Taste for seasoning and adjust as desired.

3. Stir in the shrimp. Rinse the fish and pat dry; cut into bite-sized cubes and add to the pressure cooker along with the bell pepper and beans. Lock the lid in place. Return to the heat and bring to high pressure; maintain pressure for 2 minutes. Remove from the heat and quick-release the pressure.

4. Divide the soup between 4 bowls, ladled over cooked rice if desired. Sprinkle 1 tablespoon of minced cilantro over each serving.

Tilapia with Black Olives

Serves 2

Total cost: $6.79

Serving size: 1 cup

Calories per serving: 285

Fat: 11g

Carbohydrates: 3g

Protein: 27g

Sodium: 251mg

½ cup dry white wine such as sauvignon blanc

½ cup water

1 pound tilapia fillets

Sea salt, to taste

4 thin slices white onion

6 sprigs fresh dill

3 tablespoons butter, melted

4 teaspoons freshly squeezed lime juice

6 Kalamata or black olives, pitted and chopped

Green olives are also a good option for this Mediterranean dish, and you could substitute orange roughy, red snapper, whitefish, and cod for the tilapia. Serve with a light salad of mixed greens and parmesan.

1. Pour the wine and water into the pressure cooker. Place the trivet in the cooker. Rinse the fish and pat dry. Lightly sprinkle with salt. Place 2 slices of onion on the trivet and top each onion with a sprig of dill.
2. Place the fish over the onion and dill, and then put a sprig of dill on top of each fillet and top with the remaining two onion slices. Lock the lid into place and bring to high pressure; maintain pressure for 5 minutes. Remove from the heat and allow pressure to release naturally for 5 minutes. Quick-release any remaining pressure.
3. To make the sauce, whisk together the butter, lime juice, and ½ tablespoon cooking liquid from the fish; stir in the olives. Serve the fish topped with the black olive butter sauce and garnished with the remaining 2 sprigs of dill.

Gulf Grouper with Peppers and Tomatoes

 Serves 4

$ Total cost: $6.97

Serving size: 5 ounces

Calories per serving: 172

Fat: 3g

Carbohydrates: 8g

Protein: 19g

Sodium: 186mg

2 tablespoons olive oil

1 small onion, peeled and diced

1 stalk celery, diced

1 green bell pepper, seeded and diced

1 (15-ounce) can diced tomatoes

¼ cup water

1 tablespoon tomato paste

1 teaspoon sugar

Pinch basil

½ teaspoon chili powder

1½ pounds grouper fillets

Sea salt and pepper, to taste

Grouper is found in waters all over the world and tastes delicious baked, grilled, fried, or steamed, as here. It has light flavor and texture that goes great with seasonings like lemon caper.

1. Bring the oil to temperature in the pressure cooker over medium-high heat. Add the onion, celery, and green pepper; sauté for 3 minutes. Stir in undrained tomatoes, water, tomato paste, sugar, basil, and chili powder.
2. Rinse the fish and pat dry; cut into bite-sized pieces. Sprinkle with salt and pepper, to taste. Gently stir the fish pieces into the sauce in the pressure cooker. Lock the lid into place and bring to high pressure; maintain pressure for 5 minutes. Quick-release the pressure.

Poached Salmon with Black Peppercorns and Red Wine

 Serves 6

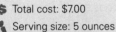

Total cost: $7.00

Serving size: 5 ounces

Calories per serving: 245

Fat: 9g

Carbohydrates: 9g

Protein: 26g

Sodium: 228mg

1 medium onion, peeled and quartered

2 cloves garlic, peeled and smashed

1 stalk celery, diced

1 bay leaf

1 teaspoon chopped fresh thyme

3½ cups water

2 cups dry red wine

2 tablespoons red wine or balsamic vinegar

½ teaspoon sea salt

½ teaspoon black peppercorns

1½ pounds salmon fillet, skin removed

1 to 2 whole lemons, sliced, for garnish/serving

For added flavor, try a little ground mustard or even a teaspoon or two of Dijon mustard.

1. Add all ingredients except the salmon and lemon to the pressure cooker. Lock the lid into place and bring to high pressure; maintain pressure for 10 minutes. Remove from the heat and allow pressure to release naturally for 15 minutes. Quick-release any remaining pressure.

2. Set the trivet in the pressure cooker. Put the pressure cooker over medium-high heat and bring the wine mixture to a high simmer.

3. Wrap the salmon in cheesecloth, leaving ends long enough to extend about 3". Use two sets of tongs to hold on to the 3" cheesecloth extensions and place the salmon on the trivet. Lock the lid into place and bring to high pressure; main-

tain pressure for 6 minutes. Remove from the heat and allow pressure to release naturally for 20 minutes.

4. Quick-release any remaining pressure. Use tongs to hold on to the 3" cheesecloth extensions to lift the salmon roast out of the pressure cooker. Set in a metal colander to allow extra moisture to drain away. When the roast is cool enough to handle, unwrap the cheesecloth. Peel away and discard any skin.

5. Transfer the salmon to a serving platter. Garnish with lemon slices or wedges if desired.

Tuna with Swiss Cheese and Gemelli Pasta

Serves 4

 Total cost: $6.59

 Serving size: 1 cup
Calories per serving: 348
Fat: 9g
Carbohydrates: 18g
Protein: 14g
Sodium: 489mg

2 cups dried gemelli pasta

1 tablespoon olive oil

2 tablespoons butter

1 yellow onion, finely chopped

1 (10-ounce) can cream of
mushroom soup

1 tablespoon curry powder

1 cup reduced fat milk

1 (12-ounce) can tuna in water,
drained

3 stalks celery, chopped

1 cup shredded Swiss cheese

1 cup red seedless grapes

2 tablespoons grated Parmesan cheese

Gemelli pasta is actually a single "s"-shaped strand of pasta that has been twisted into a spiral. It's great for pasta salads and practically any other dish you would use pasta for.

1. Cook pasta according to directions on package. Drain, drizzle with a little olive oil, toss to coat, and set aside.
2. Place butter in pressure cooker and heat over medium heat. Add onion and stir until just tender, about 1–2 minutes. Add soup and curry powder. Stir to combine and heat until bubbling, about 3 minutes.
3. Stir in milk and whisk until smooth. Add tuna and stir to combine. Latch lid of pressure cooker securely and bring to low pressure. Maintain low pressure for 5 minutes. Use quick-release method to release pressure.
4. Add celery, Swiss cheese, and grapes to cooker. Cover and bring to low pressure. Maintain low pressure for 6 minutes. Use quick-release method to release pressure. Uncover and stir in pasta until well combined. Serve with Parmesan cheese.

Other Cheeses to Try

Other cheeses that work well for this dish are provolone, mozzarella, and Monterey jack.

The $7 a Meal Pressure Cooker Cookbook

Hard Tacos with Shrimp and Potatoes

 Serves 4

 Total cost: $6.58
 Serving size: 1 taco
Calories per serving: 385
Fat: 12g
Carbohydrates: 17g
Protein: 19g
Sodium: 358mg

3 baking potatoes, peeled and cubed

1 yellow onion, chopped

3 cloves garlic, chopped

1 tablespoon butter

Sea salt and black pepper, to taste

1 tablespoon chili powder

Pinch cayenne pepper

½ pound frozen cooked bay shrimp, thawed and roughly chopped

4 hard taco shells

½ cup chopped tomatoes

1 cup shredded pepper jack cheese

You can also make fish tacos using this method—try whitefish, cod, and tilapia.

1. Place potatoes, onions, garlic, butter, salt, pepper, chili powder, and cayenne pepper in cooker and mix well. Latch lid securely and bring pressure to high pressure. Maintain high pressure for 9 minutes. Use quick-release method to release.

2. Add shrimp and resecure lid. Bring pressure to low pressure and maintain low pressure for 4 minutes. Use quick-release method to release pressure.

3. Heat tacos in a 225°F oven for 10 to 12 minutes. Serve tacos with shrimp mixture topped with tomatoes and pepper jack cheese.

What Is Pepper Jack Cheese?

Pepper jack cheese is a spicy version of Monterey jack and is perfect for tacos and casseroles including breakfast casseroles like the Veggie Breakfast Burrito or the Four Cheese Breakfast Casserole, (both from Chapter 3).

Red Snapper Risotto

Serves 6

$ Total cost: $6.89

Serving size: 1 cup

Calories per serving: 320

Fat: 9g

Carbohydrates: 25g

Protein: 15g

Sodium: 329mg

1 tablespoon olive oil

1 yellow onion, chopped

3 cloves garlic, minced

2 cups uncooked long-grain brown rice

3 carrots, sliced in ¼" thick slices

1 cup reduced fat milk

2 cups water

2 cups chicken broth

½ pound thin red snapper fillets

1 tablespoon lemon juice

1 tablespoon butter

½ cup grated Parmesan cheese

2 tablespoons chopped Italian flat-leaf parsley

If snapper isn't your favorite fish, use whitefish, cod, tilapia, or grouper. Don't use a high-end fish, however, unless you serve it on its own on the side. High-end fish is too good to be smothered with rice.

1. Heat the olive oil in the pressure cooker over medium heat. Add onion and garlic. Cook and stir for 3 minutes. Add rice and stir another 2 minutes to coat.
2. Add all ingredients except fish, Parmesan, and parsley to cooker. Latch lid securely and bring to high pressure. Once at high pressure, reduce to low pressure. Maintain low pressure for 12 minutes. Release pressure using quick-release method.
3. Add fish to cooker. Resecure lid and bring back to low pressure. Maintain low pressure for 3 minutes. Use natural-release method to release pressure.
4. Serve fish warm with Parmesan and parsley.

More on Risotto

Risotto is traditionally made with Arborio rice. This long-grain brown rice version is more fiber-filled and works great in the pressure cooker because of its hearty texture and similar moisture-absorbing properties.

The $7 a Meal Pressure Cooker Cookbook

Curried Tuna with Potatoes

 Serves 5

 Total cost: $4.84

Serving size: 1 cup

Calories per serving: 348

Fat: 14g

Carbohydrates: 16g

Protein: 15g

Sodium: 328mg

1 tablespoon butter

1 yellow onion, chopped

3 cloves garlic, chopped

3 tablespoons plain flour

1 tablespoon curry powder

Sea salt and black pepper, to taste

½ cup heavy cream

½ cup whole or reduced fat milk

4 potatoes, peeled and sliced ⅛" thick

2 stalks celery, chopped

1 (12-ounce) can light tuna in water, drained

Curry helps to bring together the flavors of the tuna and the potato.

1. In cooker, heat butter and add onion and garlic over medium heat. Add flour, curry powder, salt, and pepper. Cook until bubbly. Add cream and milk and bring to a simmer. Add potatoes by layering them with celery and tuna and pressing into the cream mixture.
2. Latch lid securely and bring to high pressure. Once at high pressure, reduce to low pressure and maintain low pressure for 12 minutes. Use natural-release method to release pressure. Serve warm.

Other Potatoes That Work

This recipe also works with sweet potatoes. The dish will have a naturally sweet flavor with a similar texture to that of baking potatoes. Or, try red potatoes.

Whitefish with Corn, Celery, and Lima Bean Medley

Serves 4

1 yellow onion, chopped

1 (10-ounce) package frozen lima beans

2 stalks celery, chopped

2 cups frozen corn kernels

Pinch sea salt and black pepper

Pinch ground ginger

¼ cup apple cider vinegar

¼ cup sugar

2 tablespoons butter

⅓ cup sour cream

½ pound whitefish

Pinch paprika

¼ cup chopped fresh cilantro

Other great fish for this dish are snapper, salmon, shrimp, and even lobster, if it fits within your budget.

1. Add onions, lima beans, celery, corn, salt, pepper, and ginger to cooker and mix well. Separately combine vinegar and sugar and blend well. Pour over bean mixture.
2. Latch lid securely and bring to low pressure. Maintain low pressure for 8 minutes. Use quick-release method to release pressure.
3. Add butter and sour cream. Add fish and season if needed with additional salt and pepper. Add paprika and cilantro. Resecure lid and bring to low pressure. Maintain low pressure for 6 minutes. Release using natural-release method.
4. To serve, flake fish and mix into veggie mixture. Serve.

Customize Your Dish
Add freshly chopped red bell pepper, diced pimientos, diced broccoli florets, or asparagus tips for added color and nutritional value.

The $7 a Meal Pressure Cooker Cookbook

Fish Burritos with Black Beans and Green Chilies

Serves 4

$ Total cost: $6.48

Serving size: 1 burrito

Calories per serving: 402

Fat: 12g

Carbohydrates: 12g

Protein: 14g

Sodium: 448mg

24 frozen fish fingers, thawed

1 tablespoon olive oil

1 yellow onion, chopped

1 green bell pepper, seeded and diced

1 (15-ounce) can black beans, drained

1 (4-ounce) can green chilies, drained

1 tablespoon chili powder

4 (10") corn tortillas

½ cup tomato salsa

1 cup shredded Monterey jack cheese

This recipe is also great with fresh fish fillet such as whitefish or cod.

1. Preheat oven to 400°F. Place fish fingers on baking sheet and bake until done, about 10 to 15 minutes or as directed on package.
2. Meanwhile, heat oil in cooker and add onion. Stir until onion is soft, about 3 minutes. Add bell pepper, beans, and chilies to cooker.
3. Latch lid securely and bring to low pressure. Maintain pressure for 5 minutes. Use quick-release method to release pressure.
4. To serve, place fish with 1 tablespoon or so of onion mixture onto tortilla. Top with salsa and cheese. Fold into a burrito by folding up one side and wrapping tortilla.
5. Place wrapped burrito on baking sheet and return to oven to melt cheese, about 10 minutes. Serve warm.

Southern Grits with Shrimp

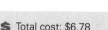 Serves 4

💲 Total cost: $6.78

🥄 Serving size: 1 cup
Calories per serving: 339
Fat: 12g
Carbohydrates: 16g
Protein: 12g
Sodium: 2811mg

2½ cups water

1½ cups whole or reduced-fat milk

1 cup quick-cooking grits

Pinch sea salt and black pepper

½ teaspoon hot sauce

1 yellow onion, chopped

2 tablespoons butter

1 cup grated sharp Cheddar cheese

2 slices bacon

1 green bell pepper, chopped

2 cloves garlic, minced

1 (8-ounce) can tomato sauce

2 teaspoons chili powder

8 ounces frozen cooked bay shrimp, thawed, drained, roughly chopped

2 tablespoons cornstarch

3 tablespoons water

Believe it or not, grits are not just for breakfast. Use this polenta-like grain for all kinds of entrées and side dishes.

1. Place water, milk, grits, salt, pepper, hot sauce, onion, and butter in pressure cooker. Latch lid securely and bring to low pressure. Maintain pressure for 5 minutes. Use quick-release method to release pressure. Stir in cheese.
2. Separately, in saucepan, cook bacon until crisp. Remove from pan and drain. Add bell pepper, garlic, tomato sauce, and chili powder. Stir to combine and bring to heat. Add shrimp and stir.
3. In small bowl, mix together cornstarch and water. Stir until well blended and then stir into tomato mixture. Bring to a simmer and stir until thickened.
4. Spoon grits into serving dish. Top with shrimp mixture and finish with crispy bacon.

Southern Grits

People often enjoy their grits with tomato sauce or salsa. This recipe incorporates that popular way of enjoying grits and adds in flavorful shrimp as well.

New Orleans–Style Shrimp with Black Beans and Rice

Serves 4

1 tablespoon olive oil

1 cup brown rice

1 yellow onion, chopped

3 cloves garlic, minced

2 cups vegetable broth

3 cups water

1 (14-ounce) can diced tomatoes

1 (15-ounce) can black beans, drained

½ teaspoon cumin

Sea salt and black pepper, to taste

Pinch cayenne pepper

8 ounces frozen bay shrimp, thawed and coarsely chopped

This dish is also great with crabmeat or, for a truly New Orleans–style dish, crawfish.

Heat oil in cooker and add rice, onion, and garlic. Stir over medium heat for 3 to 5 minutes. Add broth, water, tomatoes, beans, cumin, salt, pepper, cayenne, and shrimp. Latch lid securely and bring to low pressure. Maintain pressure for 15 minutes. Use natural-release method to release pressure. Serve warm.

Dried Beans

You can use dried beans rather than canned. However, for best results, soak them overnight in water and drain before using.

Linguini with Clams

Serves 4

1 yellow onion, chopped

3 cloves garlic, minced

2 potatoes, peeled and cubed

Sea salt and black pepper, to taste

1 (14-ounce) can diced tomatoes with herbs

1 (6-ounce) can tomato paste

2 cups water

2 (6-ounce) can clams, juice reserved

2 tablespoons lemon juice

1 (12-ounce) package linguini pasta

2 tablespoons butter

¼ cup chopped fresh Italian flat-leaf parsley

⅓ cup Parmesan cheese, grated

An Italian favorite, serve this recipe with fresh ciabatta or sourdough bread to soak up any remaining broth. If your budget allows, try other seafood that go great with linguini: lobster chunks, shrimp, and mussels.

1. Put onions, garlic, potatoes, salt, pepper, tomatoes, tomato paste, water, clams with juice, and lemon juice in pressure cooker. Bring to low pressure and maintain pressure for 10 minutes. Release using natural-release method.
2. Meanwhile, cook pasta according to directions on package in liberal amount of water. Cook until al dente. Drain and set aside.
3. When ready to serve, serve pasta and top with ¼ cup sauce or as desired and top with parsley and cheese.

Risotto with Crab and Spinach

 Serves 4

1 tablespoon olive oil

1 tablespoon butter

1 yellow onion, diced

3 cloves garlic, chopped

2 cups long-grain brown rice

3 cups chicken broth

Sea salt and black pepper, to taste

1 cup frozen chopped spinach, thawed

12 ounces imitation crab or cod

½ cup grated Parmesan cheese

½ cup grated mozzarella or Muenster cheese

Risotto can be enjoyed with many vegetable combinations, including asparagus, mushrooms, broccoli, squash, and corn—or just simply with cheese.

1. Heat olive oil in cooker over medium heat and add butter, onion, garlic, and rice. Stir until onion becomes a little tender and rice is coated, about 3 minutes.
2. Add rice and broth, season with salt and pepper, then add spinach and crab. Stir to combine. Latch lid securely and bring to high pressure. Once at high pressure, reduce pressure to low and maintain low pressure for 15 minutes.
3. Release pressure using natural-release method. Stir in cheese and serve.

Cheese and Risotto
Sometimes there is nothing more satisfying than a simple risotto with fresh Parmiggiano-Reggiano cheese and maybe a few fresh herbs, like basil or Italian parsley. Adding the cheese at the last minute helps the risotto maintain its creaminess.

CHAPTER 8

JUST SOUPS

Basil and Sun-Dried Tomato Soup / 177

Vegetable Soup with Chicken / 178

Vietnamese Pho Noodles with Beef / 179

Split Pea Soup with Bacon / 181

Cannellini Bean Soup with Kale / 182

Lentil Soup with Spinach / 183

Beef Barley Soup / 184

Black Bean Soup with Sausage / 185

Minestrone with Beef / 186

Meatball Soup with Potatoes / 187

Chicken Soup with Egg Noodles / 188

Cream of Tomato Soup / 189

Barley Soup with Chicken and Mushrooms / 190

Vegetable Soup with Turkey / 191

Beef Stroganoff Soup / 192

Classic French Onion Soup / 193

Mexican Soup with Pork / 194

Beer and Cheese Soup / 195

Chicken Soup with Corn / 196

Pumpkin Ginger Soup / 197

Broccoli Soup with Cheese / 198

Two-Potato Soup / 199

Creamy Potato Soup / 200

Butternut Squash Soup / 201

Pozole with Chicken / 202

Black Bean Soup with Sour Cream and Sherry / 203

Basil and Sun-Dried Tomato Soup

 Serves 6

2½ tablespoons unsalted butter

1 stalk celery, finely diced

1 medium carrot, peeled and finely diced

1 small sweet onion, peeled and diced

¼ cup chopped fresh basil

1 teaspoon chopped fresh marjoram

2 tablespoons unbleached all-purpose flour

2 (15-ounce) cans diced tomatoes

4 whole sun-dried tomatoes

1 teaspoon sugar

⅛ teaspoon baking soda

2½ cups vegetable or chicken broth

Salt and freshly ground black pepper, to taste

Serve this delicious soup with toasted cheese sandwiches for a modern-day twist on a classic comfort food.

1. Melt the butter in the pressure cooker over medium heat. Add the celery and carrot; sauté for 2 minutes. Stir in the onion, basil, and marjoram; sauté for 3 minutes or until the onion is soft. Add the flour; stir and cook for 2 minutes. Stir in the remaining ingredients.
2. Lock the lid into place. Bring to high pressure; maintain pressure for 8 minutes. Remove from the heat and quick-release the pressure. Remove the lid. Use an immersion blender to purée the soup. If you don't have an immersion blender, you can transfer the soup in batches to a blender or food processor, purée it, and then return it to the pot or a soup tureen. Taste for seasoning and add salt and pepper if needed.

No Sun-Dried Tomatoes?
If you can't find sun-dried tomatoes or they throw off your budget, substitute a 32-ounce can of whole stewed tomatoes, drained.

Vegetable Soup with Chicken

 Serves 4

 Total cost: $6.56

 Serving size: 1 cup

Calories per serving: 135

Fat: 3g

Carbohydrates: 9g

Protein: 23g

Sodium: 591mg

4 large carrots

2 stalks celery, finely diced

1 large sweet onion, peeled and diced

8 ounces fresh mushrooms, cleaned and sliced

1 tablespoon extra-virgin olive oil

1 teaspoon butter, melted

1 clove garlic, peeled and minced

4 cups chicken broth

4 medium potatoes, peeled and diced

1 tablespoon dried parsley

¼ teaspoon dried oregano

¼ teaspoon dried rosemary

2 strips orange zest

Sea salt and freshly ground black pepper, to taste

8 chicken thighs, skin removed

1 (10-ounce) package frozen green beans, thawed

1 (10-ounce) package frozen whole kernel corn, thawed

1 (10-ounce) package frozen baby peas, thawed

Feel free to substitute beef or turkey in this recipe.

1. Peel the carrots; dice 3 and grate 1. Add the grated carrot, celery, onion, mushrooms, oil, and butter to the pressure cooker. Stir to coat the vegetables in the oil and butter. Lock the lid into place. Bring to low pressure; maintain pressure for 1 minute. Quick-release the pressure and remove the lid.

2. Stir in the garlic. Add the broth, dice the remaining carrot. Add with the potatoes, parsley, oregano, rosemary, orange zest, salt, pepper, and chicken thighs. Lock the lid and bring to high pressure. Remove from the heat and allow pressure to release naturally for 5 minutes. Quick-release any remaining pressure and remove the lid.

3. Remove the thighs, cut the meat into bite-sized pieces, and return it to the pot. Remove and discard the orange zest. Return the uncovered pressure cooker to medium heat. Stir in the green beans, corn, and peas; cook for 5 minutes or until the vegetables are heated through. Taste for seasoning.

Creole-Style Serving Option

This soup can make another meal entirely if served over steamed white rice.

Vietnamese Pho Noodles with Beef

Serves 8

Total cost: $7.00

Serving size: 1 cup

Calories per serving: 339

Fat: 9g

Carbohydrates: 21g

Protein: 23g

Sodium: 620mg

1 (2-pound) chuck roast

3 medium yellow onions

1 (4") piece ginger

5 star anise

6 whole cloves

1 (3") cinnamon stick

¼ teaspoon sea salt

2 cups beef broth

Water, as needed to cover beef

1½ pounds small dried or fresh banh pho noodles

4 tablespoons fish sauce

1 tablespoon brown sugar

3 or 4 scallions, green part only, cut into thin rings

⅓ cup fresh cilantro, chopped

Freshly ground black pepper

Pho is a type of noodle made of rice. Use chuck roast, as indicated, or flank steak cut into cubes or strips, or meatballs.

1. Trim the roast of any fat; cut the meat into bite-sized pieces and add to the pressure cooker. Peel and quarter 2 onions. Cut the ginger into 1" pieces. Add the onion and ginger to the pressure cooker along with the star anise, cloves, cinnamon stick, salt, broth, and enough water to cover the meat by about 1". Lock the lid into place and bring to low pressure; maintain pressure for 1 hour. Remove from the heat and allow pressure to release naturally.

2. About ½ hour before serving, peel the remaining onion; cut it into paper-thin slices and soak them in cold water. For dried rice noodles: Cover them with hot water and allow to soak for 15–20 minutes or until softened and opaque white; drain in colander. For fresh rice noodles: Untangle and place in a colander, then rinse briefly with cold water.

3. Remove the meat from the broth with a slotted spoon; shred the meat. Strain the broth through a fine strainer, discarding the spices and onion; return strained broth to the pressure cooker along with the shredded meat. Bring the meat and broth to a boil over medium-high heat. Stir the fish sauce and brown sugar into the broth. (The broth should taste slightly too strong because the noodles and other ingredients are not salted. Therefore, to test for seasoning, you may want to taste the broth and meat with some noodles.

Vietnamese Pho Noodles with Beef (continued)

If you desire a stronger, saltier flavor, add more fish sauce. Add more brown sugar to make the broth sweeter if desired. If the broth is already too salty, add some additional water to dilute it.)

4. Blanch the noodles in stages by adding as many noodles to a strainer as you can submerge in the boiling broth without causing the pressure cooker to boil over. The noodles will collapse and lose their stiffness in about 15–20 seconds. Pull strainer from the broth, letting the excess broth clinging to them drain back into cooker. Empty noodles into bowls, allowing each serving to fill about ⅓ of the bowl, and then ladle hot broth and beef over the noodles. Garnish with onion slices, scallions, and chopped cilantro, and finish with freshly ground black pepper.

The $7 a Meal Pressure Cooker Cookbook

Split Pea Soup with Bacon

 Serves 6

4 strips bacon, diced

1 large sweet onion, peeled and diced

2 large potatoes, peeled and diced

2 large carrots, peeled and sliced

1 cup dried green split peas, rinsed

4 cups chicken broth

1 smoked ham hock

1 (10-ounce) package frozen peas, thawed

Sea salt and freshly ground black pepper, to taste

A popular soup for lunch or dinner, this soup is great as an entrée or to lead off your meal.

1. Add the bacon to the pressure cooker. Fry it over medium heat until the bacon begins to render its fat. Add the onion; sauté for 3 minutes or until soft. Stir in the diced potatoes; sauté for 3 minutes. Add the carrots, split peas, broth, and ham hock. Lock the lid into place and bring to low pressure; maintain pressure for 15 minutes. Remove from the heat and allow pressure to release naturally.

2. Remove the lid. Use a slotted spoon to remove the ham hock; allow to cool until the meat can be removed from the bones. Taste the split peas. If they're not cooked through, lock the lid back into place and cook at low pressure for another 5 minutes; remove from the heat and quick-release the pressure. If the split peas are cooked through and tender, stir the ham removed from the hock into the soup. If desired, use an immersion blender to purée the soup.

3. Return the soup to medium heat and bring to a simmer. If desired, stir in the peas and cook until they're heated. Taste for seasoning and add salt and pepper if needed.

Cannellini Bean Soup with Kale

 Serves 6

 Total cost: $5.65

Serving size: 1 cup

Calories per serving: 269

Fat: 10g

Carbohydrates: 24g

Protein: 12g

Sodium: 632mg

1 pound kale

1 tablespoon extra-virgin olive oil

1 large yellow onion, peeled and thinly sliced

½ pound kielbasa, sliced

4 large potatoes, peeled and diced

4 cups chicken broth

2 (15-ounce) cans cannellini beans, rinsed and drained

Sea salt and freshly ground black pepper, to taste

If kale is not your favorite or you cannot find it at the store, substitute fresh spinach leaves.

1. Trim the large ribs from the kale. Slice it into thin strips. Put the kale strips into a bowl of cold water and soak for an hour; drain well.
2. Add the oil, onions, and kielbasa to the pressure cooker; stir to combine. Place over medium heat; sauté for 5 minutes or until the onions are soft. Add the potatoes, chicken broth, drained kale, and beans. Lock the lid into place and bring to low pressure; maintain pressure for 8 minutes. Remove from the heat and allow pressure to release naturally for 5 minutes. Quick-release any remaining pressure and remove the lid. Taste for seasoning and add salt and pepper to taste.

Leaner Soups

Leave out the kielbasa and add in 1 or 2 pieces of bacon to keep the flavor but cut back on the fat and calories. Remove the bacon before eating.

The $7 a Meal Pressure Cooker Cookbook

Lentil Soup with Spinach

 Serves 6

Total cost: $4.46

Serving size: 1 cup

Calories per serving: 254

Fat: 6g

Carbohydrates: 12g

Protein: 14g

Sodium: 473mg

1 tablespoon olive oil

1 celery stalk, diced

1 large carrot, peeled and diced

1 large yellow onion, peeled and diced

2 cloves of garlic, peeled and minced

1 cup dried brown lentils, rinsed and drained

5 cups chicken broth

3 cups baby spinach, washed and dried

Sea salt and freshly ground black pepper, to taste

¼ cup Parmesan cheese, grated

If you prefer your spinach leaves fresh and crispy, leave them out of the soup and enjoy as a side salad with a simple balsamic vinaigrette.

1. Bring the oil to temperature in the pressure cooker over medium heat. Add the celery and carrot; sauté for 2 minutes. Stir in the onion; sauté for 3 minutes or until the onion is transparent. Add the garlic; sauté for 30 seconds.
2. Stir in the lentils and broth. Lock the lid into place and bring to high pressure; maintain pressure for 8 minutes. Remove from the heat and allow pressure to release naturally. Remove the lid and stir the spinach into the soup if using. Return the pressure cooker to medium heat; cook until the spinach is wilted. Taste for seasoning and season with salt and pepper, to taste. Serve in bowls, topping each one with 1 tablespoon of grated Parmesan cheese.

Great Additions to Lentil Soup

Lentil soup is a great base for adding other flavorful ingredients, such as ground sausage, diced chicken, or cubed firm tofu.

Beef Barley Soup

Serves 4

$ Total cost: $6.24

Serving size: 1 cup

Calories per serving: 322

Fat: 12g

Carbohydrates: 29g

Protein: 19g

Sodium: 461mg

2 leeks, white part only

¾ pound beef chuck, quartered

⅓ cup pearl barley

1 large carrot, peeled and diced

1 stalk celery, thinly sliced

2 medium potatoes, peeled and diced

6 cups water

Sea salt and freshly ground black pepper, to taste

Barley is a whole grain that is very good for you. It is filled with fiber and protein and has a nutty flavor when cooked. This recipe is great as an entrée soup, as it is very filling.

1. Dice the white part of the leeks; rinse well and drain. Add the leeks to the pressure cooker along with the beef, barley, carrot, celery, potatoes, water, salt, and pepper. Lock the lid into place and bring to high pressure; maintain pressure for 9 minutes.

2. Remove from the heat and quick-release the pressure. Remove the lid. Taste for seasoning and add additional salt and pepper if needed. Transfer a serving of beef to each of four bowls and ladle the soup over the meat. Garnish with parsley if desired.

Other Delicious Proteins to Try

Pork loin, lamb chops, and chicken are equally delicious proteins hearty enough to stand up to the bold flavor and texture of barley.

Black Bean Soup with Sausage

 Serves 6

½ pound bacon, chopped

1 green bell pepper, seeded and diced

1 large yellow onion, peeled and diced

8 ounces smoked sausage

3 cloves garlic, peeled and minced

2 teaspoons paprika

½ teaspoon ground cumin

½ teaspoon chili powder

¼ teaspoon coriander

6 cups chicken broth or water

1 smoked ham hock

1 pound dried black beans, soaked overnight, rinsed and drained

⅛ teaspoon cayenne pepper

½ cup dry sherry

1 tablespoon red wine vinegar

Sea salt and freshly ground black pepper, to taste

When serving, add a dollop of sour cream and some chopped green onion for the perfect finish.

1. Add bacon to the pressure cooker and fry over medium-high heat until the bacon begins to render its fat. Reduce the heat to medium and add the green pepper; sauté for 3 minutes. Stir in the onion. Slice or dice the smoked sausage and stir into the onion; sauté for 3 minutes or until the onion is tender. Stir in the garlic along with the paprika, cumin, chili powder, coriander, broth or water, ham hock, and beans. Lock the lid and bring to high pressure; maintain pressure for 30 minutes. Remove from the heat and allow pressure to release naturally, leaving the lid in place for at least 20 minutes. Remove the lid.

2. Remove the ham hock and take the meat off of the bones; return meat to the pot. Use a potato masher or immersion blender to partially purée the soup. Return the uncovered pan to medium heat and bring to a simmer. Stir in the cayenne pepper, sherry, and vinegar. Simmer for 20 minutes. Taste for seasoning; adjust the herbs as desired.

Minestrone with Beef

Serves 8

4 strips bacon, diced

1 large onion, peeled and diced

2 cloves garlic, peeled and minced

2 large carrots, peeled and diced

½ head cabbage, cored and rough chopped

2 stalks celery, diced

2 (15-ounce) cans diced tomatoes

¼ teaspoon dried rosemary

1 teaspoon dried parsley

¼ teaspoon dried oregano

4½ cups chicken broth

1 (1-pound) beef shank

½ cup elbow macaroni

Sea salt and freshly ground black pepper, to taste

½ cup grated Parmesan cheese

Enjoy this minestrone with a light salad of mixed greens and a few diced tomatoes with a simple vinaigrette.

1. Add the bacon to the pressure cooker. Fry over medium heat until it renders its fat. Add the onion and sauté until the onion is soft. Stir in the garlic, carrots, cabbage, celery, undrained tomatoes, rosemary, parsley, oregano, and chicken broth. Add the beef shank and push it down into the vegetables and liquid.

2. Lock the lid and bring to low pressure; maintain pressure for 15 minutes. Remove from the heat and quick-release the pressure.

3. Remove the beef shank. When it's cool enough to handle, remove the meat from the bone, cut it into bite-sized pieces, and return it to the pan. Stir in the macaroni.

4. Lock the lid into place and bring to low pressure; maintain pressure for 7 minutes. Remove from the heat and quick-release the pressure. Remove the lid.

5. Taste for seasoning and add salt, pepper, and additional herbs if needed. Serve in bowls topped with the grated Parmesan cheese.

To Make a Vegetarian Minestrone

Leave out the bacon and beef and add a little rice or potatoes to make this a vegetarian-friendly dish with the heartiness of protein.

The $7 a Meal Pressure Cooker Cookbook

Meatball Soup with Potatoes

Serves 6

Total cost: $6.96
Serving size: 1 cup
Calories per serving: 237
Fat: 4g
Carbohydrates: 32g
Protein: 27g
Sodium: 506mg

1 pound lean ground beef

¼ pound ground pork

1 small onion, peeled and minced

1 clove garlic, peeled and minced

6 tablespoons uncooked converted long-grain white rice

1 tablespoon dried parsley

1 teaspoon dried oregano

Sea salt and freshly ground black pepper, to taste

2 large eggs, divided

6 cups chicken or vegetable broth, or water, divided

1 medium onion, peeled and chopped

1 cup baby carrots, each sliced into thirds

2 large potatoes, peeled and cut into cubes

1 stalk celery, finely chopped

This Mediterranean-style soup is perfect as an entrée for lunch or dinner. If you are pressed for time, buy premade meatballs, which are available at affordable prices in your grocer's freezer section. Thaw before adding.

1. In a large bowl, mix the meat, onion, garlic, rice, parsley, oregano, salt, pepper, and 1 of the eggs. Shape into small meatballs and set aside.
2. Add 2 cups of broth or water to the pressure cooker. Add the meatballs, onion, carrots, potatoes, and celery, and then pour in the remaining broth or water to cover the meatballs and vegetables. Lock the lid into place and bring to low pressure; maintain pressure for 10 minutes. Remove from the heat and allow pressure to release naturally. Remove the lid. Taste for seasoning and adjust if necessary and serve.

Chicken Soup with Egg Noodles

Serves 8

$ Total cost: $6.57

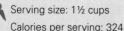
Serving size: 1½ cups

Calories per serving: 324

Fat: 14g

Carbohydrates: 26g

Protein: 24g

Sodium: 577mg

1 tablespoon butter

1 tablespoon olive oil

6 medium carrots, peeled and sliced

3 stalks celery, diced

1 large sweet onion, peeled and diced

4 pounds bone-in chicken thighs and breasts

½ teaspoon sea or kosher salt

1 teaspoon dried parsley

¼ teaspoon dried thyme

2 cups chicken broth

4 cups water

2 cups medium egg noodles

1 cup frozen baby peas, thawed

Make in batches and freeze in individual portions for quick, easy meals anytime.

1. Melt the butter and bring to temperature with the oil in the pressure cooker over medium heat. Add the carrots and celery; sauté for 2 minutes. Add the onion; sauté for 3 minutes or until the onion is soft. Add the chicken, salt, parsley, thyme, and chicken broth. Lock the lid into place and bring to low temperature; maintain pressure for 20 minutes. Remove from the heat and quick-release the pressure. Remove the lid.

2. Use tongs or a slotted spoon to transfer the chicken pieces to a cutting board. Remove and discard the skin. Once the chicken is cool enough to handle, remove the meat from the bones; shred the meat or cut it into bite-sized pieces. Return the chicken to the pressure cooker.

3. Return the pressure cooker to medium heat. Stir in the water; bring to a boil. Add the egg noodles and cook according to package directions. Stir in the thawed peas. Taste for seasoning.

Other Great Noodles to Try

If you don't have egg noodles, use fettuccini or even farfalle, or bowtie, pasta for your chicken noodle soup. Or, you can skip the noodles altogether and instead add ½ cup uncooked rice.

The $7 a Meal Pressure Cooker Cookbook

Cream of Tomato Soup

 Serves 4

Total cost: $6.74
Serving size: 1 cup
Calories per serving: 261
Fat: 18g
Carbohydrates: 18g
Protein: 8g
Sodium: 397mg

8 medium fresh tomatoes

¼ teaspoon sea salt

1 cup water

½ teaspoon baking soda

2 cups whole milk

¼ cup sour cream

Freshly ground black pepper, to taste

Creamed soups can sound intimidating to make, but this recipe proves just how easy it is. Add a few diced onions for extra flavor, if desired.

1. Wash, peel, seed, and dice the tomatoes. Add them and any tomato juice you can retain to the pressure cooker. Stir in the salt and water. Lock the lid into place. Place the pressure cooker over medium heat and bring to low pressure; maintain pressure for 2 minutes. Quick-release the pressure and remove the lid.
2. Stir the baking soda into the tomato mixture. Once it's stopped bubbling and foaming, stir in the milk. Cook and stir for several minutes or until the soup is brought to temperature. Taste for seasoning and add additional salt if needed, and pepper, to taste. Top with a tablespoon or so of sour cream when serving.

Serving Suggestions
Top this soup with some freshly chopped basil leaves, and serve with half of a grilled cheese sandwich. Or, for added flair and protein, add some diced cooked lobster meat when your budget allows.

Barley Soup with Chicken and Mushrooms

Serves 6

 Total cost: $6.64

 Serving size: 1 cup

Calories per serving: 374

Fat: 10g

Carbohydrates: 31g

Protein: 26g

Sodium: 498mg

2 tablespoons butter

1 tablespoon olive or vegetable oil

2 stalks celery, diced

1 large carrot, peeled and diced

1 large sweet onion, peeled, halved, and sliced

2 cloves garlic, peeled and minced

2 cups diced cooked chicken breasts

8 ounces cremini mushrooms, cleaned and sliced

1 bay leaf

½ cup pearl barley

6 cups water

Sea salt and freshly ground black pepper, to taste

This protein-packed soup is rich in fiber and, best of all, equally packed full of flavor. Chicken is used here, but you can add turkey breast, beef, or enjoy without the chicken as a filling vegetarian meal.

1. Melt the butter and bring the oil to temperature in the pressure cooker over medium heat. Add the celery and carrot; sauté for 2 minutes. Add the onion and sauté for 3 minutes or until the onion is soft and transparent. Stir in the garlic mushrooms; sauté for 5 minutes or until the mushrooms release their moisture and the onion begins to turn golden.
2. Stir in the chicken, bay leaf, barley, and water. Lock the lid into place and bring to high pressure; maintain pressure for 20 minutes. Remove from the heat and allow pressure to release naturally.
3. Remove the lid. Remove and discard the bay leaf. Taste for seasoning and add salt and pepper if needed. Serve.

Vegetable Soup with Turkey

 Serves 6

 Total cost: $6.94
Serving size: 1 cup
Calories per serving: 253
Fat: 6g
Carbohydrates: 19g
Protein: 25g
Sodium: 643mg

1 tablespoon extra-virgin olive oil

1 clove garlic, peeled and minced

2 (15-ounce) cans diced tomatoes

4 medium potatoes, peeled and cut into quarters

4 large carrots, peeled and sliced

1 large onion, chopped

2 stalks celery, coarsely chopped

¼ cup sliced cremini mushrooms

1 teaspoon chopped fresh oregano

1 teaspoon chopped fresh rosemary

1 bay leaf

Finely grated zest ½ an orange

Sea salt and freshly ground black pepper, to taste

¾ pound ground turkey or 1½ cups diced cooked turkey breasts

1 (10-ounce) package frozen green beans, thawed

1 (10-ounce) package frozen whole kernel corn, thawed

1 (10-ounce) package frozen baby peas, thawed

Turkey Pot Pie

Create an easy turkey pot pie by making this recipe with 4 cups of chicken broth instead of the tomatoes and add a little cornstarch mixed with water, about ½ table-spoon each mixed together. Serve over ½ a biscuit or place into a ramekin, cover top of ramekin with puff pas-try, and bake about 12 to 15 minutes until golden.

Make ahead and freeze for a quick meal.

1. Bring the oil to temperature in the pressure cooker over medium heat. Add the garlic and sauté for 10 seconds. Stir in the tomatoes, potatoes, carrots, onions, celery, mush-rooms, oregano, rosemary, bay leaf, orange zest, salt, and pepper. Add the ground turkey or cooked diced turkey.

2. Lock the lid into place and bring to high pressure; maintain pressure for 12 minutes. Remove from the heat and allow the pressure to drop naturally for 10 minutes, and then use the quick-release method for your cooker to release the remaining pressure if needed. Stir in the green beans, corn, and peas; cook over medium heat for 5 minutes. Remove and discard the bay leaf. Taste for seasoning and add salt and pepper if needed.

Beef Stroganoff Soup

Serves 6

Total cost: $6.87

Serving size: 1 cup

Calories per serving: 325

Fat: 9g

Carbohydrates: 10g

Protein: 23g

Sodium: 478mg

¾ pound sirloin, cubed

1 yellow onion, diced

3 cloves garlic, minced

3 carrots, sliced ¼" thick

Sea salt and black pepper, to taste

½ teaspoon dried thyme

3 cups beef broth

2 cups water

½ cup sour cream

2 tablespoons plain flour

2 cups egg noodles

What better way to enjoy this comfort food classic than in a simple soup? For a lighter version of this meal, substitute chicken (which is still high in protein) instead of beef and use low-fat sour cream instead of high-fat regular sour cream.

1. Place beef, onions, garlic, carrots, salt, pepper, thyme, broth, and water all in pressure cooker. Latch lid securely and bring to low pressure and maintain for 8 minutes. Use quick-release method to release pressure.
2. Stir in sour cream, flour, and noodles. Resecure lid and bring to low pressure. Maintain pressure for 5 minutes. Release using quick-release method. Stir and serve.

Classic French Onion Soup

Serves 6

 Total cost: $6.15

 Serving size: 1 cup

Calories per serving: 327

Fat: 10g

Carbohydrates: 14g

Protein: 12g

Sodium: 467mg

1 tablespoon olive oil

5 yellow onions, chopped

4 cloves garlic, minced

1 teaspoon sugar

½ cup dry red wine

4 carrots, sliced

5 cups beef broth

Sea salt and black pepper, to taste

1 (3-ounce) package cream cheese, softened

1 cup shredded Swiss cheese

6 slices French bread, toasted

This soup serves the cheese on the bread. For a cheesier soup, add additional shredded Swiss to the soup when hot immediately out of the cooker.

1. Combine olive oil with onions, garlic, and sugar in pressure cooker and heat over medium heat. Stir until onions begin to become tender, about 5 minutes.
2. Add wine, carrots, stock, salt, and pepper. Latch lid securely and bring to low pressure. Maintain pressure for 7 minutes. Release pressure using natural-release method.
3. Meanwhile, combine cheeses in mixing bowl and spread over toasted French bread slices. Place under broiler until cheese melts.
4. Serve soup in bowls with additional cheese, if desired, and cheese bread.

Mexican Soup with Pork

 Serves 4

 Total cost: $5.49

Serving size: 1 cup

Calories per serving: 289

Fat: 7g

Carbohydrates: 9g

Protein: 21g

Sodium: 635mg

1 tablespoon canola oil

1 yellow onion, chopped

½ pound boneless pork chops, diced

1 (14-ounce) can diced tomatoes

½ teaspoon dried oregano

Sea salt and black pepper, to taste

Pinch crushed red pepper flakes

1½ cups water

1 cup enchilada sauce

1 cup chicken broth

This soup can easily be turned into tortilla soup by using diced or shredded chicken and finishing with baked tortilla strips when serving. If desired, top with grated Cheddar or mozzarella, or shredded jack cheese.

1. Heat oil in cooker over medium heat and add onion. Sauté until just tender, about 3 minutes. Add pork, tomatoes, oregano, salt, pepper, red pepper flakes, water, enchilada sauce, and broth. Stir. Latch lid securely.
2. Bring to low pressure. Maintain pressure for 12 minutes. Use natural-release method to release pressure. Serve with toppings such as sour cream, tortilla chips, and cilantro.

Beer and Cheese Soup

 Serves 6

 Total cost: $5.89

Serving size: 1 cup

Calories per serving: 298

Fat: 12g

Carbohydrates: 24g

Protein: 14g

Sodium: 598mg

1 yellow onion, chopped

2 carrots, diced

3 cloves garlic, minced

1 teaspoon dried thyme or ½ tablespoon chopped fresh thyme leaves

Sea salt and black pepper, to taste

1 (16-ounce) bottle beer

3 cups chicken broth

2 cups whole milk

2 cups shredded sharp Cheddar cheese

2 tablespoons cornstarch

¼ cup grated Parmesan cheese

Remember, the lighter the soup, the lighter the beer. The heavier the soup, the heavier the beer. This light cheese soup only needs a simple beer such as Coors or Budweiser.

1. Add onion, carrots, garlic, thyme, salt, pepper, beer, and chicken broth to cooker. Latch lid securely and bring to low pressure. Maintain pressure for 8 minutes. Use quick-release method to release pressure.
2. Add milk and stir. Separately, toss cheese with cornstarch and add to cooker. Latch lid securely. Bring to low pressure. Maintain pressure for 8 minutes. Use quick-release method to release pressure.
3. Serve with Parmesan cheese.

Add Some Protein

This soup will taste great with a little added chicken breast. Simply add cooked, diced chicken at the beginning with everything else.

Chicken Soup with Corn

Serves 6

Total cost: $6.92

Serving size: 1 cup

Calories per serving: 312

Fat: 11g

Carbohydrates: 12g

Protein: 19g

Sodium: 483mg

2 tablespoons butter

1 tablespoon canola oil

1 yellow onion, chopped

3 cloves garlic, minced

2 boneless, skinless chicken breasts, cubed

1 (10-ounce) can cream of chicken soup

2 cups chicken broth

3 cups water

1 tablespoon chopped fresh basil leaves

Sea salt and black pepper, to taste

1 cup frozen kernel corn

1 (15-ounce) can cream-style corn

1 cup shredded Swiss cheese

Roasted red bell pepper would also be fabulous in this recipe, along with some diced cremini mushrooms.

1. Melt butter and oil in cooker over medium heat and add onion and garlic. Cook until fragrant. Add remaining ingredients except cheese. Latch lid securely.
2. Bring to low pressure and maintain pressure for 12 minutes. Release pressure using natural-release method.
3. Stir in cheese and serve.

Corn Chowder

Turn this corn soup into a chicken corn chowder by adding a few diced peeled potatoes, diced celery, and diced roasted red bell peppers.

The $7 a Meal Pressure Cooker Cookbook

Pumpkin Ginger Soup

 Serves 4

1 (15-ounce) can solid packed pumpkin

1 yellow onion, chopped

2 cloves garlic, minced

1 teaspoon freshly minced ginger root

4 cups chicken broth

1 cup water

Sea salt and black pepper, to taste

½ cup whole milk

½ cup sour cream

2 tablespoons cornstarch

Traditionally thought of as a fall soup, enjoy this soup anytime by using canned pumpkin and ground ginger.

1. Place pumpkin, onions, garlic, and ginger in cooker. Mash together using a potato masher. Stir in broth and water. Add a little salt and pepper.
2. Separately, whisk together milk, sour cream, and cornstarch. Pour into cooker with other ingredients.
3. Latch lid securely. Bring to low pressure. Maintain pressure for 15 minutes. Use natural-release method to release pressure.
4. Stir and serve immediately.

Don't Want Pumpkin?
Make butternut or acorn squash soup by using fresh butternut or fresh acorn squash, with the skin removed and squash cut into 1-inch cubes. Follow the same instructions. Add a small pinch of ground cinnamon for extra flavor.

Broccoli Soup with Cheese

 Serves 6

1 tablespoon olive oil

1 tablespoon butter

1 yellow onion, chopped

2 cloves garlic, chopped

Sea salt and pepper, to taste

1 tablespoon chopped fresh basil

1 (10-ounce) package frozen cut broccoli, thawed

3 cups chicken broth

1 (10-ounce) can condensed Cheddar cheese soup

2 cups low-fat milk

1 (3-ounce) package cream cheese, cubed

1 cup diced American cheese

Asparagus is another great vegetable for this recipe. In addition, substitute your favorite cheese, such as white Cheddar or Gruyère. Actually, it's so delicious as it is, you may not want to change anything!

1. Add olive oil and butter to cooker and heat over medium heat. Add onions and garlic. Cook for about 4 minutes.
2. Add salt and pepper, basil, broccoli, broth, soup, and milk. Using an immersion blender, blend until smooth.
3. Add cream and American cheeses. Latch lid securely and bring to low pressure. Maintain low pressure for 10 minutes. Use natural-release method to release pressure.
4. Stir and serve immediately.

Two-Potato Soup

 Serves 6

$ Total cost: $5.74

Serving size: 1 cup

Calories per serving: 318

Fat: 10g

Carbohydrates: 22g

Protein: 11g

Sodium: 531mg

1 sweet potato, peeled and cubed

5 russet baking potatoes, peeled and cubed

1 yellow onion, chopped

1 carrot, peeled and chopped

3 cups vegetable or chicken broth

4 cups water

Sea salt and black pepper, to taste

3 tablespoons butter, unsalted

1 (12-ounce) can evaporated milk

The sweetness comes from naturally sweet sweet potatoes with a natural starchiness from the russet potatoes.

1. Combine all ingredients in the pressure cooker. Latch lid securely and bring to high pressure. Maintain pressure for 10 minutes. Use quick-release method to release pressure.
2. Stir in butter and milk and use immersion blender to purée soup. Latch lid and return to low pressure. Maintain low pressure for 3 minutes. Use quick-release method to release pressure. Serve immediately.

Pure Potato

If you are a potato purist, add an additional baking potato and skip the carrots. A great way to add more flavor to this simple potato soup is to add both roasted garlic and fresh herbs such as basil or freshly chopped chives.

Creamy Potato Soup

 Serves 6

$ Total cost: $4.12

Serving size: 1 cup

Calories per serving: 328

Fat: 9g

Carbohydrates: 22g

Protein: 9g

Sodium: 531mg

2 tablespoons butter

1 yellow onion, finely sliced

3 potatoes, peeled and diced

2 cups chicken broth

2 cups water

2 tablespoons cornstarch

2 cups whole milk

Sea salt and white pepper, to taste

½ cup heavy cream

2 tablespoons minced fresh Italian flat-leaf parsley

Whole milk and heavy cream give this potato soup a rich creaminess. Fresh parsley added at the end gives a crisp finish to the creamy texture.

1. Melt butter in cooker and add onions. Cook about 2 minutes. Add potatoes, broth, and water and latch lid securely. Bring to high pressure and maintain pressure for 9 minutes. Use quick-release method to release pressure.
2. Purée soup using immersion blender. Separately, in small bowl combine cornstarch with milk and mix well. Add to potato mixture and stir in well with salt, pepper, and cream.
3. Resecure lid and bring to low pressure. Maintain low pressure for 5 minutes. Use quick-release method to release pressure.
4. Stir to combine and serve immediately with parsley.

White Pepper

White pepper is more spicy than cracked black pepper and should be used a little at a time. It is often used in "white" dishes like this one so as not to disrupt the white, creamy look with black pepper specks.

Butternut Squash Soup

 Serves 4

$ Total cost: $6.99

Serving size: 1 cup

Calories per serving: 318

Fat: 6g

Carbohydrates: 17g

Protein: 12g

Sodium: 256mg

4 cups chicken broth

1 yellow onion, chopped

3 cloves garlic, minced

2 slices sourdough bread, cut into cubes

2 Granny Smith apples, peeled, cored, and chopped

½ butternut squash, seeded, peeled, and cubed

1 tablespoon chopped fresh rosemary

Sea salt and black pepper, to taste

1 egg

1 cup buttermilk

Optional: pinch of nutmeg

Optional: pinch of cinnamon

Butternut squash is rich in flavor, golden in color, and makes this soup one you will be craving year round.

1. In cooker, combine broth, onion, garlic, bread, apples, and squash. Latch lid securely and bring to high pressure. Maintain high pressure for 10 minutes. Use quick-release method to release pressure.
2. Use an immersion blender to purée the soup. Add the rosemary, salt, and pepper. Separately, combine egg and buttermilk and beat together. Add all to the squash mixture and stir in well. (At this point, add nutmeg and cinnamon, if using.)
3. Latch lid securely and return to low pressure. Maintain pressure for 5 minutes. Use the quick-release method to release pressure. Stir soup and serve immediately.

Go Easy on the Nutmeg and Cinnamon

Nutmeg and cinnamon are strong, flavorful spices so use sparingly—too much can definitely ruin a good thing.

Pozole with Chicken

 Serves 4

¾-pound boneless, skinless chicken breast, cubed

1 yellow onion, chopped

2 cloves garlic, minced

1 (15-ounce) can hominy, drained

4 cups water

1 (4-ounce) can diced green chilies, undrained

1 tablespoon chili powder

1 teaspoon cumin

Sea salt, to taste

½ teaspoon dried oregano

This dish uses hearty hominy as the base, with protein-filled chicken as an added bonus alongside spices such as green chilies and cumin to round out your taste experience. This dish is also great with pork or turkey, or you could leave it without a formal protein.

1. Place chicken in cooker along with all remaining ingredients. Latch lid securely and bring to low pressure. Maintain pressure for 12 minutes.
2. Release pressure using natural-release method. Remove lid and stir. Serve hot.

Black Bean Soup with Sour Cream and Sherry

 Serves 6

1 pound dried black beans

1 yellow onion, chopped

2 cloves garlic, minced

2 stalks celery, minced

1 jalapeño pepper, seeded and minced

1 tablespoon chili powder

Sea salt and black pepper, to taste

Pinch cayenne pepper

4 cups water

4 cups chicken broth

2 tablespoons masa harina

⅓ cup water

Sour cream, for serving

Sherry wine, for serving

A popular soup in the Caribbean, finish with a dollop of sour cream and a hint of sherry for the perfect soup for lunch or dinner.

1. Soak beans overnight in water. Drain and discard water. Place all ingredients, including beans, in cooker except for masa harina, ⅓ cup water, sour cream, and sherry. Latch lid securely and bring to high pressure. Maintain pressure for 15 minutes.
2. Release using the natural-release method. Separately, mix masa harina with water and blend well. Stir into soup, mixing well. Resecure lid and return to high pressure. Maintain pressure for 7 minutes. Use quick-release method. Stir soup and serve with sour cream and a splash of sherry wine.

Masa Harina

Masa harina is made from corn kernels soaked and cooked in lime juice. Masa, or corn, is ground into a flour, which is used to make tortillas and is used in other breads and foods, as here.

CHAPTER 9

STEWS AND CHOWDERS

Quick Beef Stew with Mixed Vegetables / 205
Basic Chicken Stew / 206
Vegetable Beef Stew / 207
African-Style Beef Stew / 208
Chicken 'n' Dumplings / 209
Mexican Jalapeño Stew with Chicken / 210
White Bean Soup with Chicken and Chilies / 212
Potato Chowder with Chicken and Fennel / 213
Fish Chowder with Potatoes and Leeks / 214
Roasted Red Pepper and Corn Chowder / 215
Stew of Lima Beans, Okra, and Chicken / 216
Star of Texas Stew / 217
Jalapeño Chicken Chili / 218
Beer-Brewed Chicken Stew / 219
Beef Stew with Mushrooms and Dumplings / 221
New England Clam Chowder / 222
Manhattan Clam Chowder / 223

Quick Beef Stew with Mixed Vegetables

 Serves 8

2 cups cooked roast beef, cut into bite-sized pieces

1 (10.5-ounce) can condensed tomato soup

1 (10.5-ounce) can condensed French onion soup

1 tablespoon Worcestershire sauce

2 cups water

3 (10-ounce) boxes frozen mixed vegetables, thawed

1 tablespoon butter

1 tablespoon all-purpose flour

Sea salt and freshly ground black pepper, to taste

Leftover beef never tasted this good! Use this same recipe for leftover chicken or turkey. It's a great way to save both time and money. Throw in a few fresh frozen mixed vegetables and you have a delicious meal in minutes.

1. Add the roast beef, soups, Worcestershire sauce, water, and vegetables to the pressure cooker.
2. Lock the lid into place and bring to low pressure; maintain pressure for 3 minutes. Remove from heat, quick-release the pressure, and remove the lid.
3. In a small bowl, mix the butter into the flour to make a paste. Ladle about ½ cup of the soup broth into the bowl and whisk into the paste, then pour it into the stew.
4. Place the uncovered pressure cooker over medium-high heat and bring the stew to a boil; boil for 2 minutes, stirring occasionally.
5. Reduce the heat and simmer for an additional 2 minutes or until the stew is thickened. Taste for seasoning, and add salt and pepper if needed.

Basic Chicken Stew

 Serves 4

1 cup baby carrots, cut in half

1 stalk celery, finely diced

1 large onion, peeled and diced

4 large potatoes, peeled and diced

1 teaspoon Italian seasoning

2 tablespoons extra-virgin olive oil

2 cups chicken broth

4 bone-in chicken breast halves

Sea salt and freshly ground black pepper, to taste

Tired of the extra carbs in your soups and stews? Leave out the potatoes and add in fresh broccoli florets or protein- and fiber-filled beans, such as light and dark red kidney beans or northern beans.

1. Put the carrots, celery, onions, potatoes, seasoning blend, and oil in a pressure cooker. Pour the broth in the pot.
2. Remove and discard the skin from the chicken, then nestle the chicken pieces meat-side down on top of the vegetables.
3. Lock the pressure cooker lid and bring to high pressure; maintain pressure for 10 minutes. Remove from the heat and quick-release the pressure. Remove the lid.
4. Stir the stew. Taste for seasoning and add salt and pepper or more seasoning blend, to taste.
5. Put 1 chicken breast in each of 4 large soup bowls and ladle some carrots, potatoes, and broth over each one.

Serving Suggestions
This is a terrific recipe and can be served with baked tortilla strips, over rice, or as a pot pie.

The $7 a Meal Pressure Cooker Cookbook

Vegetable Beef Stew

Serves 4

Total cost: $6.94

Serving size: 1 cup

Calories per serving: 225

Fat: 8g

Carbohydrates: 8g

Protein: 15g

Sodium: 398mg

4 large carrots

2 stalks celery, finely diced

1 large yellow onion, peeled and diced

1 tablespoon extra-virgin olive oil

1 clove garlic, peeled and minced

4 cups beef broth

1 tablespoon chopped fresh Italian flat-leaf parsley

¼ teaspoon dried oregano

¼ teaspoon dried rosemary

1 teaspoon ground mustard

1 bay leaf

Sea salt and freshly ground black pepper, to taste

1 (1-pound) chuck roast

1 (10-ounce) package frozen green beans, thawed

1 (10-ounce) package frozen whole kernel corn, thawed

1 15-ounce jar roasted red bell peppers, drained and diced

For a purely vegetarian dish, replace beef broth with vegetable broth and replace beef with quartered potatoes.

1. Peel and dice the carrots. Add carrots, celery, onion, and oil to the pressure cooker. Stir to coat the vegetables in the oil. Lock the lid into place. Bring to low pressure; maintain pressure for 1 minute. Quick-release the pressure and remove the lid.

2. Stir in the garlic. Add the broth, potatoes, parsley, oregano, rosemary, mustard, bay leaf, salt, and pepper. Trim the roast of any fat and cut the meat into bite-sized pieces; add to the pressure cooker and stir into the vegetables. Lock the lid into place and bring to high pressure; maintain pressure for 15 minutes. Quick-release the pressure and remove the lid.

3. Remove and discard the bay leaf. Stir in the green beans, corn, and diced bell peppers; cook for 5 minutes or until the vegetables are heated through. Taste for seasoning and add additional salt, pepper, and herbs if needed.

Winter Additions

This hearty stew is great in the wintertime if served over rice, couscous, or even penne pasta.

African-Style Beef Stew

 Serves 6

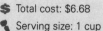
Total cost: $6.68

Serving size: 1 cup

Calories per serving: 330

Fat: 14g

Carbohydrates: 16g

Protein: 23g

Sodium: 398mg

1 tablespoon olive oil

1 pound boneless beef chuck

1 large onion, peeled and diced

2 cloves garlic, peeled and minced

1 cup dried apricots

⅓ cup raisins

⅓ cup blanched whole almonds

1 tablespoon fresh ginger, minced

½ teaspoon ground cinnamon

¾ cup red wine

¼ cup fresh orange juice

⅓ cup fresh mint leaves, packed

Sea salt and freshly ground pepper, to taste

Cinnamon, orange juice, dried apricots, and raisins are just a few of the ingredients that will make this dish one of your favorites.

1. Bring the oil to temperature in the pressure cooker over medium-high heat. Trim the beef of any fat and cut the meat into bite-sized pieces.
2. Brown the beef in 4 batches for 5 minutes each. Set aside browned meat and keep warm.
3. Reduce heat to medium. Add the onion and sauté for 3 minutes or until the onion begins to soften. Add the garlic; sauté for 30 seconds. Stir in the beef.
4. Quarter the dried apricots. Add to the pressure cooker along with the raisins, almonds, ginger, cinnamon, wine, orange juice, and mint leaves.
5. Lock the lid into place and bring to high pressure; maintain pressure for 20 minutes. Remove from the heat and allow pressure to release naturally.
6. Remove the lid and taste for seasoning. Add salt and pepper, to taste.

Chicken 'n' Dumplings

 Serves 4

$ Total cost: $6.87

Serving size: 1½ cups

Calories per serving: 469

Fat: 21g

Carbohydrates: 29g

Protein: 18g

Sodium: 639mg

¼ cup unbleached all-purpose flour

½ teaspoon sea salt

¼ teaspoon freshly ground black pepper

8 bone-in chicken thighs, skin removed

2 tablespoons unsalted butter

2 stalks celery, finely diced

1 large onion, peeled and diced

1 teaspoon dried thyme

12 ounces baby carrots, cut in half

2½ cups chicken broth

½ cup dry white wine or water

2 teaspoons chopped fresh Italian flat-leaf parsley

1 recipe dumplings

The chicken in this comfort food favorite cooks in about 10 minutes.

1. Add the flour, salt, and pepper to a large zip-closure plastic bag; shake to mix. Trim the chicken of any fat and add to the bag. Seal and shake to coat the chicken.

2. Melt the butter in the pressure cooker over medium-high heat. When the butter bubbles, add 4 chicken thighs; brown for 3 minutes on each side. Transfer chicken to a platter. Add the remaining thighs and brown them too; place on platter.

3. Add the celery; sauté for 2 minutes. Add the onion and thyme; sauté for 3 minutes or until the onion is softened.

4. Stir in the carrots, broth, wine or water, parsley, and bay leaf. Return the browned chicken thighs to the pressure cooker.

5. Lock the lid into place and bring to high pressure; maintain pressure for 10 minutes. Quick-release the pressure and remove the lid.

6. Leave the pressure cooker on the heat, adjusting it to maintain a simmer. Drop heaping teaspoons of the dumpling batter into the simmering stew.

7. Cover loosely and cook for 10 to 15 minutes or until the dumplings are puffy and cooked through. Serve.

8. For the dumplings: Mix 2 cups of unbleached all-purpose flour, 1 tablespoon baking powder, and ½ teaspoon salt to a mixing bowl. Stir to combine, then use a pastry blender or two forks to cut in 5 tablespoons of unsalted butter. Stir in 1 large beaten egg and ¾ cup of buttermilk until the mixture comes together. Drop by heaping teaspoons into simmering broth as instructed in Step 6 and cook until dumplings float to the top.

Mexican Jalapeño Stew with Chicken

Serves 8

1 cup dried pinto beans

8 cups water, divided

2 teaspoons vegetable oil

1 tablespoon olive oil

1 medium onion, peeled and diced

1 large carrot, peeled and diced

2 medium red bell peppers, seeded and diced

2 jalapeño peppers, seeded and diced

4 cloves garlic, peeled and minced

4 (4-ounce) cans chopped green chili peppers

1 chipotle pepper, seeded and diced

2 pounds mixed chicken pieces, skin removed

4 cups chicken broth

2 tablespoons butter

2 tablespoons unbleached all-purpose flour

Sea salt and freshly ground black pepper, to taste

For tortilla soup, add crispy tortilla strips and serve with grated Cheddar cheese, sour cream, and a little hot sauce.

1. Rinse the beans; soak them in 3 cups of the water overnight. Drain and add the beans, the remaining 5 cups of water, and vegetable oil to the pressure cooker.
2. Lock the lid into place and bring to high pressure; maintain pressure for 15 minutes. Remove from the heat and allow pressure to release naturally. Strain the beans; set aside. Wash and dry the pressure cooker.
3. Bring the olive oil to temperature in the pressure cooker over medium-high heat. Add the onion; sauté for 3 minutes. Stir in the carrot; sauté for 3 minutes.

Mexican Jalapeño Stew with Chicken (continued)

4. Stir in the red bell and jalapeño peppers; sauté for 5 minutes or until all vegetables are soft.
5. Add the garlic, canned peppers, chipotle peppers, chicken pieces, and chicken broth.
6. Lock the lid into place and bring to high pressure; maintain pressure for 12 minutes. Quick-release the pressure. Remove the chicken pieces to a bowl.
7. When the chicken is cool enough to handle, remove the meat from the bones, cut or tear it into bite-sized pieces, and return the meat to the pressure cooker. Stir in the beans.
8. Bring the chili to a boil. Blend the butter together with the flour to make a paste, and then whisk it into the chili.
9. Boil for 1 minute and then reduce heat to maintain a simmer for about 5 minutes or until the chili is thickened. Taste for seasoning and add salt and pepper if desired.

White Bean Soup with Chicken and Chilies

 Serves 8

 Total cost: $6.58

Serving size: 1 cup

Calories per serving: 436

Fat: 18g

Carbohydrates: 32g

Protein: 25g

Sodium: 638mg

1 tablespoon olive oil

1 large white onion, peeled and diced

4 cloves garlic, peeled and minced

2 pounds boneless, skinless chicken breasts

2 teaspoons ground cumin

2 teaspoons dried oregano

¼ teaspoon ground cayenne pepper

1 (4-ounce) can chopped green chili peppers

2 (14-ounce) cans chicken broth, divided

2 (16-ounce) cans white beans

Hot sauce, to taste

Sea salt and freshly ground white or black pepper, to taste

Feel free to use other types of beans, like black beans or navy beans. If desired, serve with chips or over steamed rice.

1. Bring the oil to temperature in the pressure cooker over medium-high heat. Add the onion; sauté for 3 minutes or until the onion is soft.
2. Stir in the garlic; sauté for 30 seconds. Cut the chicken into bite-sized pieces and add to the pressure cooker along with the cumin, oregano, and cayenne pepper; stir-fry for 1 minute.
3. Stir in the undrained can of green chilies and 1 can of the chicken broth. Lock the lid into place and bring to high pressure; maintain pressure for 6 minutes. Quick-release the pressure and remove the lid.
4. Stir in the remaining can of chicken broth and the undrained cans of beans. Bring to a simmer and allow to cook until the beans are brought to temperature. Taste for seasoning and add hot sauce, salt, and pepper to taste. Serve.

Cooked Chicken

For a quick, easy meal anytime, pressure-cook a whole chicken and then freeze light meat and dark meat separately. Then, thaw and throw into any pressure cooker recipe for a super-fast family meal.

Potato Chowder with Chicken and Fennel

 Serves 4

💲 Total cost: $6.89

Serving size: 1 cup

Calories per serving: 370

Fat: 9g

Carbohydrates: 20g

Protein: 23g

Sodium: 320mg

4 teaspoons freshly squeezed lemon juice, divided

1 pound boneless, skinless chicken breasts, diced

1 tablespoon olive oil

1 large leek

1 fennel bulb

4 medium Yukon Gold potatoes, peeled and diced

1 teaspoon sea salt

4 cups water

1 bay leaf

If desired, switch out the chicken for an equal amount of salmon fillet, beef, or even shrimp.

1. Sprinkle ½ teaspoon of lemon juice over each side of the chicken breasts. Bring the oil to temperature in the pressure cooker over medium heat.
2. Trim, thinly slice, wash, and drain the leek.
3. Add the leek to the pressure cooker; sauté for 2 minutes or until it begins to wilt.
4. Quarter the fennel bulb, then thinly slice the quarters. Add the fennel and diced potatoes to the pressure cooker along with the salt, water, and bay leaf.
5. Lock the lid into place and bring to high pressure; maintain for 7 minutes. Quick-release the pressure and remove the lid.
6. Place the chicken breasts in the pressure cooker. Lock the lid back into place and bring to high pressure; maintain pressure for 1 minute. Remove from heat and allow pressure to release naturally.
7. Remove and discard the bay leaf. Use a slotted spoon to lift each chicken breast into a bowl or, if you wish to serve the chicken separate from the chowder, to a serving plate.
8. Ladle the chowder into bowls.

Can't Find Fennel and Leeks?

Fennel and leeks are sometimes expensive and can be a little hard to find. If this happens to you, just substitute other fresh vegetables like broccoli and carrots.

Fish Chowder with Potatoes and Leeks

Serves 4

$ Total cost: $6.99

Serving size: 1 cup

Calories per serving: 324

Fat: 11g

Carbohydrates: 26g

Protein: 27g

Sodium: 1057mg

2 tablespoons butter

2 large leeks

4 cups fish broth or clam juice

2 cups water

4 medium russet or Idaho baking potatoes, peeled and diced

1 bay leaf

Sea salt and freshly ground black pepper, to taste

1 pound cod or whitefish

½ teaspoon dried thyme

½ cup whole milk

If you are not a huge fan of fish chowder, turn this into Potato Leek Chowder by leaving out the fish and adding another potato!

1. Melt the butter in the pressure cooker over medium heat. Cut off the root ends of the leeks and discard any bruised outer leaves. Slice the leeks. Rinse in running water to remove any dirt; drain and dry. Add to the pressure cooker and sauté in the butter for 2 minutes. Stir in the broth, water, and potatoes. Add the bay leaf, salt, and pepper.
2. Lock the lid into place and bring to high pressure; maintain pressure for 4 minutes. Quick-release the pressure and remove the lid. Remove and discard the bay leaf.
3. Cut the fish into bite-sized pieces and add to the pressure cooker. Simmer for 3 minutes or until the fish is opaque and flakes easily. Stir in the thyme and cream.
4. Leave the pan on the heat, stirring occasionally, until the cream comes to temperature. Taste for seasoning; add additional salt and pepper if needed.

Fish Chowder Combos

Turn this into a seafood chowder by adding mussels, clams, and shrimp, about ¼ cup each, and add about ½ cup more milk. Be aware, however, that though this will increase the cost, the recipe will also serve more people.

Roasted Red Pepper and Corn Chowder

Serves 6

2 tablespoons butter

⅓ cup chopped roasted red bell peppers, from jar

4 cups chicken broth

2 cups water

6 medium russet or Idaho baking potatoes, peeled and diced

1 bay leaf

Sea salt and freshly ground black pepper, to taste

1½ cups fresh or frozen corn (if frozen, thaw first)

½ teaspoon dried thyme

Pinch sugar

½ cup whole or evaporated milk

If desired, give this recipe a new twist by adding a can of green chilies. Serve as an entrée or with a side sandwich or salad.

1. Melt the butter in the pressure cooker over medium heat. Add red peppers to the pressure cooker and sauté in the butter for 2 minutes. Stir in the broth, water, and potatoes, Add the bay leaf, salt, and pepper.
2. Lock the lid into place and bring to high pressure; maintain pressure for 4 minutes. Quick-release the pressure and remove the lid. Remove and discard the bay leaf.
3. Stir in the corn, thyme, sugar, and milk. Leave the pan on the heat, stirring occasionally, until the corn and cream come to temperature. Taste for seasoning; add additional salt and pepper if needed.

To Make Corn Chowder with Cheese

Once the chowder comes to temperature, add in 1 cup of grated sharp Cheddar cheese and stir continually over low heat until the cheese is melted.

Stew of Lima Beans, Okra, and Chicken

Serves 6

Total cost: $6.69

Serving size: 1 cup

Calories per serving: 283

Fat: 6g

Carbohydrates: 21g

Protein: 12g

Sodium: 583mg

3 tablespoons bacon fat or canola oil

8 chicken thighs

2 cups water

1 (28-ounce) can diced tomatoes

2 large yellow onions, peeled and sliced

¼ teaspoon sugar

½ cup dry white wine or chicken broth

1 (10-ounce) package frozen lima beans, thawed

1 (10-ounce) package frozen whole kernel corn, thawed

1 (10-ounce) package frozen okra, thawed and sliced

1 cup bread crumbs, toasted

3 tablespoons Worcestershire sauce

Sea salt and freshly ground black pepper, to taste

This recipe calls for chicken thighs because they have a richer, deeper flavor than the breasts.

1. Bring the bacon fat to temperature in the pressure cooker over medium heat. Add 4 chicken thighs skin-side down and fry them until lightly browned.
2. Remove the fried thighs and fry the remaining thighs. Return the first 4 fried thighs to the pressure cooker and add the water, tomatoes, onions, sugar, and wine or chicken broth.
3. Lock the lid into place and bring to high pressure; maintain pressure for 12 minutes. Quick-release the pressure and remove the lid. Remove the chicken.
4. Once chicken is cool enough to handle, remove the meat from the bones and discard the skin and bones. Shred the chicken meat and set aside.
5. Add the lima beans, corn, and okra to the pot. Bring to a simmer and cook uncovered for 30 minutes.
6. Stir in the shredded chicken, bread crumbs, and Worcestershire sauce. Simmer for 10 minutes, stirring occasionally, to bring the chicken to temperature and thicken the stew.
7. Taste for seasoning and add salt and pepper if needed and hot sauce if desired.

Star of Texas Stew

Serves 6

Total cost: $6.79
Serving size: 1 cup
Calories per serving: 185
Fat: 9g
Carbohydrates: 8g
Protein: 18g
Sodium: 465mg

1 (2½-pound) English or chuck roast

2 tablespoons olive oil

1 (7-ounce) can green chilies

2 (15-ounce) cans diced tomatoes

1 (8-ounce) can tomato sauce

1 large sweet onion, peeled and diced

1 green bell pepper, seeded and diced

6 cloves garlic, peeled and minced

1 tablespoon ground cumin

1 teaspoon freshly ground black pepper

Cayenne pepper, to taste

2 tablespoons lime juice

2 jalapeño peppers, seeded and diced

½ cup beef broth or water

1 bunch fresh cilantro, chopped

This "star" recipe combines both Spanish and American flavors with spice, making it the perfect Texas tribute.

1. Trim the fat from the roast and cut the meat into 1" cubes. Add the oil to the pressure cooker and bring it to temperature over medium-high heat.
2. Add the beef and stir-fry for 8 minutes or until it's well browned. Stir in the chilies, tomatoes, tomato sauce, onion, bell pepper, garlic, cumin, black pepper, cayenne, lime juice, and jalapeño peppers.
3. If needed, add enough beef broth or water to cover the ingredients in the cooker, but remember not to fill the cooker more than ⅔ full.
4. Lock the lid into place and bring to low pressure; maintain pressure for 1 hour. Remove from heat and allow pressure to release naturally. Remove the lid and stir in the cilantro. Serve immediately.

Serving Suggestions
Serve this with a little grated Cheddar cheese, tortilla chips, or even over rice.

Jalapeño Chicken Chili

 Serves 4

2 pounds boneless, skinless chicken thighs

2 tablespoons vegetable oil

1 jalapeño pepper, seeded and minced

1 small red bell pepper, seeded and diced

1 small onion, peeled and diced

1 clove garlic, peeled and minced

1 (15-ounce) can diced tomatoes

1 (16-ounce) can red kidney beans

1 tablespoon paprika

1 tablespoon tomato paste

1 cup chicken broth

¼ teaspoon dried thyme

¼ teaspoon dried oregano

1 teaspoon chili powder

Sea salt and freshly ground black pepper, to taste

Avocados, sour cream, and grated cheese go great with this fun, spicy chili. Or, try ground beef or turkey, or add a few beans and make it a Chili Bean Chili.

1. Cut the chicken into bite-sized cubes. Add the oil to the pressure cooker and bring it to temperature over medium heat. Add the chicken and stir-fry for 5 minutes.
2. Add the jalapeño and red peppers; stir-fry with the chicken for 2 minutes. Stir in the onion; sauté for 3 minutes or until tender.
3. Stir in the garlic, tomatoes, rinsed and drained kidney beans, paprika, tomato paste, broth, thyme, oregano, chili powder, salt, and pepper.
4. Lock the lid into place and bring to low pressure; maintain pressure for 10 minutes. Remove the pan from the heat and let pressure release naturally for 10 minutes.
5. Quick-release any remaining pressure and remove the lid. Stir the chili and taste for seasoning; add additional salt, pepper, spices, or herbs if needed.

Beer-Brewed Chicken Stew

 Serves 6

Total cost: $6.96

Serving size: 1 cup

Calories per serving: 326

Fat: 16g

Carbohydrates: 12g

Protein: 18g

Sodium: 618mg

1 teaspoon sea salt

½ tablespoon garlic powder

½ teaspoon cayenne pepper

2 tablespoons unbleached all-purpose flour

2 pounds boneless, skinless chicken thighs

2 tablespoons olive oil

1 small green bell pepper, seeded and diced

1 small red bell pepper, seeded and diced

1 stalk celery, diced

1 medium onion, peeled and diced

1 jalapeño pepper, seeded and diced

2 cloves garlic, peeled and minced

1 bay leaf

1 teaspoon chopped fresh marjoram

1 (8-ounce) can tomato sauce

1 (12-ounce) bottle dark beer

½ cup chicken broth

2 teaspoons Worcestershire sauce

1 tablespoon bacon fat

Freshly ground black pepper, to taste

This Cajun-inspired dish is terrific over rice or with corn-bread and mashed potatoes.

1. Add the salt, garlic powder, cayenne pepper, and flour to a large zip-closure plastic bag; shake the bag to mix the spices into the flour.
2. Trim and discard any fat from the thighs and cut them into bite-sized pieces.
3. Add the thigh pieces to the bag and shake to coat them in the seasoned flour.
4. Bring the oil to temperature in the pressure cooker over medium-high heat. Add the chicken in batches; stir-fry for 3–5 minutes or until browned. Reserve leftover seasoned flour.
5. Remove the browned chicken pieces and keep warm.

Beer-Brewed Chicken Stew (continued)

6. Reduce heat to medium. Add the green bell pepper, red bell pepper, and celery; sauté for 3 minutes.
7. Stir in the onion; sauté for 3 minutes or until the onion is soft. Add the jalapeño pepper and garlic; sauté for 30 seconds.
8. Stir in the bay leaf, marjoram, tomato sauce, beer, chicken broth, and Worcestershire sauce.
9. Lock the lid into place and bring to low pressure; maintain pressure for 20 minutes. Quick-release the pressure and remove the lid. Remove and discard the bay leaf.
10. While the chicken mixture cooks under pressure, bring the bacon fat or lard to temperature in a cast-iron skillet over medium heat.
11. Whisk in the reserved seasoned flour and enough water to make a paste. Cook and stir constantly for about 10 minutes or until the roux turns the color of peanut butter.
12. Whisk some of the juices from the pressure cooker into the roux in the skillet to loosen the mixture, and then stir the roux into the mixture in the pressure cooker.
13. Bring the mixture to a simmer; simmer for 3 minutes or until thickened. Taste for seasoning; add additional salt and Worcestershire sauce, if needed, and black pepper to taste. Serve.

Want More Spice?

Fresh hot peppers are fun to cook with and create terrific spicy flavors with minimal effort. Use habanero, serrano, or any combination of your favorite peppers to create as much or as little heat as you want in this recipe.

The $7 a Meal Pressure Cooker Cookbook

Beef Stew with Mushrooms and Dumplings

Serves 6

$ Total cost: $7.00

Serving size: 1½ cups

Calories per serving: 456

Fat: 24g

Carbohydrates: 32g

Protein: 12g

Sodium: 556mg

1 (2-pound) English or chuck roast

2 (4-ounce) cans sliced mushrooms, drained

1 (10.5-ounce) can condensed cream of mushroom soup

1 (10.5-ounce) can condensed French onion soup

1 tablespoon Worcestershire sauce

2 cups water

1 (24-ounce) bag frozen vegetables for stew, thawed

4 cups frozen vegetables, thawed

Sea salt and freshly ground black pepper, to taste

Dumplings, recipe below

Before adding too much salt to any recipe, start with a little and add more after cooking.

1. Trim and discard any fat from the roast. Cut into bite-sized pieces and add meat, drained mushrooms, soups, Worcestershire sauce, and water to the pressure cooker.
2. Lock the lid into place and bring to low pressure; maintain pressure for 30 minutes. Quick-release the pressure and remove the lid.
3. Stir in the thawed frozen vegetables. Bring to a simmer and then drop tablespoon-sized dollops of the Quick and Easy Dumplings batter into the bubbling stew.
4. Lock the lid into place and bring to low pressure; maintain pressure for 5 minutes. Quick-release the pressure and remove the lid.
5. Stir the stew, being careful not to break the dumplings apart. (If dumplings aren't yet puffy and cooked through, loosely cover the pan and let the stew simmer for a few more minutes.) Taste for seasoning and add salt and pepper if needed.

Quick and Easy Dumplings

Cut 1 tablespoon shortening or butter into 1½ cups biscuit mix until crumbly. Combine ⅔ cup milk and 1 large beaten egg; add to dry mixture. Stir until just blended. When you cook the dumplings in the stew, small drops of batter will suffice; they expand in the hot liquid.

New England Clam Chowder

 Serves 4

4 (6½-ounce) cans chopped clams

4 slices bacon

1 stalk celery, finely diced

2 large shallots, peeled and minced

1 pound red potatoes, peeled and diced

2½ cups unsalted chicken or vegetable broth

1 tablespoon fresh thyme, chopped

1 cup frozen corn, thawed

2 cups whole milk

1 cup sour cream

Sea salt and freshly ground black pepper, to taste

With this recipe, you can enjoy a classic favorite chowder at home with minimal effort and cost.

1. Drain the clams. Reserve the liquid to add along with the broth. Set the clams aside.
2. Dice the bacon and add to the pressure cooker. Fry over medium-high heat until the bacon is crisp enough to crumble. Add the celery; sauté for 3 minutes.
3. Add the shallots; sauté for 3 minutes. Stir in the potatoes; stir-fry briefly in the bacon fat and vegetable mixture to coat the potatoes in the fat. Stir in the clam liquid, broth, and thyme.
4. Lock the lid into place and bring to high pressure; maintain pressure for 5 minutes. Lower the heat to warm and allow pressure to drop naturally for 10 minutes. Quick-release any remaining pressure and remove the lid.
5. Stir in the corn, milk, sour cream, and reserved clams. Bring to a simmer (but do not boil); simmer for 5 minutes or until everything is heated through. Taste for seasoning and add salt and pepper if needed.

Manhattan Clam Chowder

Serves 6

$ Total cost: $6.79

Serving size: 1 cup

Calories per serving: 376

Fat: 6g

Carbohydrates: 24g

Protein: 13g

Sodium: 518mg

4 (6.5-ounce) cans minced clams

4 slices bacon

2 stalks celery, finely diced

4 large carrots, peeled and finely diced

1 large sweet onion, peeled and diced

1 pound red potatoes, peeled and diced

1 (28-ounce) can diced tomatoes

2 cups tomato or V8 juice

1 teaspoon dried parsley

¼ teaspoon dried thyme

⅛ teaspoon dried oregano

½ teaspoon freshly ground black pepper

Sea salt, to taste

Manhattan chowder is lower in fat and calories than New England Clam Chowder, but equally delicious.

1. Drain the clams. Reserve the liquid to add along with the other liquid. Set the clams aside.
2. Dice the bacon and add to the pressure cooker. Fry over medium-high heat until the bacon is crisp enough to crumble.
3. Add the celery and carrots; sauté for 3 minutes. Add the onion; sauté for 3 minutes or until the onion is soft.
4. Stir in the potatoes; stir-fry briefly in the bacon fat and vegetable mixture to coat the potatoes in the fat.
5. Stir in the clam liquid, undrained tomatoes, tomato or V8 juice, parsley, thyme, oregano, and pepper.
6. Lock the lid into place and bring to high ptressure; maintain pressure for 5 minutes. Lower the heat to warm and allow pressure to drop naturally for 10 minutes. Quick-release any remaining pressure and remove the lid.
7. Stir in the reserved clams. Bring to a simmer (but do not boil); simmer for 5 minutes or until the clams are heated through. Taste for seasoning and add salt if needed.

Added Protein

Enjoy with the clams as directed, or turn this into a full seafood chowder by adding chopped, cooked shrimp and chunks of whitefish.

CHAPTER 10

VEGETARIAN FAVORITES

Vegetable Broth / 225

Tomato-Based Broth / 226

Mushroom Broth / 227

Risotto Primavera / 228

Pasta Fagiole / 229

Eggplant with Bell Peppers and Olives / 230

Barley Soup with Mushrooms / 231

Vegetarian Chili / 232

Chickpea Pasta with Cabbage Sauce / 233

Lentil Chili with Black Beans / 234

Dried Fruit "Chutney" / 235

Ratatouille / 236

Classic Minestrone / 237

Tortilla Chili / 238

Wild Rice with Soy Beans / 239

Wild Mushroom Risotto / 240

Pasta with Potatoes / 241

Curried Wild Rice with Apple Chutney / 242

Acorn Squash with Feta over Couscous / 243

Three-Cheese Polenta / 244

Chickpea Pilaf with Lemon / 245

Spicy Red Beans / 246

Roasted Corn and Brown Rice / 247

Indian-Spiced Rice Primavera / 248

Vegetable Broth

 Serves 8

💲 Total cost: $2.56

🥄 Serving size: ½ cup

Calories per serving: 39

Fat: 1g

Carbohydrates: 2g

Protein: <1g

Sodium: 323mg

2 large onions, peeled and halved

2 medium carrots, cleaned and cut into large pieces

3 stalks celery, cut in half

1 whole bulb garlic

10 peppercorns

1 bay leaf

4½ cups water

Vegetable stock, which is also sometimes referred to as vegetable broth, is called for in many vegetarian recipes.

1. Add the onions, carrots, and celery to the pressure cooker. Break the bulb of garlic into individual cloves; peel the garlic and add to the pressure cooker. Add the peppercorns, bay leaf, and water.
2. Add additional water if necessary to completely cover the vegetables. Lock the lid into place and bring to low pressure; maintain pressure for 10 minutes. Remove from the heat and allow pressure to release naturally.
3. Strain the stock through a fine-mesh strainer or through cheesecloth placed in a colander. Store in a covered container in the refrigerator, or freeze until needed.

Cooking with Stocks

Homemade stocks give unique and fresh flavor to many dishes, especially pressure cooker dishes that call for water. There is a "chef saying" that water is for showering. Translation: Why put liquid into your food if it is not contributing any enhanced flavor benefits? While this may not be true all the time, it is a great general rule to follow in the kitchen.

Tomato-Based Broth

 Serves 8

💲 Total cost: $3.44

Serving size: ½ cup

Calories per serving: 42g

Fat: 2g

Carbohydrates: 3g

Protein: 1g

Sodium: 323mg

2 large onions, peeled and halved

2 medium carrots, cleaned and cut into large pieces

3 stalks celery, halved

1 whole bulb garlic

4 large tomatoes, quartered

10 peppercorns

1 bay leaf

4 cups water

Tomato-based broth is a great way to add another layer of flavor to soups, sauces, and other dishes that require a liquid and have other tomato ingredients in the recipe. For example, marinara sauce, tomato bisque, tomato soup, vegetable soups, and similar dishes.

1. Add the onions, carrots, and celery to the cooker. Break the bulb of garlic into individual cloves; peel the garlic and add to the onion mixture.
2. Add the tomatoes, peppercorns, bay leaf, and water. Add additional water if necessary to completely cover the vegetables without over-filling the cooker. Latch lid securely and bring to low pressure for 10 minutes.
3. Remove from heat and release pressure using the natural-release method.
4. Strain the stock through a fine-mesh strainer or through cheesecloth placed in a colander. Store in a covered container in the refrigerator or freeze until needed.

Broth as a Base

Turn this tomato broth into tomato soup by adding more tomatoes and a little tomato paste. Or, expand it to vegetable soup by adding such fresh or fresh frozen vegetables as corn, green beans, cauliflower, carrots, and broccoli.

Mushroom Broth

 Serves 16

4 carrots, washed and cut in large pieces

2 large leeks, well cleaned and cut in large pieces

2 large onions, peeled and quartered

1 celery stalk, chopped

5 whole cloves

Pinch dried red pepper flakes

2 cups fresh mushrooms, sliced

8½ cups water

This is a good alternative to chicken broth in almost any recipe. You can use button mushrooms or, for a more intense flavor, portobello mushroom caps cleaned of the black gills or wild mushrooms like chanterelles or shiitake.

1. Put all ingredients in the pressure cooker. Lock the lid into place and bring to low pressure; maintain pressure for 15 minutes.
2. Remove from the heat and allow pressure to release naturally. Strain for a clear stock. Can be refrigerated for 2 or 3 days or frozen for 3 months.

When to Use Mushroom Broth

Use this in place of chicken or even beef broth to add flavor to pasta dishes, rice dishes, risotto, or roast beef dishes.

Risotto Primavera

Serves 4

Total cost: $4.99
Serving size: 1 cup
Calories per serving: 345
Fat: 6g
Carbohydrates: 31g
Protein: 10g
Sodium: 641mg

1 tablespoon extra-virgin olive oil

1 tablespoon unsalted butter

2 medium carrots, peeled and finely diced

1 stalk celery, finely diced

2 large shallots or 1 small red onion, peeled and diced

1 clove garlic, peeled and minced

½ teaspoon dried basil

1 teaspoon dried parsley

2 cups uncooked Arborio rice

½ cup dry white wine or vermouth

5 cups vegetable or mushroom broth, divided

½ pound asparagus

1 cup English peas, thawed

1 cup snow peas, shredded

1 cup zucchini, peeled, seeded, and diced

½ cup Fontina cheese, shredded

¼ cup Parmigiano-Reggiano or Asiago cheese, grated

This easy version combines ease and speed for a deliciously simple risotto ready in minutes without all the fuss.

1. Bring the oil and butter to temperature in the pressure cooker over medium heat. Add the carrot and celery; sauté for 3 minutes. Add the shallots or red onion; sauté for 3 minutes or until the vegetables are tender. Add the garlic, basil, and parsley; sauté for 30 seconds.

2. Stir in the rice and stir-fry for 4 minutes or until the rice becomes opaque. Add the wine or vermouth; cook and stir for 3 minutes or until the liquid is absorbed by the rice. Stir in 4½ cups broth.

3. Lock the lid into place and bring to high pressure; maintain pressure for 10 minutes. Quick-release the pressure and remove the lid.

4. Stir in the remaining ½ cup broth. Once the broth is absorbed and the rice is fluffed, adjust heat to maintain a simmer.

5. Clean the asparagus and cut it into 1" pieces. Add the asparagus, peas, snow peas, and zucchini. Stir and cook until the vegetables are bright green and cooked through. Stir in the cheese. Serve.

Pasta Fagiole

 Serves 8

Total cost: $5.76

Serving size: 1 cup

Calories per serving: 278

Fat: 5g

Carbohydrates: 43g

Protein: 14g

Sodium: 617mg

1 pound dried cannellini or white beans

1 tablespoon extra-virgin olive oil

4 medium carrots, peeled and diced

2 stalks celery, diced

2 medium onions, peeled and diced

3 cloves garlic, peeled and minced

2 teaspoons Italian seasoning, divided

6 cups water

1 bay leaf

1 teaspoon dried parsley

4 cups vegetable or mushroom broth

1½ cups small macaroni or small shell pasta

Sea salt and freshly ground black pepper, to taste

This Tuscan-style soup is an Italian favorite almost any time of year. Enjoy with Italian ciabatta slices rubbed with fresh garlic.

1. Rinse the cannellini or white beans; soak overnight in enough water to cover them by more than 1". Drain.
2. Bring the oil to temperature in the pressure cooker over medium heat. Add the carrots and celery; sauté for 3 minutes. Add the onion; sauté for 3 minutes or until the vegetables are soft. Add the garlic and a teaspoon of the Italian seasoning blend; sauté for 30 seconds.
3. Add the water, beans, and bay leaf. Lock the lid into place and bring to high pressure; maintain pressure for 35 minutes. Remove from the heat and allow pressure to release naturally for 20 minutes. Quick-release any remaining pressure and remove the lid.
4. Remove and discard the bay leaf. Add the remaining Italian seasoning blend, parsley, and vegetable or mushroom broth. Return to the heat and bring to a boil; stir in the macaroni or shells. Cook pasta to al dente according to package directions. Taste for seasoning and add salt and pepper if needed. Serve topped with grated cheese if desired.

Eggplant with Bell Peppers and Olives

Serves 8

¼ cup extra-virgin olive oil

¼ cup white wine

2 tablespoons red wine vinegar

1 teaspoon ground cinnamon

1 large eggplant, peeled and diced

1 medium onion, peeled and diced

1 medium green bell pepper, seeded and diced

1 medium red bell pepper, seeded and diced

2 cloves garlic, peeled and minced

1 (14-ounce) can diced tomatoes

3 stalks celery, diced

½ cup oil-cured olives, pitted and chopped

½ cup golden raisins

2 tablespoons capers, rinsed and drained

Sea salt and freshly ground black pepper, to taste

This versatile dish can be served hot, at room temperature, or cold. You can use it as a pasta topping, a side dish, or even a sandwich filling if you drain all the liquid.

1. Add all ingredients to the pressure cooker. Stir well to mix. Lock the lid into place and bring to low pressure; maintain pressure for 8 minutes.
2. Remove from heat and quick-release the pressure. Remove the lid and stir the contents of the pressure cooker. Taste for seasoning and add salt and pepper, to taste.

Barley Soup with Mushrooms

 Serves 8

Total cost: $5.65
Serving size: 1 cup
Calories per serving: 241
Fat: 10g
Carbohydrates: 26g
Protein: 15g
Sodium: 378mg

1 tablespoon butter

1 medium onion, peeled and diced

2 medium carrots, peeled and sliced

3 cloves garlic, peeled and minced

1 pound fresh mushrooms, cleaned and sliced

½ teaspoon dried thyme

⅓ cup sherry

¾ cup pearl barley

1 bay leaf

5 cups water or vegetable broth

½ teaspoon freshly ground black pepper

Sea salt, to taste

2 tablespoons chopped fresh Italian flat-leaf parsley

Fiber-filled and flavor-filled, this soup is perfect for lunch or dinner. Add protein to this already delicious soup by adding firm tofu, black beans, or lentils.

1. Melt the butter in the pressure cooker over medium heat. Add the onion; sauté for 3 minutes or until soft. Stir in the carrots, garlic, mushrooms, and thyme. Stir-fry for 5 minutes or until the mushrooms have released most of their moisture. Stir in the sherry, barley, bay leaf, and broth. Lock the lid into place and bring to high pressure; maintain pressure for 10 minutes. Remove from heat and allow pressure to release naturally.

2. Remove the lid. Remove and discard the bay leaf. Return to heat if necessary to bring the soup back to temperature. Stir in the pepper, salt, and parsley. Serve immediately.

Vegetarian Chili

Serves 8

2 tablespoons olive oil

1 large sweet onion, peeled and diced

3 cloves garlic, peeled and minced

1 (15-ounce) can pinto beans, rinsed and drained

1 (15-ounce) can kidney beans, rinsed and drained

1 (15-ounce) can cannellini or white beans, rinsed and drained

1 large green bell pepper, seeded and diced

2 medium zucchini

1½ cups corn

1 (28-ounce) can diced tomatoes

2 cups vegetable broth

2 tablespoons chili powder

1 teaspoon cumin

1 teaspoon dried oregano

¼ teaspoon freshly ground black pepper

⅛ teaspoon cayenne pepper

Sea salt, to taste

1 cup Monterey jack cheese, grated

For a non-vegetarian version, add ground beef or turkey-and an extra cup of broth to give it the moisture it needs to cook.

1. Bring the oil to temperature in the pressure cooker over medium heat. Add the onion; sauté for 3 minutes or until it begins to soften. Stir in the garlic; sauté for 30 seconds. Stir in the canned beans, green bell pepper, zucchini, corn, tomatoes, broth, chili powder, cumin, oregano, black pepper, and cayenne pepper. Stir to mix.
2. Lock the lid into place and bring to high pressure; maintain pressure for 5 minutes. Remove from the heat and allow pressure to release naturally.
3. Remove the lid, stir, and taste for seasoning. Add salt if desired. Serve topped with grated cheese.

Chickpea Pasta with Cabbage Sauce

Serves 8

 Total cost: $6.34

Serving size: 1 cup

Calories per serving: 312

Fat: 5g

Carbohydrates: 33g

Protein: 12g

Sodium: 739mg

⅔ cup dried chickpeas

6 dried shiitake mushrooms or 8 ounces fresh mushrooms, sliced

2 tablespoons extra-virgin olive oil

1 stalk celery, thinly sliced

1 medium red onion, peeled and sliced

1 small head Savoy cabbage, cored and shredded

4 cups water

1 pound rigatoni

Sea salt and freshly ground black pepper, to taste

Pecorino cheese, grated as desired for garnish and flavor

Chickpeas (also known as garbanzo beans) are high in carbs and protein, and make all sorts of great foods.

1. Rinse the chickpeas. Soak them overnight in enough water to cover them by more than 1". If using dried mushrooms, add them to the soaking liquid for the chickpeas. Drain.
2. Bring the oil to temperature in the pressure cooker. Add the celery; sauté for 2 minutes. Add the onion; sauté for 3 minutes. Stir in the shredded cabbage and sauté until wilted. Add the chickpeas, mushrooms, and water.
3. Lock the lid into place and bring to high pressure; maintain pressure for 20 minutes. Remove from the heat and allow pressure to release naturally while you prepare the pasta according to package directions.
4. Quick-release any remaining pressure and remove the lid. Stir the chickpea sauce and taste for seasoning, adding salt and pepper to taste. If the sauce is too thin, use a fork to mash some of the chickpeas, which will thicken the sauce.
5. Remove from the heat and allow pressure to release naturally while you cook the pasta. Top with grated cheese as desired.

Lentil Chili with Black Beans

 Serves 6

2 tablespoons vegetable oil

1 large Spanish onion, peeled and diced

1 jalapeño, seeded and minced

1 clove garlic, peeled and minced

1 cup brown or green lentils

1 (15.5-ounce) can black beans, drained and rinsed

1 cup pearl barley

3 tablespoons chili powder

1 tablespoon sweet paprika

1 teaspoon dried oregano

1 teaspoon ground cumin

1 (28-ounce) can diced tomatoes

6 cups vegetable broth

1 (12-ounce) can chipotle peppers

Sea salt and black pepper, to taste

If you prefer hotter chili, substitute a Scotch bonnet or serrano pepper for the jalapeño. Serve with cornbread.

1. Bring the oil to temperature in the pressure cooker over medium heat. Add the onion; sauté for 3 minutes. Stir in the jalapeño; sauté for 1 minute.
2. Stir in the garlic; sauté for 30 seconds. Stir in the lentils, black beans, barley, chili powder, paprika, oregano, cumin, undrained tomatoes, and vegetable broth. If using, mince 1 or more chipotle peppers and add them along with some sauce to taste.
3. Lock the lid and bring to high pressure; maintain for 10 minutes. Remove from the heat and allow pressure to release naturally for 10 minutes. Quick-release any remaining pressure. Remove the lid. Stir and check that the lentils and barley are tender. If not, lock the lid, return to the heat, and bring to pressure for the estimated time needed. Remove from heat and allow pressure to release naturally.
4. Remove the lid and return the pan to the heat. Bring to a simmer. Taste for seasoning. Simmer until slightly thickened.

Chipotle Peppers

The chipotle peppers give a rich, smoky flavor to this dish. If you prefer, use freshly diced green and red bell peppers instead. They give a crisp flavor and freshness.

Dried Fruit "Chutney"

Makes 2 quarts

½ cup butter

2 cups light brown sugar, lightly packed

2 cups fresh apple cider

1 medium orange

1 cup raisins

1 cup dried currants

1¼ cups dried figs

1 cup dried apricots

2 medium cooking apples

2 Bosc pears

⅓ cup and ¼ cup brandy, divided

⅓ cup dark rum

1 teaspoon sea salt

1 teaspoon ground cinnamon

1 teaspoon ground cloves

1 teaspoon ground allspice

1 teaspoon ground nutmeg

This chutney is really like a mincemeat, which consists of chopped dried fruit and spices combined with a liquor.

1. Melt the butter in the pressure cooker over medium heat. Stir in the brown sugar and cider. Allow the mixture to simmer while you prepare the fruit for the recipe.

2. Cut the orange into quarters, remove the seeds, and add to a food processor along with the raisins, currants, figs, and apricots; pulse to coarsely chop. Stir into the other ingredients already in the pressure cooker.

3. Peel, core, and seed the apples and pears. Add to the food processor and pulse until finely grated. Add to the pressure cooker along with ⅓ cup of the brandy, rum, salt, cinnamon, cloves, allspice, and nutmeg.

4. Bring to a simmer; skim off and discard any foam from the top. Lock the lid and bring to low temperature; maintain pressure for 10 minutes. Remove from the heat and allow pressure to release naturally.

5. Uncover, stir, and check the consistency of the chutney. To thicken it, return the pressure cooker to medium heat, and stirring occasionally, continue to cook uncovered for 10–15 minutes or until the mixture is reduced to about 2 quarts. Ladle the chutney into 2 sterilized 1-quart canning jars.

6. Top the chutney in each jar with 2 tablespoons of brandy. Screw on the 2-piece lids; allow to cool to room temperature.

Ratatouille

 Serves 4

2 tablespoons extra-virgin olive oil

2 (7") zucchini, washed and sliced

1 Japanese eggplant, peeled and sliced

1 small onion, peeled and thinly sliced

1 green bell pepper, seeded and diced

2 medium potatoes, peeled and diced

8 ounces fresh cremini mushrooms, cleaned and sliced

1 (28-ounce) can diced tomatoes

3 tablespoons tomato paste

3 tablespoons water

2 cloves garlic, peeled and minced

2 teaspoons Italian seasoning

⅛ teaspoon dried red pepper flakes

Sea salt and freshly ground black pepper, to taste

Parmigiano cheese, grated (optional)

Ratatouille is a French dish primarily consisting of stewed vegetables. Serve it with a side of pasta or bread or enjoy as an appetizer on crostini.

1. Coat the bottom and sides of the pressure cooker with oil. Add the remaining ingredients except cheese in layers in the order given. Lock the lid into place and bring to low pressure; maintain pressure for 6 minutes.
2. Remove from heat and quick-release the pressure. Remove the lid, stir, and taste for seasoning, adjusting if necessary. Serve topped with the grated cheese.

If You'd Like to Add Protein. . . .

This is an easy dish to transform into a protein-filled entrée. Add some extra-firm tofu, tempeh, or beans (such as fava or navy) and toss with penne pasta for a delicious, filling, and nutritious meal.

Classic Minestrone

 Serves 4

$ Total cost: $6.71

Serving size: 1 cup

Calories per serving: 156

Fat: 2g

Carbohydrates: 24g

Protein: 3g

Sodium: 343mg

1 small onion, peeled and diced

3 cups water

2 medium zucchini, peeled and diced

1 cup baby carrots, chopped

1 cup green beans, chopped

1 (15-ounce) can cannellini beans, rinsed and drained

2 stalks celery, diced

½ teaspoon dried basil

½ teaspoon dried oregano

Freshly ground black pepper, to taste

1 14-ounce can diced tomatoes

1 clove garlic, peeled and minced

¼ cup uncooked macaroni

4 teaspoons freshly grated Parmigiano-Reggiano cheese

When you have a variety of vegetables, chop them to similar-size portions so they cook evenly. Same goes for roasting potatoes and other vegetables. Try to keep the size about the same across the board and distribute evenly on the baking sheet.

1. Add all ingredients except the macaroni and cheese to the pressure cooker. Lock the lid into place and bring to low pressure; maintain pressure for 5 minutes. Quick-release the pressure and remove the lid.

2. At this point, you have a choice: You can either cook the macaroni separately according to package directions or you can bring the contents of the pressure cooker to a boil and stir in the uncooked macaroni, adding water or tomato juice as needed until the macaroni is cooked. If you choose the latter option, stir and watch the pot, adding more liquid as needed so that the soup doesn't boil dry.

3. Ladle the minestrone into bowls and sprinkle each serving with 1 teaspoon of the cheese, or more to taste.

Throw-in-the-Kitchen-Sink Vegetables

This is a perfect recipe for using up all the vegetables you have that need to be enjoyed. Don't let them sit and spoil. Add some basil or Italian seasoning, or use vegetable broth, tomato juice, or V8 juice instead of water.

Tortilla Chili

 Serves 4

$ Total cost: $6.09

Serving size: 1 cup

Calories per serving: 398

Fat: 14g

Carbohydrates: 20g

Protein: 17g

Sodium: 799mg

1 tablespoon canola oil

1 yellow onion, chopped

2 jalapeño peppers, seeded and minced

1 (8-ounce) can tomato sauce

1 cup tomato juice

1 (15-ounce) can black beans, drained

1 tablespoon chili powder

Sea salt and black pepper, to taste

6 (6") corn tortillas

1 cup grated Cheddar cheese

½ cup sour cream

Layers of beans, corn, and tortillas make this simple recipe a favorite for tailgate parties, appetizer parties, or family night. Add a can of green chilies, use a Mexican four-cheese blend, or add a little taco seasoning or sauce to add your own twist to what will be a family favorite.

1. Heat oil in pressure cooker over medium heat and add onions and jalapeños. Sauté about 3 minutes. Add tomato sauce, juice, black beans, and seasonings. Simmer for about 5 minutes.
2. Remove all but about ½ cup of sauce, layer with 1 tortilla, 2 tablespoons of cheese, and repeat layers of sauce, tortilla, and cheese, ending with cheese.
3. Latch lid securely and bring to low pressure. Maintain pressure for 8 minutes. Use quick-release method to release pressure.
4. Serve with sour cream, if desired.

Wild Rice with Soy Beans

 Serves 4

$ Total cost: $4.08	
Serving size: 1 cup	
Calories per serving: 253	
Fat: 4g	
Carbohydrates: 18g	
Protein: 13g	
Sodium: 198mg	

1 cup wild rice

1 yellow onion, chopped

3 cloves garlic, minced

2 cups vegetable broth

2 cups frozen soy beans, thawed

Sea salt and pepper, to taste

⅓ cup grated Parmesan cheese

1 tablespoon butter

A refreshing twist on an Italian favorite, this version of Risi e Bisi uses wild rice and soy beans instead of the usual white rice and peas.

1. Combine rice, onion, garlic, and broth in a pressure cooker. Latch lid securely and bring to high pressure. Once at high pressure, reduce to low pressure and maintain for 12 minutes. Use quick-release method to release pressure.
2. Stir in soy beans, season with salt and pepper, and resecure lid. Bring to low pressure and maintain about 5 minutes. Use natural-release method to release pressure.
3. When serving, stir in cheese and butter. Fluff with fork and serve.

More on Soy Beans

Soy beans have more protein and fiber than English peas. They are also a bit larger and more firm and crisp than traditional peas.

Wild Mushroom Risotto

Serves 6

2 tablespoons olive oil

1 yellow onion, chopped

2 cloves garlic, minced

2 cups cremini mushrooms, sliced

2 carrots, sliced

Sea salt and black pepper, to taste

½ tablespoon chopped fresh tarragon

1 cup long-grain brown rice

2 cups vegetable broth

⅓ cup grated Parmesan cheese

This recipe calls for cremini mushrooms, but you can use any combination of mushrooms you prefer and as your budget allows. Experiment with a few porcini, shiitake, or oyster mushrooms, keeping the total amount the same.

1. Heat oil in cooker and add onion and garlic over medium heat for about 2 minutes, until fragrant. Add all remaining ingredients except cheese.
2. Latch lid securely and bring to high pressure. Once at high pressure, reduce to low pressure and maintain for 13 minutes. Release pressure using natural-release method.
3. Uncover and stir in cheese. Serve warm.

Brown Rice

Brown rice is higher in fiber than most other rice grains and has a heartier flavor and texture. It's perfect for earthy mushrooms.

Pasta with Potatoes

 Serves 5

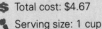

Total cost: $4.67

Serving size: 1 cup

Calories per serving: 364

Fat: 6g

Carbohydrates: 32g

Protein: 6g

Sodium: 269mg

5 russet potatoes, peeled and cubed

1 yellow onion, chopped

4 cloves garlic, minced

Sea salt and black pepper, to taste

1 teaspoon dried thyme

1 cup water

1 (12-ounce) package spaghetti pasta

3 tablespoons olive oil

½ cup grated Parmesan cheese

3 tablespoons chopped fresh Italian flat-leaf parsley

A carb lover's dream, this is the perfect dish for the active person who needs extra energy boosts throughout the day. Add protein by tossing in 1 cup diced cooked turkey or sausage.

1. Combine all ingredients except pasta, olive oil, cheese, and parsley in the pressure cooker. Latch lid securely and bring to low pressure. Maintain pressure for 10 minutes.
2. Separately, bring large pot of water to a boil. Add spaghetti and a dash of salt, cooking as directed on package. Drain pasta but reserve ½ cup of the liquid.
3. Release pressure from cooker using quick-release method. Add pasta, potatoes, olive oil, and ¼ cup of the reserved water. Toss to coat. If needed, add additional water but be careful not to add too much.
4. Add cheese and toss again. Sprinkle with parsley when serving.

Curried Wild Rice with Apple Chutney

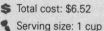 Serves 4

1 tablespoon olive oil

1 yellow onion, chopped

2 cloves garlic, chopped

1 tablespoon fresh ginger root, minced

2 teaspoons curry powder

1 cup wild rice

1 pear, peeled, cored, and chopped

1 apple, peeled, cored, and chopped

½ cup black currants

¼ cup dark raisins

Sea salt and black pepper, to taste

1 (15-ounce) can chickpeas, drained

2 cups vegetable broth

½ cup prepared apple chutney

Chickpeas add a soft crunch to this recipe, which is packed full of fiber and natural sweetness from fruits, both fresh and dried.

1. Heat oil in cooker over medium heat and add onion and garlic. Sauté until fragrant, about 2 minutes. Add ginger, curry powder, and rice. Then, layer pears, apples, currants, and raisins. Add salt and pepper, chickpeas, broth, and chutney.
2. Latch lid securely and bring to low pressure. Maintain low pressure for 15 minutes. Release pressure using natural-release method.
3. When ready to serve, stir to combine and serve.

Other Rice Options
This fruit combination is great with more than just wild rice. Try it over long-grain white rice or even pasta.

Acorn Squash with Feta over Couscous

Serves 4

 Total cost: $6.47

Serving size: 1 cup

Calories per serving: 285

Fat: 9g

Carbohydrates: 12g

Protein: 8g

Sodium: 267mg

1 acorn squash, peeled and cubed

1 yellow onion, chopped

2 cloves garlic, chopped

2 carrots, peeled and sliced

3 cups vegetable broth, divided

4 cups water, divided

Sea salt and black pepper, to taste

1 (15-ounce) can chickpeas, drained

½ cup golden raisins

1½ cups couscous

⅓ cup crumbled feta cheese

Feta is common in Greek cuisine. Butternut squash also works well for this recipe. Serve this over long-grain white rice or baked polenta.

1. Combine all ingredients except 1 cup broth, 2 cups water, couscous, and feta in cooker. Latch lid securely and bring to high pressure. Maintain pressure for 15 minutes. Release using natural-release method.
2. Place 1 cup broth and 2 cups of water in large saucepan and bring to a boil over high heat. Stir in couscous, cover, and remove from heat. Let stand for 5 minutes and then fluff with fork.
3. Stir acorn squash mixture and serve over couscous sprinkled with feta cheese.

Three-Cheese Polenta

Serves 6

Total cost: $6.44

Serving size: 1 cup

Calories per serving: 299

Fat: 5g

Carbohydrates: 12g

Protein: 9g

Sodium: 234mg

1 tablespoon olive oil

1 yellow onion, chopped

1 red bell pepper, chopped

1 (8-ounce) can tomato sauce

1 (15-ounce) can chickpeas, drained

½ teaspoon dried oregano

Black pepper, to taste

1½ cups yellow cornmeal

2½ cups vegetable broth

1 cup water

1 tablespoon butter

Sea salt, to taste

1 cup shredded sharp Cheddar cheese

1 (3-ounce) package cream cheese, cubed

¼ cup grated Parmesan cheese

Cheddar, cream, and Parmesan cheeses give this a rich flavor that will make this polenta your favorite.

1. Make sauce first by heating olive oil over medium heat and adding onion. Cook about 2 minutes and then add bell pepper, tomato sauce, chickpeas, oregano, and pepper. Simmer and then transfer to bowl. Set aside.
2. Then in cooker, add cornmeal, broth, water, butter, salt, and pepper. Stir together. Latch lid securely and bring to high pressure. Once at high pressure, reduce to low pressure and maintain for 6 minutes. Use quick-release method to release pressure. Stir in Cheddar and cream cheeses.
3. Then, layer chickpea mixture over polenta mixture and top with Parmesan cheese. Resecure lid and bring to low pressure. Maintain low pressure for 7 minutes. Release using quick-release method. Serve warm.

Polenta

Polenta gets firm when it "sits" or rests. You can then mold it into squares or triangles and grill it, bake it, or use it as a base for sauces such as this one or even proteins like seared tuna.

Chickpea Pilaf with Lemon

Serves 4

$ Total cost: $4.89

Serving size: 1 cup

Calories per serving: 295

Fat: 4g

Carbohydrates: 13g

Protein: 13g

Sodium: 319mg

1 cup cracked wheat

1 (15-ounce) can chickpeas, drained

Sea salt and black pepper, to taste

2 cups vegetable broth

1 yellow onion, chopped

3 cloves garlic, minced

Finely grated zest of ½ lemon

1 red bell pepper, seeded and diced

1 tablespoon olive oil

Pinch ground cumin

¼ cup fresh lemon juice

⅓ cup chopped fresh Italian flat-leaf parsley

Lemon is one of the easiest ways to add flavor to foods as it complements most everything, including vegetables and proteins such as fish, chicken, and turkey.

1. Combine all ingredients except lemon juice and parsley in cooker. Latch lid securely and bring to high pressure. Once at pressure, reduce to low pressure and maintain for 15 minutes. Release using the natural-release method.
2. Stir in lemon juice and parsley to combine. If needed, heat over medium heat for 10 minutes or until mixture has thickened slightly. Serve warm.

Cracked Wheat

Cracked wheat has a rich, earthy, almost nutty flavor. It is super-high in fiber and is also a good source of protein.

Spicy Red Beans

Serves 6

$ Total cost: $4.55

Serving size: 1 cup

Calories per serving: 312

Fat: 5g

Carbohydrates: 15g

Protein: 7g

Sodium: 328mg

1 pound dried red beans

5 cups water

1 yellow onion, chopped

6 cloves garlic, minced

3 stalks celery, sliced

½ cup ketchup

1 red bell pepper, seeded and chopped

1 tablespoon olive oil

1 tablespoon Worcestershire sauce

1 teaspoon hot sauce

1 bay leaf

½ teaspoon dried thyme leaves

Sea salt and black pepper, to taste

¼ cup chopped fresh Italian flat-leaf parsley

Red beans and rice is a Carribbean classic. Serve these over long-grain white rice, brown rice, or wild rice. You could also add some cooked diced or sliced andouille or other sausage.

1. Soak beans overnight in water. Drain and discard the water. Place beans in cooker and add the water. Latch lid securely and bring to high pressure. Maintain pressure for 20 minutes. Release using quick-release method.
2. Add remaining ingredients to cooker. Resecure lid and return to low pressure. Maintain low pressure for 9 minutes. Release using the natural-release method.
3. Discard bay leaf and serve.

Roasted Corn and Brown Rice

 Serves 4

2 cups frozen corn kernels, thawed

1 tablespoon olive oil

1 yellow onion, chopped

3 cloves garlic, chopped

1 cup uncooked long-grain brown rice

2 cups vegetable broth

Sea salt and black pepper, to taste

Pinch nutmeg

1 (3-ounce) package cream cheese, cut into cubes

2 green onions, chopped

A great base dish to which you can add ½ cup roughly chopped shrimp, diced chicken, or ground sausage.

1. Roast corn by preheating oven to 400°F. Place corn on parchment-lined baking sheet and place in oven for 20 minutes. Remove from oven and transfer to cooker.
2. Heat olive oil over medium heat. Add onion, garlic, and rice to cooker along with corn and stir together for about 3 minutes. Add in broth, salt, pepper, and nutmeg and latch lid securely. Bring to high pressure and maintain for 1 minute. Then, adjust pressure to low and maintain for 9 minutes. Use quick-release method to release pressure.
3. Add in cheese and green onion and mix to combine. Rese-cure lid and bring back to low pressure for 9 minutes. Stir and serve.

Roasting Vegetables

Roasting vegetables, or any food product, creates a richer flavor that permeates the entire dish. Try this for simple salad ingredients, ingredients for soups and pizzas, and almost any rec-ipe that includes vegetables.

Indian-Spiced Rice Primavera

Serves 4

2 tablespoons canola oil

2 teaspoons sweet paprika

2 teaspoons turmeric

2 teaspoons garam masala

Cayenne pepper, to taste

1 medium onion, peeled and sliced

4 ounces fresh mushrooms, sliced

1 small green bell pepper, seeded and diced

1 cup basmati rice, uncooked

½ cup small cauliflower florets

½ cup diced carrots

2 tablespoons dried apricots, diced

2 tablespoons raisins

2 cups vegetable broth

½ cup frozen peas, thawed

Sea salt, to taste

Serve as a main course or a side dish. Either way, this recipe has something for everyone in your family.

1. Bring the oil to temperature in the pressure cooker over low heat. Add the paprika, turmeric, garam masala, and cayenne; sauté for 1 minute.
2. Stir in the onion, mushrooms, and green pepper. Increase the heat to medium and sauté for 3 minutes. Stir in the rice, cauliflower, carrots, apricots, raisins, and broth or water.
3. Lock the lid into place and bring to high pressure; maintain pressure for 7 minutes. Remove from the heat and allow pressure to release naturally for 5 minutes. Quick-release any remaining pressure.
4. Remove the lid and stir in the peas. Cover the pressure cooker (but don't lock the lid into place) and allow to rest for 5 minutes.
5. Uncover and fluff the rice with a fork. Taste for seasoning and add salt if desired. Serve.

Added Protein

Make this an easy one-pot entrée by substituting chicken broth or beef broth for the vegetable broth when you pressure-cook the rice and then stir in a cup of diced, cooked chicken or beef when you add the peas.

CHAPTER 11

PASTA, RICE, BEANS, AND GRAINS

Steamed Vegetable Salad with Wheat Berries / 250

Cannellini Bean Salad with Dried Cranberries and Asian Chilies / 251

Classic American Baked Beans / 252

New Orleans Red Beans and Rice / 253

Curried Chicken Salad with Lentils / 254

Chicken Alfredo with Mushrooms / 255

Farfalle with Italian Sausage / 256

Smoked Salmon Fettuccine / 257

Salad of Bell Peppers and Garbanzo Beans / 258

Risotto of Barley and Mushrooms / 259

Three-Cheese Mac 'n' Cheese / 260

Salad of Artichoke Hearts and Quinoa / 261

Cheese Tortellini with Chicken / 262

Risotto with Shrimp and Fennel Seed / 263

Green Onion Rice Pilaf with Carrot and Toasted Almonds / 264

Swiss Chard with Brown Rice and Water Chestnuts / 265

Chicken with Mushrooms and Rice / 266

Fresh Vegetable Risotto with Basil / 267

Chicken and Brown Rice Salad / 268

Cinnamon Brown Rice with Dried Apricots and Plums / 269

Chicken and Rice Casserole with Vegetables / 270

Spiced Rice with Coconut / 271

Cajun-Style Chicken with Rice / 272

Long-Grain Rice with Mixed Vegetables and Lemon / 273

Southern Black-Eyed Peas / 274

Brown Rice Risotto with Fontina Cheese / 275

Rice Pilaf with Cauliflower, Peppers, and Almonds / 276

Steamed Vegetable Salad with Wheat Berries

Serves 8

Total cost: $5.36
Serving size: ½ cup
Calories per serving: 218
Fat: 9g
Carbohydrates: 28g
Protein: 6g
Sodium: 258mg

1½ tablespoons olive oil

6¾ cups water

1½ cups wheat berries

1½ teaspoons Dijon mustard

1 teaspoon sugar

1 teaspoon sea salt

½ teaspoon freshly ground black pepper

¼ cup white wine vinegar

½ cup extra-virgin olive oil

½ small red onion, peeled and diced

1⅓ cups frozen corn or peas, thawed

1 medium zucchini, peeled, grated, and drained

2 stalks celery, finely diced

1 red bell pepper, seeded and diced

4 green onions, diced

¼ cup sun-dried tomatoes, diced

¼ cup chopped fresh Italian flat-leaf parsley

Wheat berries are the entire kernel of the wheat.

1. Add the oil, water, and wheat berries to the pressure cooker. Lock the lid into place and bring to high pressure; maintain pressure for 50 minutes. Remove from the heat and quick-release the pressure. Fluff with a fork. If the grains aren't yet as tender as you'd like, simmer and stir the mixture for a few minutes, adding more liquid if necessary. When done to your liking, drain and transfer to a large bowl.

2. Make the dressing by puréeing the mustard, sugar, salt, pepper, vinegar, olive oil, and red onion in a food processor or blender. Start by stirring ½ cup dressing into the cooled wheat berries. Toss the seasoned wheat berries with remaining ingredients. Taste for seasoning; add additional salt, pepper, or dressing if needed. Cover and refrigerate any leftover dressing for up to 3 days.

Tasty Additions

As with most any recipe, add more flavor by using tomato broth, mushroom broth, or any preferred cooking liquid instead of water. As well, use your favorite veggies in place of the ones here. Recipes are guidelines, not hard-and-fast rules. Don't be afraid to experiment with the flavors you love.

Cannellini Bean Salad with Dried Cranberries and Asian Chilies

 Serves 8

Total cost: $5.91

Serving size: 1 cup

Calories per serving: 269

Fat: 2g

Carbohydrates: 16g

Protein: 9g

Sodium: 432mg

1 cup dried pinto, black, or cannellini beans

3 tablespoons sherry vinegar

2 tablespoons fresh lime juice

1½ tablespoons low-sodium soy sauce

1½ teaspoons honey

1½ teaspoons fresh ginger, grated

1 teaspoon Asian chili paste

1 clove garlic, peeled and minced

3 cups water

2 teaspoons olive oil

1 cup fresh corn or frozen corn, thawed

8 ounces green beans, cut into ½" pieces, steamed, and chilled

1 cup frozen baby peas, thawed

4 stalks celery, thinly sliced

1 red bell pepper, seeded and diced

¾ cup dried cranberries

1 medium red onion, peeled and diced

Sea salt and freshly ground black pepper, to taste

Asian chili paste can be found in the Asian section of most grocery markets.

1. Rinse and drain the beans, then soak them overnight in enough water to cover them by several inches.
2. To make the dressing, add the vinegar, lime juice, soy sauce, honey, ginger, chili paste, and garlic in a bowl; whisk to mix. Cover and refrigerate overnight to allow the flavors to blend.
3. Drain the soaked beans and add them to the pressure cooker along with 3 cups of water and the olive oil. Lock the lid into place and bring to high pressure; maintain pressure for 25 minutes. Remove from the heat and allow pressure to release naturally.
4. Drain the beans and transfer them to a large bowl. Stir in half of the dressing; chill.
5. Add the corn, green beans, peas, celery, bell pepper, cranberries, onion, salt, and pepper. Toss, adding more dressing if desired. Serve.

Classic American Baked Beans

Serves 8

$ Total cost: $4.78	1 pound dried small white beans
Serving size: ½ cup	4 slices bacon, diced
Calories per serving: 198	2 medium sweet onions, peeled and diced
Fat: 8g	4 cloves garlic, peeled and minced

Total cost: $4.78
Serving size: ½ cup
Calories per serving: 198
Fat: 8g
Carbohydrates: 15g
Protein: 4g
Sodium: 693mg

1 pound dried small white beans

4 slices bacon, diced

2 medium sweet onions, peeled and diced

4 cloves garlic, peeled and minced

3½ cups chicken broth

2 teaspoons dried mustard

¼ teaspoon freshly ground black pepper

¼ cup molasses

½ cup ketchup

¼ brown sugar

1 teaspoon Worcestershire sauce

1 teaspoon cider vinegar

Sea salt, to taste

Usually, beans this good take hours to prepare. Here, the pressure cooker gives you a time advantage, cooking them in minutes without sacrificing flavor.

1. Wash and drain the dried beans. Soak them overnight in 6 cups water, or enough to cover them by more than 1".

2. Fry the bacon in the pressure cooker over medium-high heat until the bacon begins to render its fat. Lower the heat to medium and add the onion; sauté for 3 minutes or until the onions are soft. Stir in the garlic; sauté for 30 seconds. Add the drained soaked beans, broth, dry mustard, and pepper.

3. Lock the lid into place and bring to low pressure; maintain pressure for 20 minutes. Remove from the heat and allow pressure to release naturally.

4. Remove the lid; the beans should still be somewhat soupy at this point. Stir in the molasses, ketchup, brown sugar, Worcestershire sauce, and vinegar. Stir to mix. Taste and add another ¼ cup of molasses if you prefer a heartier taste. Return the pan to the heat, lock the lid into place, and bring to low pressure; maintain pressure for 5 minutes. Remove from the heat and allow pressure to release naturally.

5. Remove the lid. Stir the beans and taste for seasoning. Add salt to taste and additional Worcestershire sauce if needed. If the beans are still too soupy, return to the heat and simmer them, stirring occasionally, until thickened. Serve.

New Orleans Red Beans and Rice

 Serves 8

1 cup dried red beans

3 cups water

2 teaspoons olive oil

1 pound ham hocks

1 pound smoked sausage, diced

4 stalks celery, finely diced

1 large green bell pepper, seeded and diced

1 medium onion, peeled and diced

3 bay leaves

1 teaspoon freshly ground white pepper

1 teaspoon dried thyme

1 teaspoon garlic powder

¼ teaspoon cayenne pepper

¼ teaspoon freshly ground black pepper

Hot sauce, as desired

Sea salt, to taste

Soaking beans in water ensures your beans will be tender when cooked.

1. Wash and drain the beans; soak them overnight in water.
2. Drain the beans and add them to the pressure cooker along with 3 cups of water and the olive oil. Lock the lid into place and bring to low pressure; maintain pressure for 15 minutes. Remove from heat and allow pressure to release naturally for 10 minutes. Quick-release any remaining pressure and remove the lid.
3. Add the remaining ingredients except for the hot sauce and salt. Lock the lid into place and bring to high pressure; maintain pressure for 15 minutes. Remove from the heat and allow pressure to release naturally. Remove the lid.
4. Remove and discard the bay leaves. Remove the ham hocks; when cool enough to handle, remove the meat from the bones and shred naturally. Stir ham into the beans. Discard any pork skin, fat, and bones. Taste for seasoning and add salt and hot sauce, to taste.

Sausage Substitute

If you are worried about the fat content in sausage clogging up your arteries, substitute turkey sausage or turkey bacon. It's flavorful yet saves on both fat and calories. Use as you would regular sausage and bacon.

Curried Chicken Salad with Lentils

 Serves 6

2 small Golden Delicious apples, peeled and diced, divided

1 teaspoon lemon juice

1 teaspoon olive oil

1½ pounds boneless, skinless chicken breasts

1 cup dried lentils

2 cups water

2½ teaspoons curry powder, divided

1 cup seedless grapes, cut in half

½ cup roasted cashews

2 stalks celery, diced

½ small red onion, peeled and diced

¾ cup plain yogurt or sour cream

¼ cup mayonnaise

6 cups mixed salad greens

Serve on lettuce cups for brunch, lunch, or dinner.

1. Toss the apples with the lemon juice to prevent browning. Bring the oil to temperature in the pressure cooker over medium-high heat. Cut the chicken into bite-sized pieces; add to the pressure cooker and stir-fry for 5 minutes or until browned. Stir in the lentils, water, and 1 teaspoon of the curry powder. Add half the apples.
2. Lock the lid and bring the pressure cooker to low pressure; maintain pressure for 8 minutes. Remove from the heat and allow pressure to release naturally.
3. Transfer the contents of the pressure cooker to a bowl. Once it's cooled, stir in the remaining diced apple, grapes, cashews, celery, and red onion.
4. To make the dressing, mix together the yogurt or sour cream, mayonnaise, and remaining 1½ teaspoons curry powder.
5. For each serving, place 1 cup of the salad greens on a plate. Add the lentil mixture on top of the lettuce and drizzle with the dressing.

Adding Sugar

For a sweeter taste, add a pinch or two of sugar to the dressing, if you like. It highlights the other flavors of the dish and gives it a nice sweet taste. Don't overdo it, however. You don't want your lunch to taste like dessert.

The $7 a Meal Pressure Cooker Cookbook

Chicken Alfredo with Mushrooms

 Serves 6

2 tablespoons olive oil

1½ pounds boneless, skinless chicken breasts

1 small onion, peeled and diced

1 red bell pepper, seeded and diced

8 ounces fresh mushrooms, cleaned and sliced

4 cloves garlic, peeled and minced

1 tablespoon dried basil

1 teaspoon dried thyme

⅛ teaspoon freshly ground nutmeg

¼ teaspoon freshly ground black pepper

1 (14-ounce) can chicken broth

8 ounces sugar snap peas, sliced diagonally

½ cup sliced carrots

1½ cups broccoli florets

1½ cups cauliflower segments

¼ cup Parmesan cheese, grated

1 stick butter, softened

1 cup whole milk

8 ounces uncooked linguini

For a more classic Alfredo, cut back on some of the vegetables in this dish and stick with a simple, classic sauce.

1. Bring the oil to temperature in the pressure cooker over medium heat. Cut the chicken into bite-sized pieces and add to the pressure cooker; stir-fry for 5 minutes or until they begin to brown. Add the onion and red bell pepper; sauté for 3 minutes. Add the sliced mushrooms; sauté for 3 minutes. Add the garlic, basil, thyme, nutmeg, pepper, and broth. Stir to combine. Lock the lid and bring to low pressure; maintain pressure for 3 minutes. Remove from the heat and quick-release the pressure. Remove the lid.

2. Add the sugar snap peas, carrots, broccoli, and cauliflower to the pressure cooker. Return the pressure cooker to the heat, lock the lid, and bring to low pressure; maintain 3 minutes. Remove from the heat and quick-release the pressure.

3. Whip the cheese into the butter and then blend with the milk. Return the pressure cooker to medium heat. Stir in the cream mixture; cook and stir for 3 minutes.

4. Cook the linguini according to package directions. Top the noodles with the sauce and additional grated cheese if desired.

Farfalle with Italian Sausage

 Serves 6

 Total cost: $6.19

Serving size: 1 cup

Calories per serving: 461

Fat: 14g

Carbohydrates: 26g

Protein: 21g

Sodium: 870mg

1 pound ground Italian sausage, spicy or mild

1 tablespoon olive oil

1 large onion, peeled and diced

3 cloves garlic, peeled and minced

3 cups chicken broth

1 cup tomato sauce

2 teaspoons dried parsley

½ teaspoon ground fennel

1 teaspoon dried basil

½ teaspoon sugar

¼ teaspoon freshly ground black pepper

⅛ teaspoon dried red pepper flakes

3 cups bow tie pasta

¼ cup whole milk

Sea salt, to taste

½ cup Parmesan cheese, grated

Lighten up this dish with diced chicken breasts or ground turkey. Follow the same instructions for cooking. Serve with a tossed salad and garlic bread.

1. Add the sausage to the pressure cooker over medium-high heat; break the sausage apart as you stir-fry it for 5 minutes or until it is cooked through and has rendered its fat. Drain and discard the fat. Stir in the oil and onion; sauté for 3 minutes or until the onion is soft. Stir in the garlic; sauté for 30 seconds.

2. Stir in the broth, tomato sauce, parsley, fennel, basil, sugar, pepper, red pepper flakes, and pasta. Reduce the heat to medium, lock the lid into place, and bring to low pressure; maintain pressure for 9 minutes. Quick-release the pressure and remove the lid.

3. Stir in the milk. Taste for seasoning and adjust if necessary. Add salt to taste. Transfer to a serving bowl or platter. Top with the cheese. Serve.

Smoked Salmon Fettuccine

 Serves 6

¼ cup olive oil

2 cups fettuccine

4 cups chicken broth

½ teaspoon sea salt

¼ teaspoon freshly ground white pepper

1 teaspoon dried thyme

3 tablespoons butter

½ cup sour cream

2 green onions, cleaned and diced

1 pound smoked salmon, in bite-sized pieces

⅓ cup Parmesan cheese, grated

You can substitute smoked trout, smoked whitefish, or crisp bacon for the smoked salmon.

1. Bring the oil to temperature in the pressure cooker over medium heat. Stir in the fettuccine, broth, salt, pepper, and thyme. Lock the lid in place and bring to high pressure; maintain pressure for 8 minutes. Quick-release the pressure and remove the lid.
2. Drain the pasta if necessary. Transfer to a serving bowl. Cut the butter into small chunks and toss with the pasta. Add the sour cream; stir to combine. Add the green onion and smoked salmon; toss to mix. Top with the grated cheese. Serve.

Other Pastas to Try
Penne pasta, linguini— really, almost any pasta would work well for this dish. For a healthier version, try whole-wheat pasta. You may be pleasantly surprised how tasty it is.

Salad of Bell Peppers and Garbanzo Beans

 Serves 12

1 pound chickpeas

10 cups water, divided

1½ tablespoons olive oil

Sea salt, to taste

4 green onions, sliced

1 medium red onion, peeled and diced

1 small green bell pepper, seeded and diced

1 small red bell pepper, seeded and diced

½ cup fresh parsley, minced

1 large carrot, peeled and grated

¼ cup extra-virgin olive oil

2 teaspoons fresh lemon juice

2 teaspoons white wine vinegar

1 tablespoon mayonnaise

1 clove garlic, peeled and minced

⅛ teaspoon freshly ground white pepper

½ teaspoon dried oregano

¼ cup Parmesan cheese, grated

For warmer months, put the salad in an aluminum baking pan and cook it over indirect heat on a covered grill. Or skip the baking part, chill the salad, and serve cold.

1. Rinse and drain the chickpeas. Soak them in 6 cups of water for at least 4 hours. Drain. Add chickpeas to the pressure cooker along with 4 cups of water and the vegetable oil. Lock the lid and bring to high pressure; maintain for 20 minutes. Remove from heat and allow pressure to release naturally. Drain the beans and transfer them to an ovenproof 9" × 13" casserole dish. Sprinkle salt to taste over the beans.

2. Add the green onion, red onion, green and red bell peppers, parsley, and carrot to the casserole and toss with the beans.

3. Preheat the oven to 375°F.

4. To prepare the dressing, add the oil, lemon juice, vinegar, mayonnaise, garlic, pepper, and oregano to a small bowl or measuring cup. Whisk to mix. Pour the dressing over the beans mixture; stir to combine. Sprinkle the cheese over the dressed beans. Bake for 6 minutes. Stir before serving.

Risotto of Barley and Mushrooms

 Serves 4

1 tablespoon butter

1 tablespoon olive oil

1 large onion, peeled and diced

1 clove garlic, peeled and minced

1 stalk celery, finely minced

1½ cups pearl barley, picked over and rinsed

⅓ cup dried mushrooms

4 cups chicken or vegetable broth

2¼ cups water

1 cup Parmesan cheese, grated

2 tablespoons chopped fresh Italian flat-leaf parsley

Sea salt, to taste

Parmigiano-Reggiano cheese is another great option if it fits into your budget and appeals to your tastebuds. Crumbled blue cheese and cheddar are also delicious.

1. Bring the butter and oil to temperature in the pressure cooker over medium heat. Add the onion; sauté for 3 minutes or until the onion is soft. Add the garlic; sauté for 30 seconds. Stir in the celery and barley until the barley is coated with the fat. Add the mushrooms, broth, and water. Lock the lid into place and bring to high pressure; maintain pressure for 18 minutes. Quick-release the pressure and remove the lid.
2. Drain off any excess liquid not absorbed by the barley, leaving just enough for a slightly soupy risotto. Reduce heat to low and stir in the cheese and parsley. Taste for seasoning and add salt if needed.

Three-Cheese Mac 'n' Cheese

 Serves 6

$ Total cost: $6.12

Serving size: 1 cup

Calories per serving: 325

Fat: 7g

Carbohydrates: 15g

Protein: 9g

Sodium: 285mg

1 tablespoon olive or vegetable oil

1 medium sweet onion, peeled and diced

1 clove garlic, peeled and minced

2 cups elbow macaroni

3 cups chicken broth

1 teaspoon sea salt

⅛ teaspoon freshly ground white pepper

½ cup whole milk

½ cup heavy cream

½ cup Cheddar cheese, grated

½ cup mozzarella cheese, grated

½ cup Colby cheese, grated

¼ cup dried bread crumbs

2 tablespoons butter, melted

You can speed up the process by cooking and stirring the cheese into the macaroni over very low heat until it's melted. Then follow the directions in Step 2, except preheat the broiler and brown the bread crumbs under the broiler.

1. Bring the oil to temperature in the pressure cooker over medium heat. Add the onion; sauté for 3 minutes or until the onion is soft. Add the garlic; sauté for 30 seconds. Add the macaroni and stir to coat it in the oil. Stir in the broth, salt, and pepper. Lock the lid into place and bring to high pressure; maintain pressure for 6 minutes. Quick-release the pressure and remove the lid.

2. Preheat the oven to 350°F. Drain the macaroni. Transfer to a 9" × 13" ovenproof baking dish. Stir in the milk, cream, and cheeses. Mix the bread crumbs together with the melted butter and sprinkle over the top of the macaroni and cheese. Bake for 30 minutes or until the cheeses are melted and the bread crumbs are golden brown. Remove from the oven and let rest for 5 minutes. Serve.

More Cheese

If your budget allows, add a little flavorful Gruyère or blue cheese and take this already delicious cheesy recipe to the next cheese level. If you do, I suggest substituting the Cheddar cheese for one of these.

Salad of Artichoke Hearts and Quinoa

 Serves 4

Total cost: $6.36
Serving size: 1 cup
Calories per serving: 348
Fat: 10g
Carbohydrates: 31g
Protein: 7g
Sodium: 298mg

1 cup pecans

1 cup uncooked quinoa

2½ cups water

2 cups frozen artichoke hearts

2 cups cherry or grape tomatoes, halved

2 shallots or ½ small red onion, thinly sliced

¼ cup Italian or Caesar salad dressing

2 heads Belgian endive

Make your own simple vinaigrette with 1 part balsamic or apple cider vinegar and 1½ parts olive oil. Whisk well with a little sea salt, pepper, a pinch of sugar, and a few freshly chopped herbs like cilantro.

1. Roughly chop the pecans and add them to the pressure cooker over medium heat. Dry roast for several minutes, stirring continuously to prevent the nuts from burning. The pecans are sufficiently toasted when they're fragrant and slightly brown. Transfer to a bowl and set aside to cool.

2. Add the quinoa and water to the pressure cooker. Lock the lid into place and bring to high pressure; maintain pressure for 2 minutes. Remove from the heat and allow pressure to release naturally for 10 minutes. Quick-release any remaining pressure. Transfer to a colander; drain and rinse under cold water. Transfer to a large bowl.

3. While the quinoa is cooking, prepare the artichoke hearts according to package directions and then plunge into cold water to cool and stop the cooking process. When cooled, cut into quarters.

4. Stir the artichoke hearts into the quinoa along with the tomatoes and shallots or red onion. Toss with the salad dressing. At this point, the quinoa mixture can be covered and refrigerated until ready to serve. This allows the flavors to blend. However, if you'll be refrigerating the quinoa mixture for more than 1 hour, leave the cherry or grape tomatoes whole rather than halving them.

5. To prepare the salad, separate the endive leaves. Rinse, drain, and divide them between 4 plates. Top each with ¼ of the quinoa mixture. Sprinkle ¼ cup of the toasted pecans over the top of each salad.

Cheese Tortellini with Chicken

Serves 6

Total cost: $6.97

Serving size: 1½ cups

Calories per serving: 423

Fat: 10g

Carbohydrates: 42g

Protein: 29g

Sodium: 861mg

3 slices bacon, diced

¼ cup plus 3 tablespoons butter, divided

2 shallots, peeled and minced

1 tablespoon chopped fresh Italian flat-leaf parsley

1 pound boneless, skinless chicken breasts

1 small carrot, peeled and finely sliced

1 (8-ounce) package dried cheese tortellini

1 teaspoon chopped fresh tarragon

2 cups chicken broth

1 cup coarsely chopped broccoli florets

2 teaspoons all-purpose flour

½ cup whole milk

½ cup Parmesan cheese, grated

Sea salt and freshly ground black pepper, to taste

Other delicious veggies for this dish include asparagus and spinach.

1. Fry the bacon in the pressure cooker over medium heat until it is crisp. Stir in ¼ cup of the butter, shallots, and parsley; sauté for 3 minutes. Cut the chicken into bite-sized pieces and add it to the pressure cooker along with the carrot, tortellini, tarragon, and broth. Stir. Lock the lid into place and bring to high pressure; maintain pressure for 6 minutes.

2. Quick-release the pressure and remove the lid. Add the broccoli to the pressure cooker. Lock the lid into place and bring to low pressure; maintain pressure for 2 minutes.

3. Quick-release the pressure and remove the lid. Combine the remaining 3 tablespoons of butter with the flour and then whisk it into the milk; stir in the cheese. Bring the contents of the pressure cooker to a simmer and slowly stir in the flour mixture. Cook and stir for 3 minutes or until the sauce is thickened and the flour taste is cooked out of the sauce. Taste for seasoning and add salt and pepper to taste. Transfer to a serving bowl or platter. Top with additional cheese if desired.

Risotto with Shrimp and Fennel Seed

 Serves 4

$ Total cost: $6.99

Serving size: 1 cup

Calories per serving: 305

Fat: 6g

Carbohydrates: 22g

Protein: 12g

Sodium: 382mg

2 tablespoons extra-virgin olive oil

1 small onion, peeled and diced

1 teaspoon fennel seeds

3 cloves garlic, peeled and minced

1½ cups Arborio rice

½ teaspoon cayenne pepper

2 tablespoons tomato paste

¼ cup dry white vermouth

3 cups chicken broth

1 pound medium shrimp, peeled and deveined

Sea salt and freshly ground black pepper, to taste

Risotto is a creamy favorite and is perfect served as first course or as an entrée. When serving as either one, add a little freshly chopped asparagus, broccoli, or spinach. A little risotto goes a long way, so even just a ¼ cup should do the trick.

1. Bring the oil to temperature in the pressure cooker over medium-high heat. Add the onion and fennel seeds; sauté for 3 minutes or until the onions are softened.
2. Add the garlic, rice, cayenne pepper, and tomato paste. Stir until the rice is evenly colored. Stir in vermouth and broth.
3. Lock the lid into place and bring to high pressure; maintain pressure for 6 minutes. Quick-release the pressure and remove the lid.
4. Stir in the shrimp; simmer for 2 minutes or until the shrimp are pale pink and cooked through.
5. Taste for seasoning and add salt and pepper if needed. Serve immediately.

Switch out the Shrimp

When your budget allows, try lobster instead of shrimp or skip the fish altogether and go for chopped Italian sausage. Risotto is delicious with just about any combination.

Green Onion Rice Pilaf with Carrot and Toasted Almonds

 Serves 4

1½ tablespoons unsalted butter

1 medium carrot, peeled and diced

1 stalk celery, finely diced

1 bunch green onion, coarsely chopped

2 cups long-grain white rice

¼ teaspoon sea salt

3 cups chicken broth

¼ cup whole toasted almonds

For a truly vegetarian version, skip the chicken broth and use Vegetable Broth (Chapter 10) or Mushroom Broth (Chapter 10).

1. Melt the butter in the pressure cooker over medium heat. Add the carrot and celery; sauté for 3 minutes.
2. Add the onion; sauté for 3 minutes or until the onion is tender. Add the rice and stir into the vegetables. Add the salt, broth, and almonds. Stir.
3. Lock the lid into place and bring to high pressure; maintain pressure for 3 minutes. Remove from the heat and allow pressure to release naturally for 5 minutes.
4. Quick-release any remaining pressure and remove the lid. Fluff the rice with a fork. Serve.

Swiss Chard with Brown Rice and Water Chestnuts

 Serves 6

1 cup brown rice

1½ cups water or chicken broth

1 small turnip, peeled and diced

1 pound banana squash, peeled and diced

½ cup baby carrots, quartered

1 small zucchini, peeled, quartered lengthwise, and sliced

3 stalks Swiss chard, leafy greens chopped and stems diced

1 cup broccoli florets, coarsely chopped

⅓ cup water chestnuts, diced

Sea salt and freshly ground black pepper, to taste

This recipe combines many flavorful but often overlooked vegetables. If you prefer, use your favorite vegetables instead.

1. Rinse and drain the rice. Bring the rice and water or broth to a boil in the pressure cooker over high heat.
2. Lock the lid into place and adjust heat to bring to low pressure; maintain pressure for 10 minutes.
3. Remove from the heat and allow pressure to release naturally. Remove the lid.
4. Add the turnip, squash, carrots, zucchini, chard, broccoli, and water chestnuts. Stir to mix with the rice.
5. Lock the lid into place, return the pan to the heat, and bring to low pressure; maintain pressure for 1 minute.
6. Remove from the heat and allow pressure to release naturally. Remove the lid.
7. Fluff the rice and vegetables with a fork. Taste for seasoning and add salt and pepper to taste. Serve.

Water Chestnuts

Water chestnuts are actually an aquatic vegetable. Their crispy crunch is pleasing to the palate and adds dimension to foods. As an alternative, use "real" nuts by substituting almonds, pecans, walnuts, pine nuts, or even cashews.

Chicken with Mushrooms and Rice

Serves 6

2 tablespoons extra-virgin olive oil

1 pound boneless chicken breast, cut into bite-sized pieces

1 large green pepper, seeded and diced

1 teaspoon chili powder

1 teaspoon smoked paprika

¼ teaspoon dried thyme

⅛ teaspoon dried oregano

¼ teaspoon freshly ground black pepper

Pinch cayenne pepper

1 medium white onion, peeled and diced

4 ounces fresh cremini mushrooms, sliced

2 cloves garlic, peeled and minced

2 cups chicken broth

1 cup long-grain rice

½ cup black olives, pitted and halved

Adjust the spice by using mild, medium, or hot chili powder, according to your tastes.

1. Bring the oil to temperature in the pressure cooker over medium heat. Add the chicken, green pepper, chili powder, paprika, thyme, oregano, black pepper, cayenne, and onion; stir-fry for 5 minutes or until the onion is transparent and the chicken begins to brown.
2. Stir in the mushrooms; sauté for 2 minutes. Add the garlic, broth, rice, and olives.
3. Lock the lid into place and bring to high pressure; maintain pressure for 3 minutes. Remove from the heat and allow the pressure to release naturally for 7 minutes.
4. Quick-release any remaining pressure. Uncover and fluff with a fork. Taste for seasoning and add salt and other seasoning if needed.

Olives

Olives are good for you in that they contain vitamins, minerals, and protein. This recipe calls for black olives, but you can use green olives or a combination of both.

The $7 a Meal Pressure Cooker Cookbook

Fresh Vegetable Risotto with Basil

 Serves 4

Total cost: $6.89
Serving size: 1 cup
Calories per serving: 335
Fat: 8g
Carbohydrates: 26g
Protein: 7g
Sodium: 276mg

¼ cup extra-virgin olive oil

1 clove garlic, peeled and minced

1 portobello mushroom

1 small zucchini, sliced

1 large red bell pepper, seeded and cut in quarters

1 medium onion, peeled and thickly sliced

Sea salt and freshly ground black pepper, to taste

¼ cup butter

1 cup Arborio rice

½ cup dry white wine

2 cups chicken broth

¼ cup fresh basil, sliced

½ cup Parmesan cheese, grated

For even more flavor, roast the peppers first and then dice and add.

1. Ten minutes before you'll be grilling the vegetables, add the oil and garlic to a small bowl; stir to mix and set aside to infuse the flavor of the garlic into the oil.
2. Preheat the grill or a grill pan over medium-high heat. Remove the stem and black gills from the mushroom cap; slice the cap.
3. Brush all sides of the zucchini slices, bell pepper quarters, mushroom slices, and onion with the oil.
4. Place vegetables on the grill rack or in the grill pan. Sprinkle with salt and pepper.
5. Turning once, grill the vegetables for several minutes on each side or until softened and slightly charred. Set aside to cool, and then coarsely chop.
6. Bring the remaining garlic-infused oil and 3 tablespoons of the butter to temperature in the pressure cooker over medium heat.
7. Add the rice and stir it to coat it in the oil-butter mixture. Stir in the wine and broth.
8. Lock the lid into place and bring to high pressure; maintain pressure for 7 minutes. Remove from the heat, quick-release the pressure, and remove the lid.
9. Add the chopped grilled vegetables and basil. Cover the pressure cooker (but do not lock the lid into place).
10. Let rest, covered, for 5 minutes. Stir in cheese and remaining butter. Taste for seasoning and add additional salt and pepper to taste.

Chicken and Brown Rice Salad

Serves 6

 Total cost: $6.79

Serving size: 1 cup

Calories per serving: 376

Fat: 7g

Carbohydrates: 24g

Protein: 21g

Sodium: 268mg

2 cups long-grain brown rice, rinsed and drained

4½ cups chicken broth

1 whole chicken breast, skin removed

1½ teaspoons sea salt

3 green onions, finely diced

2 large carrots, peeled and diced

2 stalks celery, sliced

1 small red bell pepper, seeded and diced

3 tablespoons mayonnaise

1 teaspoon Dijon mustard

1 teaspoon honey

2 tablespoons butter, melted

2 tablespoons apple cider vinegar

½ cup extra-virgin olive oil

2 hard-boiled eggs, peeled and chopped

Freshly ground white pepper, to taste

2 tablespoons chopped fresh Italian flat-leaf parsley

Toss with a simple dressing or drizzle with balsamic vinegar.

1. Add the rice, broth, chicken, and salt to the pressure cooker. Lock the lid into place and bring to high pressure; maintain pressure for 12 minutes.
2. Remove from heat, quick-release the pressure, and remove the lid. Transfer the chicken to a cutting board. Fluff the rice with a fork and transfer it to a bowl. Once rice has cooled, toss it with the onions, carrots, celery, and bell pepper.
3. To make the dressing, whisk together the mayonnaise, mustard, honey, melted butter, and vinegar, and then slowly whisk in the olive oil.
4. Fold in the chopped boiled egg. Taste for seasoning.
5. Pour half of the dressing over the rice salad mixture in the bowl. Stir to mix, adding more dressing if desired. Sprinkle the fresh parsley over the salad. Serve.

Dijon Mustard

Dijon mustard—or any mustard, really—adds such great sharp flavors to foods with little to no calories. Its spicy and creamy texture are a complement to the sweet and silky texture of honey.

The $7 a Meal Pressure Cooker Cookbook

Cinnamon Brown Rice with Dried Apricots and Plums

 Serves 6

💲 Total cost: $6.37

Serving size: ½ cup

Calories per serving: 355

Fat: 8g

Carbohydrates: 29g

Protein: 6g

Sodium: 410mg

2 tablespoons butter oil

2 stalks celery, thinly sliced

2 large carrots, peeled and diced

1 large sweet potato, peeled and diced

1½ cups long- or short-grain brown rice, rinsed and drained

⅓ cup pitted prunes, chopped

⅓ cup dried apricots, chopped

½ teaspoon ground cinnamon

2 teaspoons orange zest, grated

3 cups water or chicken broth

1 bay leaf

½ teaspoon sea salt

To dice a large peeled carrot, quarter the carrot length-wise and then slice the resulting strips into cubes.

1. Melt the butter in the pressure cooker. Add the celery, carrots, sweet potato, and rice. Stir to coat in the butter.
2. Stir in the prunes, apricots, cinnamon, and orange zest. Bring the water or broth to a boil and pour it into the pressure cooker; stir to mix it into the rice mixture. Add the bay leaf and salt.
3. Lock the lid into place and bring to high pressure; maintain pressure for 16 minutes. Remove from the heat and allow pressure to release naturally for 10 minutes.
4. Quick-release any remaining pressure and remove the lid. Use a fork to fluff the rice.
5. Taste to make sure the rice is cooked through. If it isn't, add additional water or broth if needed and simmer or cook under pressure until tender.
6. If the rice is already cooked through, drain off any excess moisture. Remove and discard the bay leaf. Taste for seasoning and adjust if necessary. Transfer to a serving bowl. Serve hot.

Chicken and Rice Casserole with Vegetables

 Serves 6

$ Total cost: $6.99

Serving size: 1 cup

Calories per serving: 358

Fat: 8g

Carbohydrates: 29g

Protein: 25g

Sodium: 467mg

2 tablespoons olive oil

1½ pounds boneless, skinless chicken breasts

1 cup long-grain white rice, rinsed and drained

1 (14-ounce) can chicken broth

½ cup bottled Caesar salad dressing

4 cloves garlic, peeled and minced

1 tablespoon dried Italian herb blend

1 cup frozen broccoli florets, thawed

1 cup frozen cauliflower pieces, thawed

1 cup frozen sliced carrots, thawed

½ cup pimiento-stuffed olives, sliced

½ cup Parmesan cheese, grated

This dish is made super-easy with bottled Caesar salad dressing.

1. Bring the oil to temperature in the pressure cooker over medium heat. Cut the chicken into bite-sized pieces and add to the pressure cooker.
2. Stir-fry for 5 minutes or until lightly browned. Stir in the rice, broth, dressing, garlic, and Italian herb blend.
3. Lock the lid into place and bring to high pressure; maintain pressure for 8 minutes. Quick-release the pressure and remove the lid.
4. Stir the mixture in the pressure cooker. Add the thawed frozen vegetables and olives to the top of the chicken and rice mixture.
5. Lock the lid back into place and bring to high pressure; maintain pressure for 2 minutes.
6. Remove from the heat and allow pressure to release naturally. Remove the lid. Stir in the cheese, fluffing the rice with a fork. Transfer to a serving bowl. Serve hot.

Variations

This dish is great with pork, beef, or turkey. Or, leave out the pimiento-stuffed olives entirely or replace with black olives or another of your favorite olives.

The $7 a Meal Pressure Cooker Cookbook

Spiced Rice with Coconut

 Serves 4

2 tablespoons butter

1 cup extra long-grain white rice, rinsed and drained

½ cup unsweetened coconut, flaked or grated

2¼ cups water

¼ cup currants

½ teaspoon ground cinnamon

1 teaspoon anise seed

⅛ teaspoon ground cloves

½ teaspoon sea salt

The combination of coconut, currants, and spices trans- forms this rice into a succulent dish. It's perfect as a sur- prise dish for guests, as it's not every day you are served this type of dish. It goes great with jerk chicken or Cajun shrimp. Add the chicken or shrimp right after cooking for a full meal.

1. Bring the butter to temperature in the pressure cooker over medium heat. Add the rice, stirring well to coat it in the fat.
2. Add the coconut, water, currants, cinnamon, anise seeds, cloves, and salt. Lock the lid into place and bring to high pressure; maintain the pressure for 3 minutes. Turn off the heat and let the pressure drop naturally for 7 minutes.
3. Quick-release any remaining pressure and remove the lid. Fluff the rice with a fork. Drain off any excess moisture. Taste for seasoning and adjust if necessary. Serve.

Cajun-Style Chicken with Rice

Serves 6

2 tablespoons olive oil

1½ pounds boneless, skinless chicken breasts

1 medium white onion, peeled and diced

1 large green bell pepper, seeded and diced

4 cloves garlic, peeled and minced

1 teaspoon dried rosemary, crushed

1 teaspoon dried thyme

1 teaspoon paprika

¼ teaspoon dried red pepper flakes

½ cup white wine

1 (28-ounce) can diced tomatoes

1 (14-ounce) can chicken broth

2 cups frozen okra, thawed and sliced

1 cup frozen whole kernel corn, thawed

2 large carrots, peeled and sliced

1 cup long-grain white rice, rinsed and drained

½ cup chopped fresh cilantro, packed

1 bay leaf

Sea salt and freshly ground black pepper, to taste

Serve with steamed broccoli, sautéed green beans, or grilled artichoke hearts.

1. Bring the oil to temperature in the pressure cooker. Cut the chicken into bite-sized strips.
2. Add to the oil along with the onion and green pepper; sauté for several minutes or until the chicken is slightly browned.
3. Add the garlic, rosemary, thyme, paprika, and red pepper flakes; sauté for 2 minutes or until the herbs begin to release their aroma.

4. Pour in the wine; deglaze the pan, scraping up any bits stuck to the bottom of the pan.
5. Add the remaining ingredients. Stir to mix. Lock the lid and bring to high pressure; maintain pressure for 7 minutes.
6. Remove from the heat and allow pressure to release naturally. Remove the lid. Remove and discard the bay leaf. Fluff the rice with a fork. Taste for seasoning and adjust if necessary. Serve.

Long-Grain Rice with Mixed Vegetables and Lemon

 Serves 6

3 tablespoons butter

1 small red onion, peeled and diced

2 cloves garlic, peeled and diced

1 cup long-grain white rice, rinsed and drained

3 cups frozen mixed vegetables, thawed

1 (14-ounce) can chicken broth

¼ cup fresh lemon juice

1 tablespoon ground cumin or herb blend

½ teaspoon sea salt

½ teaspoon freshly ground black pepper

Mix it up a bit by using wild rice pilaf, brown rice, or even basmati rice. For true wild rice (not the quick-cooking kind) and brown rice, add an additional 3 minutes of cooking time.

1. Melt the butter in the pressure cooker over medium heat. Add the onion; sauté for 3 minutes or until soft. Add the garlic; sauté for 30 seconds.
2. Add the rice and stir to coat it in the butter; sauté until the rice becomes translucent. Add the remaining ingredients. Stir to mix.
3. Lock the lid into place and bring to high pressure; maintain pressure for 7 minutes. Remove from the heat and allow pressure to release naturally. Remove the lid. Fluff the rice with a fork. Taste for seasoning and adjust if necessary.

Adding Protein

You can easily turn this side dish into a meal by adding diced chicken breasts, lean turkey sausage, or ground beef.

Southern Black-Eyed Peas

 Serves 6

 Total cost: $5.32

Serving size: ¾ cup

Calories per serving: 318

Fat: 5g

Carbohydrates: 12g

Protein: 8g

Sodium: 359mg

½ pound thick-cut bacon, diced

1 stalk celery, finely diced

1 (1-pound) bag baby carrots, divided

1 large onion, peeled and diced

2 (15-ounce) cans black-eyed peas, rinsed and drained

1 cup long-grain white rice, rinsed and drained

4 cups chicken broth

Sea salt and freshly ground black pepper, to taste

In the South, black-eyed peas are a tradition on New Year's Day. The tradition is to eat modestly on the first day of the year to symbolize prosperity every day thereafter. If you are not a fan of black-eyed peas, use lentils or black beans for this recipe.

1. Fry the bacon in the pressure cooker over medium heat until the fat begins to render out of the bacon. Add the celery; sauté for 2 minutes.
2. Shred 4 baby carrots and add them to the pan with the celery; sauté for another minute. Add the onion and sauté for 3 minutes or until the onions are soft.
3. Dice the remaining baby carrots and add them to the pressure cooker. Stir in the black-eyed peas, rice, and chicken broth.
4. Lock the lid into place and bring to high pressure; maintain pressure for 7 minutes. Remove from the heat and allow pressure to release naturally. Remove lid and stir. Taste for seasoning; add salt and pepper if needed.

Brown Rice Risotto with Fontina Cheese

 Serves 8

$ Total cost: $6.74

Serving size: 1 cup

Calories per serving: 325

Fat: 7g

Carbohydrates: 29g

Protein: 6g

Sodium: 251mg

1 medium leek

½ small fennel bulb

3 tablespoons butter

2 cups short-grain brown rice, rinsed and drained

½ teaspoon sea salt

2¾ cups water

1 tablespoon frozen white grape juice concentrate

¾ cup Fontina cheese, grated

1½ teaspoons freshly ground or cracked black pepper

Using grape juice gives this risotto a slight sweetness and is an alternative to using the traditional white wine. If cooking with alcohol does not bother you, use a white wine, such as a sauvignon blanc, instead.

1. Cut the leeks into quarters lengthwise, and then slice into ½" slices; wash thoroughly, drain, and dry.
2. Clean the fennel. Trim the fronds from the fennel and chop. Dice the bulb.
3. Melt the butter in the pressure cooker over medium heat. Add the leeks and diced fennel bulb; sauté for a minute or until the leeks begin to wilt.
4. Add the rice and stir-fry into the leeks until the rice begins to turn golden brown. Stir in the salt, water, and white grape juice concentrate.
5. Lock the lid into place and bring to high pressure; maintain pressure for 20 minutes. Remove from the heat and allow pressure to release naturally for 10 minutes. Quick-release any remaining pressure. Remove the lid.
6. Fluff the rice with a fork. Stir in the cheese, fennel fronds, and pepper. Taste for seasoning and add additional salt if needed. Serve.

Shrimp Risotto

If your budget allows, add ½ cup coarsely chopped cooked shrimp to this recipe for a delicious shrimp risotto.

Rice Pilaf with Cauliflower, Peppers, and Almonds

 Serves 4

1 tablespoon butter

1 tablespoon olive oil

½ small yellow onion, peeled and thinly sliced

2 cloves garlic, peeled and minced

1 (1½") piece fresh ginger, peeled and grated

1 serrano pepper, seeded and minced

1½ cups cauliflower florets, quartered

1 cup green beans, cleaned and cut into 1" pieces

1 large carrot, peeled and sliced diagonally

1 teaspoon ground cumin

½ teaspoon ground turmeric

¼ teaspoon cardamom seeds

1 teaspoon chili powder

⅛ teaspoon ground cloves

⅛ teaspoon hot paprika

½ teaspoon sea salt

1 cup long-grain white rice, rinsed and drained

1½ cups water

¼ cup slivered almonds, toasted

Add chicken or turkey to make this a nutrition-packed meal.

1. Melt the butter in the pressure cooker over medium heat. Add the oil and bring to temperature.
2. Add the onion, garlic, ginger, and serrano pepper; sauté for 2 minutes. Stir in the cauliflower, green beans, carrot, cumin, turmeric, cardamom seeds, chili powder, ground cloves, paprika, salt, rice, and water.
3. Lock the lid into place and bring to high pressure; maintain pressure for 6 minutes. Remove from the heat and allow pressure to release naturally for 15 minutes. Quick-release any remaining pressure and remove the lid.
4. Fluff rice with a fork. Transfer to a serving bowl. Top with toasted almonds.

CHAPTER 12

SAVORY CASSEROLES AND SIDE DISHES

Red Potato Casserole with Ham / 278

Potato Sausage Casserole / 279

Wild Rice Mushroom Casserole / 280

Spicy Beef with Jalapeño and Cheddar / 281

Ziti and Summer Sausage with Cream Cheese / 282

One-Pot "Paella" / 283

Barley with Ham and Bell Pepper / 284

Scalloped Potatoes with Ham and Onion / 285

Ham Stuffed with Potato, Spinach, and Red Bell Pepper / 286

Casserole of Beef, Bell Pepper, and Tomato / 287

Turkey with Mixed Vegetables and Potatoes / 288

Ham and Cabbage Casserole / 289

Yam and Potato with Curry / 290

Herbed New Potatoes / 291

Simple Red Beets / 292

Beet and Carrot Salad / 293

Cabbage with Merlot Apples / 294

Southern Lima Beans with Bacon / 295

Steamed Broccoli with Caesar Dressing / 296

Dijon Broccoli with Lemon / 297

Sweet Potatoes and Bell Peppers with Coconut / 298

Herb Garlic Polenta / 299

Creamy Root Vegetables / 300

Easy Asparagus with Olive Oil and Shallots / 301

Simple Corn on the Cob with Lime / 302

Garlic Mashed Potatoes with Chives / 303

Fresh Celery with Lemon / 304

Brussels Sprouts with Parmesan / 305

Parsnip Purée with Nutmeg / 306

Curried Green Tomatoes / 307

Pressure-Braised Kale with Potatoes / 308

Poached Fennel with Onion in White Wine / 309

Beet Greens with Shallots and Balsamic Vinegar / 310

Buttered Baby Turnips / 311

Fresh Radishes with Italian Parsley and Light Cream Sauce / 312

Creamy Turnip Purée with Lemon / 313

Turnip Greens with Toasted Pine Nuts / 314

Purée of Carrot with Turnip and Nutmeg / 315

Creamed Rutabagas with Parsnips / 316

Red Potato Casserole with Ham

Serves 4

$ Total cost: $6.12

Serving size: 1 cup

Calories per serving: 315

Fat: 5g

Carbohydrates: 21g

Protein: 9g

Sodium: 265mg

4 smoked ham hocks, about ½ pound each

1 tablespoon gin

1 medium sweet onion, peeled and quartered

2 stalks celery, tops only

1 large carrot, peeled and quartered

1 cup chicken broth

3 cups water

4 large red potatoes, scrubbed and quartered

4 Belgian endives, rinsed, drained, and cut in half lengthwise

¾ cup heavy cream

1 tablespoon herb dry soup mix, optional

Gin adds flavor but also enhances the flavor in the other ingredients. Don't add too much or the strong juniper influence of gin will overpower the dish.

1. Add the ham hocks, gin, onion, celery tops, carrot, broth, and water to the pressure cooker.
2. Lock the lid into place and bring to low pressure; maintain pressure for 30 minutes. Remove from the heat and allow pressure to release naturally. Remove the lid.
3. Transfer the ham hocks to a serving platter; keep warm. Strain the pan juices. Discard the cooked vegetables.
4. Skim off any fat from the top of the strained juices and discard. Pour the strained, defatted juices back into the pressure cooker.
5. Add the potatoes to the pressure cooker, cut-side down. Lock the lid into place and bring to low pressure; maintain pressure for 7 minutes.
6. Quick-release the pressure and remove the lid. Adjust heat to maintain a low simmer and add the endives.
7. Loosely cover the pan and simmer for 4 minutes to steam the endives. Transfer the endives and potatoes to the serving platter with the ham hocks; keep warm.
8. Stir the cream into the pan juices remaining in the pressure cooker. Bring to a boil over medium-high heat; boil hard for 5 minutes. Remove from heat and whisk in herb soup mix, if using.
9. To assemble, place a ham hock, 4 potato quarters, and 2 endive pieces on each plate. Generously spoon the sauce over all.

Potato Sausage Casserole

 Serves 8

Total cost: $6.34

Serving size: ¾ cup

Calories per serving: 381

Fat: 16g

Carbohydrates: 29g

Protein: 19g

Sodium: 730mg

1 pound smoked sausage, sliced

1 (1-pound) bag frozen Tater Tots, thawed

1 (1-pound) bag broccoli and cauliflower, thawed

1 (10.75-ounce) can condensed cream of mushroom soup

1 (10.75-ounce) can condensed cream of chicken soup

1 (12-ounce) can evaporated milk

This simple and delicious casserole uses breakfast sausage. If desired, substitute ground beef or ground turkey for the sausage.

1. Treat the inside of the pressure cooker with nonstick spray. Arrange a layer of smoked sausage slices over the bottom of the pressure cooker. Top with a layer of Tater Tots and a layer of broccoli and cauliflower.
2. In a large measuring cup, mix together the soups and evaporated milk. Working in thirds, pour the soup-milk mixture over the layers in the pressure cooker.
3. Continue to layer until all of the smoked sausage, vegetables, and soup-milk mixture have been added to the pressure cooker, ending with a layer of smoked sausage.
4. Lock the lid into place and bring to low pressure over medium heat; maintain pressure for 10 minutes. Remove from the heat and allow pressure to release naturally. Serve.

Adding Cheese

Grated Cheddar cheese or mozzarella is also good with this recipe. If using quick-release method, stir in immediately after cooking. To use the natural-release method, place cheese on top of cooked dish, resecure lid, and return to pressure for 2½ minutes to melt cheese. Melt over top or stir into cheese and then melt.

Wild Rice Mushroom Casserole

 Serves 4

 Total cost: $6.22
Serving size: ½ cup
Calories per serving: 306
Fat: 11g
Carbohydrates: 23g
Protein: 9g
Sodium: 469mg

2 tablespoons butter

1 small sweet onion, peeled and diced

4 ounces fresh cremini mushrooms, cleaned and sliced

1 cup wild rice, rinsed and drained

½ cup pecans, chopped and toasted

2 teaspoons herb seasoning blend

2 cups chicken broth

Sea salt and freshly ground black pepper, to taste

A natural side dish for roast turkey or chicken. Add flavor dimension by using shiitake mushrooms along with the fresh button mushrooms.

1. Melt the butter in the pressure cooker over medium heat. Stir in the onion and mushrooms; sauté for 5 minutes or until the mushrooms have given off their moisture and begin to brown. Stir in the wild rice, pecans, seasoning blend, and broth.
2. Lock the lid into place and bring to high pressure; maintain pressure for 20 minutes. Remove from the heat and allow pressure to release naturally.
3. Fluff rice with a fork and drain off any excess moisture. Taste for seasoning and add salt and pepper if needed.

Nuts

This recipe calls for chopped pecans but is equally delicious with chopped walnuts, pistachios, or pine nuts.

Spicy Beef with Jalapeño and Cheddar

Serves 6

1 pound lean ground beef

1 tablespoon olive oil

1 small yellow onion, peeled and diced

1 jalapeño pepper, seeded and minced

2 cloves garlic, peeled and minced

2 cups bottled salsa

1 (3-ounce) can tomato paste

2 tablespoons chili powder

3 cups uncooked penne or ziti pasta

Water, enough to cover all ingredients

1¼ cups grated sharp Cheddar cheese

This dish is popular served with avocado and baked tortilla chips. As with many recipes, you can easily substitute Italian sausage, shredded chicken, or pork for the beef.

1. Add the ground beef to the pressure cooker. Fry over medium-high heat and break apart until it is cooked through. Drain off and discard fat.
2. Stir in the oil, onion, and jalapeño; sauté for 3 minutes or until onion is tender. Stir in the garlic and sauté for 30 seconds.
3. Stir in the salsa, tomato paste, chili powder, and pasta. Pour in enough water to cover all of the ingredients.
4. Lock the lid into place and bring to low pressure; maintain pressure for 6 minutes. Remove from the heat and allow pressure to release naturally. Remove the lid. Drain off and discard any excess moisture.
5. Stir in the cheese. Cover the pressure cooker for 3 minutes to allow time for the cheese to melt. Stir again. Taste for seasoning and adjust if necessary. Serve.

Ziti and Summer Sausage Casserole with Cream Cheese

 Serves 6

$ Total cost: $6.99

Serving size: 1 cup

Calories per serving: 461

Fat: 14g

Carbohydrates: 29g

Protein: 21g

Sodium: 870mg

1 tablespoon butter

1 stalk celery, finely diced

2 baby carrots, grated

1 small onion, peeled and diced

1½ pounds summer or smoked sausage, diced

1 (8-ounce) can mushroom stems and pieces, drained

3 cups uncooked penne or ziti pasta

Water, enough to cover ingredients

1 (8-ounce) package cream cheese, cubed

¼ cup heavy cream

1 cup frozen baby peas, thawed

Sea salt and freshly ground black pepper, to taste

The cream cheese and cream in this recipe serves as a quick and easy substitute for using canned condensed soup.

1. Melt the butter and bring it to temperature over medium heat. Add the celery and carrot; sauté for 2 minutes.
2. Add the onion; sauté for 3 minutes or until the onion is tender. Stir in the sausage and mushrooms; sauté for 2 minutes. Stir the pasta into the other ingredients already in the pressure cooker.
3. Pour in enough water to cover all of the ingredients. Lock the lid into place and bring to low pressure; maintain pressure for 6 minutes.
4. Remove from heat and allow pressure to release naturally. Remove the lid. Drain off and discard any excess moisture.
5. Add the cream cheese and cream to a microwave-safe bowl. Heat on high for 30 seconds or long enough to soften the cream cheese so that it can be whisked into the cream.
6. Add the cream cheese mixture to the pressure cooker and stir into the pasta mixture along with the baby peas.
7. Cover the pressure cooker for 3 minutes to allow time to warm the peas. Taste for seasoning and add if needed. Serve.

One-Pot "Paella"

 Serves 6

3 slices bacon, diced

¼ cup olive oil

2 large yellow onions, sliced

4 cloves garlic, peeled and minced

1¾ cups long-grain white rice

½ pound boneless, skinless chicken thighs

½ pound boneless, skinless chicken breasts

5 cups chicken broth

6 tablespoons tomato paste

½ cup bottled clam juice

3 tablespoons fresh lemon juice

2 tablespoons sherry

1 tablespoon light brown sugar

2 tablespoons dried parsley

1 teaspoon sea salt

½ teaspoon sweet paprika

¼ teaspoon red pepper flakes, crushed

2 teaspoons dried oregano

1 small green bell pepper, seeded and sliced

¼ pound bay scallops

¼ pound uncooked, cleaned shrimp

1 cup frozen peas, thawed

1 cup black olives, pitted and sliced

6 lemon slices

You can stretch this recipe to 8 servings by adding additional chopped vegetables.

1. Add the bacon to the pressure cooker and fry it over medium-high heat until crisp. Add the oil and bring it to temperature.
2. Stir in the onions; sauté for 3 minutes. Add the garlic; sauté for 30 seconds. Stir in the rice, sautéing it until the rice is coated in the oil and translucent.
3. Cut the chicken into bite-sized pieces. Add to the cooker, stirring it into the contents of the pan along with the broth, tomato paste, clam juice, lemon juice, sherry,

brown sugar, parsley, salt, paprika, pepper flakes, and oregano.
4. Lock the lid and bring to high pressure; maintain for 8 minutes. Remove from heat, quick-release the pressure, and remove the lid.
5. Stir in the bell pepper, scallops, and shrimp. Return to heat, lock the lid, and bring to low pressure; maintain for 3 minutes. Remove from the heat, quick-release the pressure, and remove the lid.
6. Stir in the peas and olives. Taste for seasoning. Serve garnished with lemon slices.

Barley with Ham and Bell Pepper

 Serves 8

Total cost: $6.98
Serving size: 1 cup
Calories per serving: 430
Fat: 20g
Carbohydrates: 31g
Protein: 16g
Sodium: 730mg

4 tablespoons butter

1 cup pearl barley, rinsed and drained

1 teaspoon sea salt

4 cups water or chicken broth

1 tablespoon olive oil

2 teaspoons fresh ginger, peeled and grated

2 cloves garlic, peeled and minced

1 large green bell pepper, seeded and diced

1 large red bell pepper, seeded and diced

1 stalk celery, sliced

1 (5-ounce) can sliced water chestnuts, drained

8 ounces fresh cremini mushrooms, cleaned and sliced

8 green onions, chopped and whites and greens separated

½ pound bean sprouts, rinsed and well drained

¾ pound cooked ham, diced

1 tablespoon toasted sesame oil

Soy sauce, to taste

This goes well with cooked chicken, sausage, or turkey. Add as you would the ham.

1. Melt the butter in the pressure cooker over medium-high heat. Stir in the barley and salt. Add the water.
2. Lock the lid and bring to high pressure; maintain for 4 minutes. Reduce to low pressure; maintain for 20 minutes.
3. Remove from heat and allow pressure to release naturally for 10 minutes. Quick-release any remaining pressure.
4. Unlock the lid, but leave the cooker covered with the lid slightly ajar for 10 minutes.
5. If necessary, drain or place the pan over low heat for a few minutes to remove any excess moisture.
6. Bring the oil to temperature in a large, deep nonstick skillet over medium-high heat. Add the ginger and garlic; sauté for 30 seconds.
7. Add the peppers, celery, water chestnuts, mushrooms, and the whites of the green onions; sauté an additional 2 minutes, stirring frequently.
8. Stir in the bean sprouts, barley, and ham; stir-fry for 3 minutes or until the ingredients are hot and most of the liquid given off by the vegetables has evaporated.
9. Stir in the scallion greens. Stir in the toasted sesame oil. Taste for seasoning and add soy sauce to taste.

The $7 a Meal Pressure Cooker Cookbook

Scalloped Potatoes with Ham and Onion

Serves 6

1 cup chicken broth

6 medium potatoes, peeled and cut into ½" slices

¼ teaspoon sea salt

⅛ teaspoon freshly ground white or black pepper

1 tablespoon fresh chives, chopped

½ thinly sliced yellow onion

½ cup whole milk

2 tablespoons butter, softened

2 tablespoons all-purpose flour

½ cup sour cream

¾ pound cooked ham, diced

¾ cup grated medium or sharp Cheddar cheese

You can easily increase the number of servings to 8 by adding a thinly sliced sweet onion and a sliced bell pepper to the potatoes.

1. Add the broth, potatoes, salt, pepper, chives, and onion to the pressure cooker. Lock the lid into place and bring to high pressure; maintain pressure for 5 minutes.

2. Remove the pressure cooker from the heat, quick-release the pressure, and remove the lid.

3. Treat a 9" × 13" ovenproof casserole dish with nonstick spray. Use a slotted spoon to transfer the potatoes to the casserole dish. Preheat the oven to 350°F.

4. Place the uncovered pressure cooker over medium-high heat. Stir the milk into any broth left in the pressure cooker and bring to a boil.

5. Add the butter and flour to a small bowl; mash into a paste, then stir in 1–2 tablespoons boiling liquid from the pressure cooker.

6. Whisk the butter-flour mixture into liquid in the pressure cooker; boil and stir for 1 minute, then continue to cook and stir until the mixture begins to thicken.

7. Remove from heat and stir in the sour cream. Pour over the potatoes in the casserole dish.

8. Evenly sprinkle the ham over the potatoes. Top with cheese. If desired, evenly sprinkle paprika to taste over the cheese.

9. Bake for 15 minutes or until the cheese is melted and bubbly.

Ham Stuffed with Potato, Spinach, and Red Bell Pepper

Serves 4

1½ cups fresh spinach, chopped

1 medium onion, peeled and diced

1 stalk celery, finely diced

Pinch dry red pepper flakes, crushed

⅓ cup instant mashed potato flakes

2 (1"-thick) ham steaks

1 cup chicken broth

½ cup water

1 large red or green bell pepper, seeded and diced

2 tablespoons butter, softened

2 tablespoons all-purpose flour

Instant potato flakes are an easy way to add substance to stuffing. For a lighter yet still flavorful alternative, leave out potato flakes and just use the chopped vegetables.

1. Add the spinach, onion, celery, red pepper, and potato flakes to a bowl and mix together.
2. If necessary, trim ham steaks so they'll fit onto the rack of the pressure cooker.
3. Pour the broth and water into pressure cooker. Add the diced bell pepper. Place 1 ham steak on rack.
4. Spread the spinach mixture evenly over the ham steak. Place the other ham steak on top of the mixture. Place the rack in the pressure cooker.
5. Lock the lid into place and bring to high pressure; maintain pressure for 5 minutes.
6. Remove from heat and allow pressure to release naturally. Remove lid. Transfer ham to a heated serving platter and keep warm.
7. Add enough water or broth to the pressure cooker to bring the remaining pan juices to 1 cup.
8. Place the pressure cooker over medium-high heat and bring the pan juices and cooked bell pepper mixture to a boil.
9. Mash the butter and flour into a paste, then thin it with some of the boiling pan juices. Whisk the thinned butter-flour mixture into the pan and boil for 1 minute.
10. Reduce heat and simmer and stir until the mixture thickens into a gravy. Pour over the stuffed ham steaks. Cut into 4 portions and serve.

Casserole of Beef, Bell Pepper, and Tomato

 Serves 4

1 pound lean ground beef

1 tablespoon olive oil

1 medium onion, peeled and chopped

2 large green bell peppers, seeded and diced

2½ cups herb-seasoned bread crumbs

1 (8-ounce) can whole-kernel corn, drained

1 (14-ounce) can diced tomatoes

½ cup beef broth

1 tablespoon butter, melted

Use canned whole tomatoes if you prefer. Crush or chop them when adding to the casserole.

1. Add the ground beef to the pressure cooker. Fry over medium-high heat until cooked through. Drain and discard fat. Stir in the oil, onion, and green bell pepper. Sprinkle 1½ cups of the bread crumbs over the beef-onion-pepper mixture.
2. Add the corn in a layer over the bread crumbs and the can of undrained diced tomatoes in a layer over the corn. Drizzle with the beef broth.
3. Lock the lid into place and bring to high pressure; maintain pressure for 3 minutes. Remove from the heat, quick-release the pressure, and remove the lid. Stir well. Taste for seasoning and adjust if necessary.
4. Preheat the oven to 400°F. In a small bowl, mix the remaining bread crumbs with the melted butter.
5. Transfer the contents of the pressure cooker to an ovenproof casserole treated with nonstick spray and sprinkle the buttered bread crumbs over the top.
6. Bake for 10 minutes or until the bread crumbs are golden brown. Remove from the oven and let rest for 10 minutes. Serve.

Seasoned Bread Crumbs

Bread crumbs are a versatile addition to many foods, adding both flavor and texture and making your dish more filling. Using seasoned bread crumbs works well for most dishes, as they add more flavor.

Turkey with Mixed Vegetables and Potatoes

Serves 6

Total cost: $6.94

Serving size: 1 cup

Calories per serving: 335

Fat: 6g

Carbohydrates: 19g

Protein: 26g

Sodium: 845mg

1 tablespoon extra-virgin olive oil

1 clove garlic, peeled and minced

4 cups chicken broth

6 medium potatoes, peeled and diced

6 large carrots, peeled and sliced

1 large sweet onion, peeled and diced

2 stalks celery, finely diced

½ ounce dried mushrooms

¼ teaspoon dried oregano

¼ teaspoon dried rosemary

1 bay leaf

2 strips orange zest

Sea salt and freshly ground black pepper, to taste

2 (1¼-pound) turkey drumsticks, skin removed

1 (10-ounce) package frozen green beans, thawed

1 (10-ounce) package frozen whole kernel corn, thawed

1 (10-ounce) package frozen baby peas, thawed

This recipe also works well with rice or pasta. Simply serve with 2 cups of cooked rice or 1 cup of cooked pasta.

1. Add the oil to the pressure cooker and bring to temperature over medium heat. Add the garlic and sauté for 10 seconds.
2. Stir in the broth, potatoes, carrots, onions, celery, mushrooms, oregano, rosemary, bay leaf, orange zest, salt, and pepper. Stand the 2 drumsticks meaty-side down in the pan.
3. Lock the lid and bring to high pressure; maintain pressure for 12 minutes. Remove from heat and allow pressure to drop naturally.
4. Remove the drumsticks. Cut the meat from the bone and into bite-sized pieces, and return it to the pot.
5. Stir in the green beans, corn, and peas; cook over medium heat for 5 minutes. Remove and discard the orange zest and bay leaf. Taste for seasoning and add salt and pepper if needed.

Turkey Drumsticks

Turkey drumsticks are a pressure cooker's friend. The turkey gets very tender, to the point where it naturally falls off the bone. Measure the depth of your pressure cooker before buying to be sure they will fit easily.

The $7 a Meal Pressure Cooker Cookbook

Ham and Cabbage Casserole

 Serves 6

💲 Total cost: $6.79

Serving size: 1 cup

Calories per serving: 299

Fat: 13g

Carbohydrates: 9g

Protein: 19g

Sodium: 435mg

3 slices bacon, cut into pieces

1 medium yellow onion, peeled and diced

1 zucchini, grated

3 large potatoes, scrubbed and diced

4 ounces cooked ham, diced

1 small head cabbage, cored and chopped

Sea salt and freshly ground black pepper, to taste

This flavorful meal is delicious as is, or switch out ham for boneless pork chops.

1. Add the bacon pieces to the pressure cooker; fry until just beginning to crisp over medium-high heat.
2. Reduce heat to medium and add the onion; sauté for 3 minutes or until the onion is softened. Add the zucchini and potatoes and stir into the onion and bacon.
3. Lock the lid into place and bring to low pressure; maintain pressure for 3 minutes. Remove from heat, quick-release the pressure, and remove the lid.
4. Mash the potatoes into the bacon and onions. Spread the ham over the potato mixture, then spread the cabbage over the ham.
5. Lock the lid into place and bring to high pressure; maintain pressure for 3 minutes. Remove from the heat and allow pressure to release naturally. Remove the lid.
6. If necessary, place the pan over low heat until any excess moisture from the cabbage and zucchini evaporates. Add salt and pepper, to taste. To serve, invert onto a serving plate.

Subbing and Serving

Substitute green beans or broccoli for the zucchini, if you like, or other vegetables such as diced bell pepper. Also, when serving, serve with spicy mustard for the perfect final flavor on this easy dish.

Yam and Potato with Curry

 Serves 8

1 tablespoon butter

1 small onion, peeled and finely diced

2 tablespoons curry paste

3 cloves garlic, peeled and minced

4 large yams, peeled and diced

1 large potato, peeled and diced

¼ cup applesauce

¼ cup water

1 cup frozen baby peas, thawed

Use this recipe as a base for making Indian vegetable samosas. Simply form a pastry pocket and place about 1 tablespoon of mixture inside. Bake at 400°F for about 10 to 15 minutes or until pastry is golden and puffed. Serve with plain or vanilla yogurt and strips of zucchini or fresh cucumber.

1. Melt the butter in the pressure cooker and bring to temperature over medium-high heat. Add the onion; sauté for 3 minutes.
2. Stir in the curry paste and garlic; sauté for 2 minutes. Stir in the diced yams and potatoes; sauté for several minutes or until the pan is sticky and the mixture is about to burn. Stir in the applesauce and water.
3. Lock the lid into place and bring to low pressure; maintain pressure for 5 minutes. Remove from the heat and allow pressure to release naturally.
4. Remove the lid. Stir and slightly mash the potato mixture. Add the peas. Stir into the potatoes. Cover and let rest for a few minutes to bring the peas to temperature. Serve.

The $7 a Meal Pressure Cooker Cookbook

Herbed New Potatoes

 Serves 8

$ Total cost: $5.21

Serving size: 1 cup

Calories per serving: 236

Fat: 3g

Carbohydrates: 19g

Protein: 2g

Sodium: 78mg

2 tablespoons olive oil

1 medium onion, peeled and diced

8 large red new potatoes, scrubbed and quartered

¼ cup water

1 teaspoon Italian seasoning

Sea salt and freshly ground black pepper, to taste

This is a great side dish for chicken, beef, and pork entrées. Serve with your desired protein and some grilled or steamed colorful veggies such as zucchini, red bell pepper, and corn.

1. Bring the oil to temperature over medium heat in the pressure cooker. Add the onion; sauté for 3 minutes or until the onion is softened.
2. Add the potatoes, cut-side down. Fry uncovered for 5 minutes or until the potatoes begin to brown.
3. Pour in the water. Sprinkle the herb blend over the potatoes. Season with salt and pepper.
4. Lock the lid into place and bring to high pressure; maintain pressure for 5 minutes. Remove from the heat and allow pressure to release naturally. Remove the lid. Serve.

Fresh Herbs

Use Italian seasoning, as suggested here, or try 1 teaspoon each of fresh herbs such as chopped rosemary and thyme. Adjust salt and pepper seasoning as needed, because most herb blend seasonings also contain salt and pepper.

Simple Red Beets

 Serves 8

$ Total cost: $4.27

Serving size: 1 cup
Calories per serving: 145
Fat: 2g
Carbohydrates: 14g
Protein: 3g
Sodium: 76mg

4 large golden or red beets

1 cup water

Butter, to taste

Sea salt and freshly ground
   black pepper, to taste

Beets are beautiful in color, which means they are also rich in nutrients. Serve them with practically anything including spinach, broccoli, kale, and zucchini.

1. Scrub the beets and trim both ends. Place the rack in the pressure cooker. Pour in the water. Place the beets on the rack.
2. Lock the lid into place and bring to high pressure; maintain pressure for 25 minutes.
3. Remove the pressure cooker from the heat, quick-release the pressure, and remove the lid. Transfer the beets to a cutting board. Test for doneness. If beets aren't cooked, simmer or cook, covered, in the microwave for a few extra minutes after Step 4.
4. When the beets are cool enough to handle, use a paring knife to remove the peel. Slice the beets. Reheat the beets and melt butter to taste over the heated beets.
5. Season with salt and pepper to taste.

Easy, Flavorful Additions
A simple, affordable addition to these already delicious vegetables: Toss with ¼ cup of feta or goat cheese. You'll transform ordinary beets into a dish everyone will love.

Beet and Carrot Salad

 Serves 8

$ Total cost: $6.62

Serving size: 1 cup

Calories per serving: 176

Fat: 3g

Carbohydrates: 10g

Protein: 3g

Sodium: 125mg

8 small red beets

1 (1-pound) bag peeled baby carrots

¼ cup water

Butter, to taste

Sea salt and freshly ground black pepper, to taste

Colorful beet juice will transform the color of the carrots. Be careful when handling beets that you don't get the juice on your clothes; the color can sometimes be hard to get out.

1. Scrub and peel the beets and trim the ends; quarter the beets. Add the baby carrots to the pressure cooker and put the beets on top. Pour in the water.
2. Lock the lid into place and bring to high pressure; maintain pressure for 8 minutes.
3. Remove the pressure cooker from heat, quick-release the pressure, and remove the lid.
4. Test the beets and carrots to determine whether or not they're cooked through.
5. If they're not yet tender, return the pan to medium heat. Add more water if necessary, and bring to a simmer. Simmer loosely covered until the vegetables are tender.
6. Once they're cooked through, drain off any excess moisture and transfer to a serving bowl. Top with butter, salt, and pepper to taste.

More with Carrots and Beets

Once cooked, chill this colorful healthy combination in the refrigerator for about 25 minutes. Toss lightly with Italian or honey mustard dressing and add in some freshly diced onion and herbs such as parsley or cilantro.

Cabbage with Merlot Apples

Serves 8

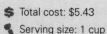
2 slices bacon, diced

2 Granny Smith apples

1 medium onion, peeled and diced

½ cup merlot wine or apple juice

⅓ cup light brown sugar, packed

3 tablespoons red wine vinegar

1 (2½-pound) red cabbage

Sea salt and freshly ground black pepper, to taste

Substitute Bartlett or d'Anjou pears for the apples if you prefer.

1. Add the bacon to the pressure cooker; fry over medium-high heat until crisp. Use a slotted spoon to remove the bacon to paper towels; set aside.
2. Peel the apples, remove the cores, and slice them. Reduce the heat to medium and add the apple slices and onion. Sauté for 3 minutes or until the onion is soft. Stir in the wine, brown sugar, and vinegar.
3. Wash the cabbage and remove and discard the outer leaves. Quarter the cabbage. Remove and discard the core. Slice the quarters into thin strips.
4. Gradually add to the pressure cooker, at first filling the pressure cooker to the top and loosely covering until the cabbage wilts, freeing up more space in the pan.
5. Stir in enough of the remaining cabbage to bring the pressure cooker to the fill line.
6. Lock the lid and bring to high pressure; maintain for 8 minutes.
7. Remove the pressure cooker from the heat, quick-release the pressure, and remove the lid. Stir and then use a slotted spoon to transfer the cabbage to a serving bowl. Stir in the reserved crisp bacon. Season with salt and pepper to taste.

Southern Lima Beans with Bacon

 Serves 4

2 slices bacon, diced

1 small onion, peeled and diced

1 clove garlic, peeled and minced

1 (1-pound) bag frozen lima beans

¼ cup water

¼ teaspoon freshly ground black pepper

2 tablespoons fresh parsley, minced

You can easily change the flavor of this dish by adding a (14-ounce) can of diced tomatoes. Add protein by adding cooked diced ham or sausage.

1. Add the bacon to the pressure cooker and fry over medium-high heat until almost crisp. Add the onion and sauté for 3 minutes or until soft.
2. Stir in the garlic; sauté for 30 seconds. Stir in the lima beans, water, and pepper.
3. Lock the lid into place and bring to high pressure; maintain pressure for 10 minutes.
4. Remove the pressure cooker from the heat and allow the pressure to release naturally for 10 minutes.
5. Quick-release any remaining pressure and remove the lid. Stir in the parsley. Transfer to a serving bowl. Serve immediately.

Steamed Broccoli with Caesar Dressing

Serves 6

Total cost: $5.82

Serving size: 1 cup

Calories per serving: 228

Fat: 4g

Carbohydrates: 8g

Protein: 3g

Sodium: 179mg

4 cups broccoli florets

¼ teaspoon sea salt

1 cup water

2 large hard-boiled eggs

2 cloves garlic, peeled and sliced

1 canned anchovy, rinsed and drained

1 tablespoon fresh lemon juice

¼ teaspoon Dijon mustard

2 tablespoons mayonnaise

2 tablespoons Parmesan cheese, grated

¼ cup extra-virgin olive oil

Additional salt and pepper, to taste

For a true salad, toss all with chopped romaine lettuce leaves. Serve with cooked chicken breasts, steak strips, or grilled fish as your budget allows.

1. Put the broccoli in the pressure cooker along with the salt and water. Lock the lid into place and bring to low pressure; maintain pressure for 2 minutes.
2. Remove the pressure cooker from heat, quick-release the pressure, and remove the lid. Drain and transfer the broccoli to a serving bowl.
3. Chop the egg whites and add to the serving bowl with the broccoli. Add the egg yolks to a blender or food processor along with the garlic, anchovy, lemon juice, mustard, mayonnaise, and cheese; process until smooth.
4. Gradually drizzle in the olive oil and process until oil is completely incorporated into the dressing.
5. Pour the dressing over the broccoli and chopped egg whites. Stir to mix. Season with salt and pepper to taste. Serve.

Dijon Broccoli with Lemon

 Serves 6

$ Total cost: $4.20

Serving size: 1 cup

Calories per serving: 108

Fat: 1g

Carbohydrates: 2g

Protein: 4g

Sodium: 139mg

4 cups broccoli florets

¼ teaspoon sea salt

1 cup water

4 tablespoons butter, melted

1 tablespoon fresh lemon juice

¼ teaspoon Dijon mustard

Broccoli is not only delicious, it packs in nutritious anti-oxidants, vitamins, minerals, and fiber.

1. Put the broccoli, salt, and water in the pressure cooker. Lock the lid into place and bring to low pressure; maintain pressure for 2 minutes.
2. Remove the pressure cooker from the heat, quick-release the pressure, and remove the lid. Drain and transfer the broccoli to a serving bowl.
3. While the broccoli cooks, whisk together the butter, lemon juice, and mustard. Pour over the cooked broccoli and toss to mix.

Serve as an Entrée
Simply toss this dish with cooked penne pasta and serve as an entrée. Add a cup of cooked diced chicken breast for more protein, if you like.

Sweet Potatoes and Bell Peppers with Coconut

Serves 6

Total cost: $6.72

Serving size: 1 cup

Calories per serving: 286

Fat: 12g

Carbohydrates: 21g

Protein: 12g

Sodium: 319mg

1 tablespoon peanut oil

1 red bell pepper, seeded and sliced

1 yellow bell pepper, seeded and sliced

1 large onion, peeled and sliced

2 cloves garlic, peeled and minced

1 tablespoon Thai green curry paste

3 large sweet potatoes, peeled and diced

1 (14-ounce) can unsweetened coconut milk

¼ cup water

1 teaspoon fresh lemon or lime juice

1½ cups frozen green beans, thawed

1½ tablespoons fresh cilantro, minced

Adjust the spice as you desire by using Thai red curry paste instead of green curry paste.

1. Bring the oil to temperature over medium heat. Add the bell pepper slices; sauté for 2 minutes.
2. Add the onion slices; sauté for 3 minutes or until the vegetables are soft. Add the garlic and curry paste; sauté for 1 minute.
3. Stir in the sweet potatoes, coconut milk, water, and lemon or lime juice. Lock the lid into place and bring to high pressure; maintain pressure for 3 minutes.
4. Remove the cooker from heat, quick-release the pressure, and remove the lid. Taste for and adjust seasoning.
5. Cut the snow peas or green beans into 1" segments. Stir into the sweet potato mixture in the pressure cooker.
6. Return the pressure cooker to medium heat and bring to a simmer. Maintain the simmer for 3 minutes or until the vegetables are cooked to tender-crisp. Stir in the cilantro. Serve.

Herb Garlic Polenta

 Serves 4

💲 Total cost: $2.56

🥄 Serving size: ½ cup

Calories per serving: 126

Fat: <1g

Carbohydrates: 27g

Protein: 3g

Sodium: 25mg

1 cup yellow cornmeal

4 cups cold water, divided

2 cloves garlic, minced

1 tablespoon chopped fresh cilantro

½ teaspoon sea salt

1 tablespoon butter

Polenta is delicious as a side dish or served under a protein such as grilled chicken breasts.

1. In a bowl or measuring cup, mix together the cornmeal, 1 cup cold water, and salt. Set aside.
2. Bring the remaining 3 cups water to a boil in the pressure cooker over medium heat. Stir in the moistened cornmeal mixture and the butter.
3. Continue to cook and stir until the mixture comes to a low boil or begins to bubble.
4. Lock the lid into place and bring to low pressure; maintain pressure for 10 minutes.
5. Remove the pressure cooker from heat, quick-release the pressure, and remove the lid. Stir in the garlic and cilantro. Taste for seasoning; add additional salt if needed. Serve warm.

Other Versions of Polenta

Use fresh basil, grated Parmesan cheese, and low-fat milk instead of water to give polenta a richer flavor. Serve with proteins such as chicken, as mentioned above, or grilled fish or pork chops.

Creamy Root Vegetables

Serves 8

1 cup water

2 pounds potatoes, peeled and diced

½ pound carrots, peeled and diced

1½ pounds white turnips, peeled and diced

1 teaspoon sea salt

4 tablespoons butter

½ cup whole milk

½ cup sour cream

2 teaspoons prepared horseradish

Freshly ground black pepper, to taste

Serve this unique dish as a substitute for mashed potatoes. The carrots add a touch of sweetness.

1. Add the water, potatoes, carrots, turnips, and salt to the pressure cooker in that order.
2. Lock the lid into place and bring to high pressure; maintain pressure for 7 minutes. Remove from the heat and allow pressure to release naturally for 10 minutes.
3. Quick-release any remaining pressure and remove the lid. Drain the vegetables and put them in a large serving bowl. Set aside and keep warm.
4. Wipe out the pressure cooker. Melt the butter and add ¼ cup of the milk and ¼ cup of the sour cream. Heat to low simmer over medium heat.
5. Mash the vegetables, stirring in the heated butter-cream mixture. Gradually add the remaining ¼ cup of milk and ¼ cup of sour cream.
6. Stir in 1 teaspoon horseradish; taste for seasoning and add additional salt and the remaining horseradish if needed. Season to taste with pepper. Serve.

Mashing Vegetables

Run the cooked vegetables through a food mill or mash with a handheld potato masher for best results.

The $7 a Meal Pressure Cooker Cookbook

Easy Asparagus with Olive Oil and Shallots

 Serves 4

$ Total cost: $6.56

Serving size: ½ cup

Calories per serving: 89

Fat: 1g

Carbohydrates: 3g

Protein: 2g

Sodium: 12mg

1½ pounds fresh asparagus

½ cup water

2 tablespoons shallot or red onion, minced

1 tablespoon fresh lemon juice

3 tablespoons extra-virgin olive oil

Sea salt and freshly ground white or black pepper, to taste

Using fresh asparagus is the way to go. This easy pressure cooker version couldn't be simpler!

1. Clean the asparagus and snap off the ends. If necessary, peel the stems. Lay flat in the pressure cooker and add the water.
2. Lock the lid into place and bring to high pressure; maintain pressure for 3 minutes. Remove from the heat and allow pressure to release naturally for 2 minutes.
3. In a small bowl or measuring cup, whisk together the shallot or onion, lemon juice, oil, salt, and pepper.
4. Quick-release any remaining pressure and remove the lid. Drain the asparagus and transfer to a serving platter. Pour the dressing over the asparagus. Serve.

Asparagus

Asparagus are great grilled, or cooked easily as here in the pressure cooker. You can also use broccoli, zucchini, or Brussels sprouts for this recipe. If using Brussels sprouts, cook an additional 3 minutes.

Simple Corn on the Cob with Lime

 Serves 4

 Total cost: $4.12

 Serving size: 1 ear

Calories per serving: 59

Fat: <1g

Carbohydrates: 14g

Protein: 2g

Sodium: 3g

4 ears fresh sweet corn, shucked

½ cup water

1 lime, quartered

Freshly ground black pepper,
   to taste

Lime adds a great crisp, fresh flavor to this dish. If desired, mix a little lime zest in with softened butter for an easy lime butter and spread onto cooked corn.

1. Place the rack in the pressure cooker and place the corn on the rack. Pour in the water.
2. Lock the lid into place and bring to low pressure; maintain pressure for 3 minutes.
3. Remove the pressure cooker from heat, quick-release the pressure, and remove the lid.
4. Transfer the corn to 4 serving plates. Place a lime wedge beside each ear of corn.
5. Have diners squeeze the lime juice over the corn and grind black pepper to taste over each ear of corn.

Corn Goes with Everything!
Delicious and colorful vegetables such as sliced red bell pepper, tomatoes, and cucumber are all great complements to corn. Corn is also a favorite with grilled burgers, pork loin, and of course, barbecue chicken.

The $7 a Meal Pressure Cooker Cookbook

Garlic Mashed Potatoes with Chives

 Serves 6

6 medium potatoes, peeled and quartered

2 cups water

½ teaspoon sea salt

2 tablespoons butter

3 cloves garlic, peeled and minced

¼ cup sour cream

¼ cup chopped fresh chives

Freshly ground white or black pepper, to taste

Garlic mashed potatoes are a favorite at dinner parties. Serve with grilled steak, chicken, pork, or fish.

1. Add the potatoes, water, and salt to the pressure cooker. Lock the lid into place and bring to high pressure; maintain pressure for 7 minutes.
2. While the potatoes cook, melt the butter in a small skillet over medium heat. Add the garlic; sauté for 2 minutes, being careful not to burn the garlic. Stir the garlic-infused butter into the sour cream.
3. Remove the pressure cooker from the heat, quick-release the pressure, and remove the lid. Drain the potatoes.
4. Return the potatoes to the pressure cooker and set it at low heat for 1–2 minutes to evaporate any residual moisture.
5. Mash the potatoes. Stir in the sour cream mixture, chives, and pepper. Taste for seasoning and add more salt if needed. Transfer to a bowl and serve.

Roasting Garlic

Roasting garlic gives it a richer, deeper flavor and a soft—almost creamy—texture. Simply place garlic in aluminum foil, drizzle with a little olive oil, fold aluminum foil around the garlic, and place in oven for 30 minutes at 400°F. You can roast a whole head of garlic this way, too; just leave it in the oven for about 45 minutes. Squeeze into mashed potatoes or spread on crostini for a separate appetizer altogether.

Fresh Celery with Lemon

 Serves 4

2 bunches celery

1 cup chicken broth

3 tablespoons butter, divided

1 tablespoon fresh lemon juice

Celery

Celery is most often thought of as for celery sticks, as an appetizer with dips, and for adding flavor to soups and stews. Here, celery is the featured vegetable and goes great with practically any dish. Add to Three-Cheese Mac 'n' Cheese (Chapter 11) or to Cajun-Style Chicken with Rice (Chapter 11) for a slightly crunchy or al dente texture and subtle flavor.

For added flavor, add a teaspoon of chopped fresh mint or Italian flat-leaf parsley.

1. Remove the outer stalks from the celery. Cut off the ends and the tops. Quarter the remaining celery. Rinse, drain, and add to the pressure cooker with broth and 1 tablespoon butter. Lock the lid into place and bring to high pressure; maintain pressure for 5 minutes. Reduce to low pressure and maintain for 5 minutes. Remove from heat and allow pressure to release naturally for 5 minutes. Quick-release any remaining pressure and remove the lid. Use a slotted spoon to transfer the cooked celery to a serving platter; keep warm.

2. Discard all but ½ cup of the liquid in the pressure cooker. Return the pressure cooker to the heat and bring to a boil over medium-high heat. Boil until reduced by half. Stir in the lemon juice. Whisk in the remaining 2 tablespoons of butter a teaspoon at a time. Remove from heat. Pour over the celery.

Brussels Sprouts with Parmesan

 Serves 6

Total cost: $6.53

Serving size: 1 cup

Calories per serving: 168

Fat: 4g

Carbohydrates: 19g

Protein: 5g

Sodium: 131mg

½ cup water

1 onion, peeled and sliced

3 stalks celery, diced

2 carrots, sliced on the diagonal

1 pound Brussels sprouts

1 cauliflower

4 tablespoons butter

4 cloves garlic, peeled and minced

½ cup Parmesan cheese, grated

⅛ teaspoon dried red pepper flakes, crushed

¼ cup whole milk

¼ cup sour cream

Get your family and friends to finally try Brussels sprouts with this simple and delicious recipe. The pressure cooker makes them perfectly tender.

1. Add the water to the pressure cooker.
2. Layer the onion, celery, and carrots into the pressure cooker. Wash and drain Brussels sprouts. Remove and discard the outer leaves. Cut in half and add on top of the carrots. Divide the cauliflower into large florets and add to top of vegetables.
3. Lock the lid into place and bring to high pressure; maintain pressure for 3 minutes. Remove the pressure cooker from the heat, quick-release the pressure, and remove the lid. Drain the vegetables and transfer them to a serving bowl.
4. Melt the butter in the pressure cooker over medium heat. Stir in the garlic and sauté for 30 seconds to 1 minute, being careful not to let the garlic burn. Stir in the cheese and pepper flakes. Slowly whisk in the milk and sour cream.
5. Continue to cook and stir until the sauce is smooth and bubbling. Pour over the vegetables. Toss to coat the vegetables. Serve.

Other Vegetables

Using a pressure cooker helps cook foods evenly, so use a medley of vegetables, if you like, with combinations like zucchini, Swiss chard, and bok choy.

Parsnip Purée with Nutmeg

 Serves 4

2 pounds parsnips

½ cup chicken broth

½ teaspoon sea salt

½ cup bread crumbs

¼ cup whole milk

¼ cup heavy cream

2 large eggs

2 tablespoons butter, divided

Freshly grated nutmeg, to taste

This dish requires a three-step preparation process: first, cooking the parsnips in the pressure cooker; second, puréeing the parsnips and assembling the dish; and third, baking the purée.

1. Clean and peel the parsnips, and then quarter them. Add the rack to the pressure cooker and pour in the broth. Place the chopped parsnips on the rack and sprinkle them with the salt. Lock the lid into place and bring to high pressure; maintain pressure for 4 minutes. Remove the pressure cooker from heat, quick-release the pressure, and remove the lid.
2. Preheat the oven to 350°F.
3. Drain and transfer the parsnips to a food processor. Add the bread crumbs, milk, cream, and eggs. Process until the parsnips are puréed.
4. Use 1 tablespoon butter to grease an ovenproof casserole dish large enough to hold the parsnip mixture; the mixture should only come up about 1" in the dish. Pour in the parsnip mixture.
5. Dot the top of the parsnip mixture with remaining butter and grate nutmeg over the top of the pudding. Bake for 1 hour or until firm and lightly browned on top.

Curried Green Tomatoes

 Serves 4

 Total cost: $5.24

Serving size: ¾ cup

Calories per serving: 96

Fat: 3g

Carbohydrates: 13g

Protein: 2g

Sodium: 87mg

2 tablespoons butter

2 tablespoons onion, minced

4 large green tomatoes, sliced

¼ cup water

½ teaspoon sugar

½ teaspoon sea salt

¼ teaspoon paprika

½ teaspoon curry powder

2 slices "day old" white bread, crusts removed

1 tablespoon fresh Italian flat-leaf parsley leaves, chopped

Though green tomatoes are unripe, they are great to eat. In the south, traditionally these are breaded and fried. Enjoy this leaner version with entrées such as sliced flank steak, pork loin or chops, and chicken.

1. Melt the butter in the pressure cooker over medium heat. Add the onion and sauté for 2 minutes. Add the tomatoes, water, sugar, salt, paprika, and curry powder. Stir to mix.
2. Lock the lid into place and bring to low pressure; maintain pressure for 8 minutes. Remove from the heat and allow pressure to release naturally.
3. Process the white portion of the bread in a blender or food processor to make fresh bread crumbs.
4. Remove the lid from the pressure cooker. Return the pan to medium heat and bring to a simmer. Stir in the fresh bread crumbs.
5. Simmer and stir until the mixture is thickened. Transfer to a serving bowl and sprinkle the parsley on top. Serve.

Add Some Red Tomatoes

If you desire, add 1 can of whole stewed red tomatoes for a simple twist on this easy dish. Serve with diced cooked chicken over rice.

Pressure-Braised Kale with Potatoes

 Serves 4

$ Total cost: $5.97

Serving size: 1 cup

Calories per serving: 165

Fat: 4g

Carbohydrates: 21g

Protein: 5g

Sodium: 175mg

2 cups water

½ teaspoon sea salt

2 bunches kale, washed and drained

2 tablespoons olive oil

1 small onion, peeled and diced

1 clove garlic, minced

1½ cups chicken broth

4 medium potatoes, peeled and diced

1 stalk celery, diced

Additional sea salt and freshly ground black pepper, to taste

Sour cream, for garnish, about 1 tablespoon per serving

This dish provides all the starch and vegetables needed for a meal. Kale is a leafy green vegetable that is both colorful and nutritious.

1. Add the water to the pressure cooker and bring to a boil over high heat. Stir in the salt. Cut the kale leaves into ½"-wide strips. Add the kale to the pressure cooker and blanch for 1 minute. Drain the kale in a colander and set aside.
2. Wipe out the pressure cooker and add the oil. Bring the oil to temperature in the pressure cooker over medium heat. Add the onion; sauté for 5 minutes or until it begins to brown. Add the garlic; sauté for 30 seconds.
3. Add the broth, potatoes, celery, and blanched kale. Lock the lid into place and bring to high pressure; maintain pressure for 6 minutes. Remove from the heat and allow pressure to release naturally. Remove the lid.
4. Stir, slightly mashing the potatoes into the mixture. Taste for seasoning and add additional salt and pepper, to taste. Garnish each serving with a dollop of sour cream.

Poached Fennel with Onion in White Wine

 Serves 4

4 fennel bulbs

1 tablespoon butter

1 tablespoon olive oil

1 small onion, peeled and diced

1 cup white wine

Sea salt and freshly ground black pepper, to taste

After the fennel has simmered uncovered in Step 2, use a slotted spoon to transfer it to a food processor. Pulse until smooth, adding some of the cooking liquid if necessary. The light anise flavor of fennel makes it a perfect companion for roast pork.

1. Cut off the tops and bottoms of the fennel bulbs and remove the two outer leaves. Thoroughly rinse the bulbs under cold running water. Dice the bulbs. Set aside.
2. Bring the butter and oil to temperature in the pressure cooker over medium heat. Add the onion; sauté for 3 minutes. Stir in the diced fennel; sauté for 3 minutes. Stir in the wine. Lock the lid into place and bring to low pressure; maintain pressure for 8 minutes.
3. Quick-release the pressure and remove the lid. Leave on the heat and simmer until the fennel is cooked through and soft and the alcohol is cooked out of the wine. This will mellow the flavor. Taste for seasoning and add salt and pepper, to taste. Serve.

Fennel

Fennel has a licorice-type flavor that is not a favorite for some people. If that's you, try a potato/spinach combination or carrots with cauliflower.

Beet Greens with Shallots and Balsamic Vinegar

 Serves 4

1 tablespoon olive oil

1 large shallot or small red onion, peeled and minced

1 pound beet greens

Sea salt and freshly ground black pepper, to taste

¼ cup chicken broth or water

Balsamic vinegar, for drizzling, approximately 2 teaspoons per serving

Young, fresh greens will cook quicker than older, tougher ones. Always use the freshest greens possible.

1. Bring the oil to temperature in the pressure cooker over medium heat. Add the shallot or onion; sauté for 3 minutes. Add the beet greens. Sprinkle with salt and pepper. Stir the greens to coat them in the oil. Once they're slightly wilted, add the broth or water, making sure not to exceed the fill line in your pressure cooker.

2. Lock the lid into place and bring to low pressure; maintain pressure for 1–3 minutes. Quick-release the pressure and remove the lid. Simmer and stir for a minute or until the remaining moisture in the pan evaporates. Taste for season-ing and add more salt and pepper if needed. Serve warm, with a splash of balsamic vinegar if desired.

Preparing Beet Greens

Cut the greens off of the beets starting at about 1" above the root part of the vegetable. Hold the stems and use the other hand to tear off the greens; discard the stems. Tear into pieces or cut into strips. Rinse thoroughly and drain. Weigh them. Eight to ten beets with greens yields approximately 1 pound.

Buttered Baby Turnips

 Serves 4

Total cost: $4.31
Serving size: ½ cup
Calories per serving: 27
Fat: 1g
Carbohydrates: 5g
Protein: 1g
Sodium: 20mg

4 baby turnips

½ cup water

½ teaspoon sea salt

3 tablespoons butter

1 small onion, peeled and sliced

½ teaspoon sugar

¼ teaspoon freshly ground black pepper

¼ teaspoon ground allspice

2 tablespoons fresh lemon juice

1 tablespoon fresh Italian flat-leaf parsley, minced

Root vegetables are a pressure cooker's friend, as the even steam of pressure makes them tender while the spices add the flavor.

1. Clean, peel, and quarter the turnips. Place the rack in the pressure cooker. Pour in the water. Place the turnips on the rack and sprinkle them with the salt.
2. Lock the lid into place and bring to low pressure; maintain pressure for 8 minutes. Remove the pressure cooker from the heat, quick-release the pressure, and remove the lid.
3. Transfer the turnips to a serving bowl; set aside. Remove the rack and discard any water remaining in the pressure cooker. Wipe out the pressure cooker; add the butter and melt over medium heat. Add the onion; sauté for 3 minutes. Stir in the sugar, pepper, allspice, and lemon juice. Whisk and cook until the sugar is dissolved into the sauce. Add the turnips and toss to coat them in the sauce. Transfer back to the serving bowl. Sprinkle the parsley over the top if using.

Turnips

Turnips traditionally have a stronger flavor than, say, potatoes. Serve with hearty proteins like beef, ham, or sausage.

Fresh Radishes with Italian Parsley and Light Cream Sauce

 Serves 4

24 large red radishes

2 tablespoons butter

2 tablespoons all-purpose flour

1 cup chicken broth or water

1 tablespoon chopped fresh Italian flat-leaf parsley

⅓ cup heavy cream

Sea salt and freshly ground white or black pepper, to taste

Braised radishes are another easy side dish. Just cover your radishes in water, add some butter, sugar, salt, and pepper, and bring to a boil. Simmer for 10–12 minutes or until radishes are tender.

1. Rinse and drain the radishes. Cut off the tops, leaving about 1" of the stem. Reserve some of the small leaves for garnish. Cut the radishes in half lengthwise.
2. Melt the butter in the pressure cooker over medium heat. When the butter begins to foam, whisk in the flour and then gradually whisk in the broth or water. Stir in the radishes.
3. Lock the lid into place and bring to low pressure; maintain pressure for 5 minutes. Remove from the heat and allow pressure to release naturally for 5 minutes. Quick-release any remaining pressure and remove the lid.
4. Use a slotted spoon to transfer the radishes to a serving bowl and toss with the parsley. Return the pressure cooker to medium heat and bring to a boil. Whisk in the cream; boil and stir for 2 minutes or until thickened.
5. Pour over the radishes. Add salt to taste and sprinkle liberally with pepper. Garnish with the reserved radish leaves, if desired.

Creamy Turnip Purée with Lemon

 Serves 4

4 medium turnips, peeled and diced

1 small onion, peeled and diced

½ cup beef or chicken broth

Fresh juice of ¼ lemon

¼ cup sour cream

1 tablespoon chopped fresh Italian flat-leaf parsley

Sea salt and freshly ground black pepper, to taste

Serve this low-carb dish in place of mashed potatoes using vegetable broth, if desired, for a truly vegetarian dish.

1. Add the turnips, onion, broth, and lemon to the pressure cooker. Lock the lid into place and bring to high pressure; maintain pressure for 5 minutes. Remove from the heat and allow pressure to release naturally for 10 minutes.
2. Drain the turnips or use a slotted spoon to transfer them to a serving bowl. Use a handheld mixer or immersion blender to purée the turnips, adding some of the broth from the pressure cooker if necessary.
3. Stir in the sour cream and parsley. Taste for seasoning and add salt and pepper, to taste.

Turnip Greens with Toasted Pine Nuts

Serves 4

Total cost: $6.12

Serving size: ½ cup

Calories per serving: 57

Fat: 4g

Carbohydrates: 3g

Protein: 3g

Sodium: 71mg

10 cups turnip greens, shredded

½ cup chicken broth or water

1 clove garlic, peeled and crushed

½ teaspoon sea salt

4 teaspoons extra-virgin olive oil

Freshly ground black pepper, to taste

½ cup pine nuts, pecans, or pistachios, toasted

Try using 1 shallot in place of the garlic to give the turnips a different flavor. Serve in place of a salad or as a vegetable side dish.

1. Rinse and drain the turnip greens. Add to the pressure cooker along with the broth or water, garlic, and salt.
2. Lock the lid into place and bring to low pressure; maintain pressure for 3 minutes. Remove from heat and allow pressure to release naturally for 5 minutes. Quick-release any remaining pressure and remove the lid.
3. Drain the turnip greens and transfer to a serving bowl. Toss with the oil. Add the pepper.
4. Taste for seasoning and add additional salt if needed. Stir in the toasted nuts.

Purée of Carrot with Turnip and Nutmeg

Serves 6

3 large turnips, peeled and quartered

4 large carrots, peeled and cut into 2" pieces

2 cups water

1 teaspoon sea salt

2 tablespoons extra-virgin olive oil

½ teaspoon nutmeg, freshly grated

2 tablespoons sour cream

1 tablespoon chopped fresh Italian flat-leaf parsley, for garnish

This is a good side dish to serve with leftover turkey. The nutmeg will put you in the mood for some leftover pumpkin pie or eggnog.

1. Put the turnips, carrots, water, and salt in the pressure cooker. Lock the lid into place and bring to high pressure; maintain pressure for 8 minutes. Remove the pressure cooker from the heat, quick-release the pressure, and remove the lid.

2. Drain the vegetables. Return them to the pressure cooker and put it over low heat for 1–2 minutes to evaporate any residual moisture. Mash the vegetables together with the oil, nutmeg, and sour cream. Taste for seasoning and add additional salt if needed. Serve with a little chopped parsley.

Sweet Carrots and Sour Cream

All dishes should ideally blend sweet, sour, and salty elements, and combine both smooth and al dente textures. This purée gets its sweetness from the carrots, its sourness from the sour cream, and its al dente texture from the added parsley at the end.

Creamed Rutabagas with Parsnips

Serves 4

$ Total cost: $6.28

Serving size: ½ cup

Calories per serving: 226

Fat: 5g

Carbohydrates: 20g

Protein: 4g

Sodium: 297mg

1 (¾-pound) rutabaga, peeled, quartered, and sliced

2 parsnips, peeled and sliced

2 tablespoons butter

¼ teaspoon sea salt

¼ water

¼ cup heavy cream

¼ cup sour cream

Nutmeg, freshly grated

Unlike many mashed root vegetable dishes where you can substitute milk for the cream or sour cream, this dish needs the added fat to offset the strong flavors of the vegetables.

1. Add the rutabaga, parsnips, butter, salt, and water to the pressure cooker. Lock the lid into place and bring to low pressure; maintain pressure for 8 minutes.
2. Remove from heat and allow pressure to release naturally for 10 minutes. Quick-release any remaining pressure and remove the lid.
3. Drain any excess moisture from the vegetables or put the pressure cooker over low heat for few minutes. Transfer to a food processor; pulse to purée the vegetables. Gradually add the cream as you pulse the vegetables until they reach their desired consistency. Once the vegetables are puréed, transfer them to a serving bowl and stir in the sour cream. Taste for seasoning and add additional salt and sour cream if desired. Garnish with the nutmeg.

Rutabagas

Rutabagas are a root vegetable that are best harvested in the fall (although they can be grown year round). Since they are essentially a cross between a cabbage and a turnip, they have a strong flavor. You can substitute beets for them, if desired.

CHAPTER 13

DESSERTS: BUTTERS, GLACÉS, COMPOTES, AND MORE

Cinnamon Apple Butter / 318

Fresh Cranberry Chutney / 319

Wine-Poached Pears / 320

Egg Custard with Lemon / 321

Compote of Wild Berries, Apples, and Pears / 322

Balsamic Peaches / 323

Banana Cream "Pie" / 324

Fruit Compote of Apricots, Peaches, and Golden Raisins / 325

Cinnamon Apples with Walnuts / 326

Cream Sherry Poached Pears / 327

Pear Butter with Vanilla Beans / 328

Lemon Glacé / 329

Cinnamon Apple Butter

Yield: About 2 cups

$ Total cost: $4.98

Serving size: ¼ cup

Calories per serving: 175

Fat: 1g

Carbohydrates: 39g

Protein: 1g

Sodium: 7mg

1 cup apple juice or cider

12 medium apples (about 3 pounds)

1½ teaspoons ground cinnamon

½ teaspoon ground allspice

⅛ teaspoon ground cloves

Finely grated zest of ½ lemon

1½ cups sugar

Apple butter is a great-tasting, easy, and healthy substitute for traditional butter on foods such as chicken, pork, and turkey. Use as a spread for breakfast or even on pita pockets with deli-sliced turkey for lunch.

1. Add the apple juice or cider to the pressure cooker. Wash, peel, core, and dice the apples.
2. Lock the lid into place, bring to high pressure, and immediately remove from heat; let the pressure release naturally for 10 minutes. Quick-release any remaining pressure.
3. Once the apples have cooled, press through a fine sieve or food mill, or process in a food processor or blender. Return the apples and cooking liquids to the pressure cooker and stir in the cinnamon, allspice, cloves, zest, and sugar.
4. Return the pan to medium heat and bring to a simmer. Simmer uncovered and stir until the sugar is dissolved and reduce heat.
5. Continue to simmer and stir for 1 hour or until the mixture is very thick. Note that it's important that you frequently stir the apple butter from the bottom of the pan to keep it from burning.

More Than Just Apple
This is a great recipe to try with other fruits, such as pears and mangoes. Substitute them for the fresh apples here but keep the apple juice as is. The apple juice will actually be a nice complement to almost any fruit.

The $7 a Meal Pressure Cooker Cookbook

Fresh Cranberry Chutney

 Serves 6

 Total cost: $5.78
 Serving size: ½ cup
Calories per serving: 281
Fat: <1g
Carbohydrates: 45g
Protein: 2g
Sodium: 10mg

1 (12-ounce) bag fresh cranberries

1 cup sugar

1 fresh clove

Small pinch of cinnamon

½ cup water, apple juice, or pineapple juice

Pinch sea salt

1 tablespoon frozen orange juice concentrate

As with the Cinnamon Apple Butter recipe (this chapter), other fruits pair nicely with this simple recipe. Try fresh cherries when fresh cranberries are not in season; just be sure to pit them beforehand.

1. Rinse and drain the cranberries. Remove and discard any stems or blemished cranberries.
2. Add the cranberries to the pressure cooker along with the sugar, clove, cinnamon, water or juice, and salt. Lock the lid into place and bring to high pressure; maintain pressure for 6 minutes.
3. Remove from heat and allow pressure to release naturally for 10 minutes. Remove the lid.
4. Stir in the orange juice concentrate. Stir well, breaking the cranberries apart with a spoon or mashing them slightly with a potato masher.
5. Taste for seasoning and adjust if necessary, stirring in additional sugar if needed. Add a little additional ground cinnamon and cloves if desired, being careful not to overseason. Serve warm or chilled.

Chutneys Are a Good Base!
Mix chutneys and thick sauces and jams with low-fat or nonfat cream cheese for an instant spread for crackers or toast points or as a dip for fresh celery sticks.

Wine-Poached Pears

Serves 4

$ Total cost: $5.69

Serving size: 1 pear

Calories per serving: 164

Fat: 4g

Carbohydrates: 33g

Protein: 1g

Sodium: 91mg

4 pears

1 lemon

¼ cup water

¼ cup white wine

Firm pears are best for this dish, which can be served as a dessert on its own or with a dollop of vanilla bean ice cream, crème fraîche, or freshly whipped cream.

1. Rinse and dry the pears. Halve them lengthwise. Use a melon baller to remove the core from each half. Cut the lemon in half and rub the cut end of the lemon over the cut ends of the pears or brush the pear halves with fresh lemon juice.
2. Add the water and wine to the pressure cooker. Place the rack in the pressure cooker and place a heatproof plate onto the rack. Arrange the pears on the plate. Lock the lid into place and bring to high pressure; maintain pressure for 4 minutes. Remove the pressure cooker from the heat, quick-release the pressure, and remove the lid. Use a slotted spoon to carefully transfer the pears to a serving plate. Serve warm or allow to cool slightly and then cover the plate and refrigerate until needed.

Cooking with Wine
Cooking with wine adds flavor and dimension to foods. For this recipe, either red or white wine works. If using white, go for sauvignon blanc or chenin blanc. For reds, try merlots and pinot noirs.

Egg Custard with Lemon

 Serves 6

½ cup sugar

1 tablespoon cornstarch

2 large eggs

2 egg yolks

1½ cups milk

1 cup heavy cream

2 medium lemons

2 cups water

Serve these custards dusted with powdered sugar or topped with fresh or cooked fruit.

1. Add the sugar and cornstarch to a bowl. Stir to combine well. Whisk in the eggs and egg yolks. Stir in the milk and cream. Grate the zest from one of the lemons and add it to the batter along with the juice from both lemons (about ¼ cup). Evenly divide between 6 (½-cup) custard cups. Tightly cover the top of each custard cup with aluminum foil to prevent any water from getting into the cups.

2. Set the rack in the bottom of the pressure cooker and pour in the water. Place the custard cups on the rack, stacking them if you need to.

3. Lock the lid into place and bring to high pressure; maintain pressure for 12 minutes. Remove the pressure cooker from the heat, quick-release the pressure, and remove the lid.

4. Carefully lift the custard cups from the pressure cooker and place them on a wire rack. Remove the foil.

5. Let custard cool to room temperature. Once cooled, cover each cup with plastic wrap and chill overnight in refrigerator.

Add More Flavor!

As with many recipes, a little flavored liqueur or wine will add volumes to the flavor and make your guests go "wow." Try 1 or 2 teaspoons of marsala wine or orange liqueur.

Compote of Wild Berries, Apples, and Pears

Serves 6

1 cup apple juice

1 cup dry white wine

2 tablespoons honey

1 cinnamon stick

¼ teaspoon ground nutmeg

Zest of 1 lemon

Zest of 1 orange

2 apples

3 pears

1 cup mixed blackberries, raspberries, and strawberries

Tired of apples and pears? Make a true wild berry compote by using 1 cup blackberries, 1 cup blueberries, 1 cup raspberries, and 1 cup strawberries.

1. Add the apple juice and wine to the pressure cooker over medium-high heat. Bring to a boil. Stir in the honey until dissolved. Add the cinnamon stick, nutmeg, lemon zest, and orange zest. Reduce heat to maintain a simmer.

2. Wash, peel, core, and chop the apples and pears. Add to the pressure cooker. Stir. Lock the lid into place and bring to high pressure; maintain pressure for 1 minute. Remove the pressure cooker from heat, quick-release the pressure, and remove the lid.

3. Use a slotted spoon to transfer the cooked fruit to a serving bowl. Return the pressure cooker to the heat and bring to a boil; boil and stir until reduced to a syrup that will coat the back of a spoon. Stir the berries in with the cooked fruit in the bowl and pour the syrup over the fruit mixture. Stir to mix. Allow to cool slightly, then cover with plastic wrap and chill overnight in the refrigerator.

Berries Are Good for You

Berries are a great source of fiber and antioxidants. Their natural water content helps replenish water in your body and, therefore, your skin! Berries are naturally low in calories and fat, making them a great food for any occasion.

Balsamic Peaches

 Serves 6

2 (15-ounce) cans sliced peaches in syrup

¼ cup water

1 tablespoon white wine vinegar

1 teaspoon balsamic vinegar

½ tablespoon chopped fresh Italian flat-leaf parsley

Finely grated zest of one lemon

1 cinnamon stick

2 whole cloves

¼ teaspoon ground ginger

Pinch cayenne pepper

To make spiced peach butter, after Step 2, process the peaches and liquid in a blender or food processor until smooth and return to the pressure cooker. Simmer and stir over low heat for 30 minutes or until thickened enough to coat the back of a spoon.

1. Add all of the ingredients to the pressure cooker. Stir to mix. Lock the lid into place and bring to low pressure; maintain pressure for 3 minutes. Remove the pressure cooker from the heat, quick-release the pressure, and remove the lid.
2. Remove and discard the cinnamon stick and cloves.
3. Return the pressure cooker to medium heat. Simmer and stir for 5 minutes to thicken the syrup.
4. Serve warm or chilled. To store, allow to cool and then refrigerate for up to a week.

Balsamic Vinegar

Believe it or not, balsamic vinegar is not just for salads! Its natural sweet and tangy flavor adds depth and flavor to fruits, vegetables, meats, and fish. To use as a syrup, just simmer 1 cup of balsamic until it reaches about ¼ cup. Use as you would honey and drizzle over fresh strawberries or steamed broccoli.

Banana Cream "Pie"

Serves 6

Butter, approximately 1 tablespoon

2 slices sourdough bread, crusts removed

2 ripe bananas

2 tablespoons fresh lemon juice

1 cup heavy cream

2 large eggs

½ cup dark brown sugar, packed

1 teaspoon ground nutmeg

2 tablespoons dark rum

1 tablespoon vanilla

1 cup water

Ripe bananas and dark rum fill the flavor in this easy-as-pie custard-like recipe. It's perfect for a ladies' brunch or an at-home buffet.

1. Butter the inside of a 5-cup casserole dish that will fit inside the pressure cooker on the rack; set aside. Add the bread to a blender or food processor; pulse to create soft bread crumbs. Remove and set aside.

2. Add the bananas and lemon juice to the blender or food processor; purée while gradually adding in the cream. Add the eggs; pulse to mix.

3. Add the brown sugar, nutmeg, rum, and vanilla; pulse until mixed. Stir in the reserved bread crumbs.

4. Pour the banana mixture into the prepared casserole dish. Cover and wrap tightly in aluminum foil.

5. Pour the water into the pressure cooker. Place the rack in the cooker. Set the foil-covered casserole dish on the rack. Lock the lid into place and bring to low pressure; maintain pressure for 22 minutes. Remove from the heat and allow pressure to release naturally.

6. Transfer the casserole dish to a cooking rack and remove the foil. Serve warm or chilled.

Try Adding Chocolate!
For a truly decadent finish to this already rich dessert, add a drizzle of melted chocolate. For pure presentation, slice a banana in half, then half again. Dip a banana quarter in the melted chocolate and serve as a garnish.

Fruit Compote of Apricots, Peaches, and Golden Raisins

 Serves 6

1 (8-ounce) package dried
apricots

1 (8-ounce) package dried
peaches

1 cup golden raisins

1½ cups orange juice

1 cinnamon stick

4 whole cloves

If you like more sugar, use powdered sugar, as it dissolves easily. Otherwise, use honey as a sweetener when serving.

1. Cut the dried apricots and peaches into quarters and add them to the pressure cooker along with the raisins, orange juice, cinnamon stick, and cloves. Lock the lid into place and bring to high pressure; maintain pressure for 3 minutes. Remove from heat and allow pressure to release naturally. Remove the lid.

2. Remove and discard the cinnamon stick and cloves. If you wish to thicken the fruit, return to medium heat and simmer for several minutes. Serve warm or allow to cool, and then cover and store in the refrigerator until needed. Use within a week.

More on Dried Fruits

Dried fruits are great for cooking over long periods of time with meat dishes such as pork loin, a whole turkey, and Cornish hens. Another benefit is that you can make this ahead of time and pour over your finished product. Keep in the refrigerator until ready to use and reheat in a small boiler on the stovetop over low heat.

Cinnamon Apples with Walnuts

Serves 4

$ Total cost: $6.57

Serving size: 1 apple

Calories per serving: 185

Fat: 14g

Carbohydrates: 30g

Protein: 3g

Sodium: 95mg

½ cup apple juice

¼ cup golden raisins

¼ cup walnuts, toasted and chopped

2 tablespoons sugar

½ teaspoon finely grated lemon zest

½ teaspoon finely grated orange zest

½ teaspoon ground cinnamon

4 Golden Delicious apples, firm and not overripe

4 teaspoons butter

1 cup water

Enjoy baked apples without the baking! These apples come out tender and moist with all the flavors you love.

1. Put the apple juice in a microwave-safe container; heat for 1 minute on high or until steaming and hot. Pour over the raisins. Soak the raisins for 30 minutes. Drain, reserving the apple juice. Add the nuts, sugar, orange and lemon zest, and cinnamon to the raisins and stir to mix.

2. Rinse and dry the apples. Cut off the top fourth of each apple. Peel the cut portion and chop it, then stir the diced apple pieces into the raisin mixture. Hollow out and core the apples by cutting to, but not through, the apple bottoms.

3. Place each apple on a piece of aluminum foil that is large enough to wrap the apple completely. Fill the apple centers with the raisin mixture.

4. Top each with a teaspoon of the butter. Wrap the foil around each apple, folding the foil over at the top and then pinching it firmly together.

5. Pour the water into the pressure cooker. Place the rack in the cooker. Place the apples on the rack. Lock the lid into place and bring to high pressure; maintain pressure for 10 minutes.

6. Remove pressure cooker from heat, quick-release the pressure, and remove the lid. Carefully lift the apples out of the pressure cooker. Unwrap and transfer to serving plates. Serve hot, at room temperature, or chilled.

Cream Sherry Poached Pears

 Serves 4

4 ripe, but still firm, pears such as d'Anjou

2 tablespoons fresh lemon juice

1¼ cups dry white wine such as sauvignon blanc

½ cup cream sherry

¼ cup sugar

1 (3") cinnamon stick, halved

¼ teaspoon ground ginger

2 teaspoons orange zest, grated

Soft yet firm pears work best for this recipe. Look for Bartlett, d'Anjou, or Bosc pears, as opposed to more hearty pears such as Asian.

1. Rinse and peel the pears and cut them in half. Use a spoon or melon baller to remove the cores. Brush the pears with the lemon juice.
2. Combine the wine, sherry, sugar, cinnamon, ginger, and orange zest in the pressure cooker. Bring to a boil; stir to blend and dissolve the sugar. Carefully place the pears cut-side down in the pressure cooker. Lock the lid into place and bring to low pressure; maintain pressure for 3 minutes. Remove the pressure cooker from the heat, quick-release the pressure, and remove the lid.
3. Use a slotted spoon to transfer the pears to a serving bowl or to place them on dessert plates. If desired, return the pressure cooker to medium heat and simmer uncovered for several minutes to thicken the sauce. Remove and discard the cinnamon stick pieces. Spoon the sauce over the pears. Serve.

Cooking with Wine

A good rule of thumb to remember when cooking with wine is the heartier the dish, the heartier the wine; the lighter the dish, the lighter the wine. Meaning, a recipe with robust flavor needs a wine that can stand up to that. That's why beef roasts usually have a Cabernet sauce as opposed to a Beaujolais sauce. The same is relevant here. Pears love the flavors of sauvignon blanc or chenin blanc as opposed to heavier-flavored chardonnay wines.

Pear Butter with Vanilla Beans

Makes about 2 cups

Total cost: $5.83
Serving size: 2 tablespoons
Calories per serving: 81
Fat: 1g
Carbohydrates: 20g
Protein: 1g
Sodium: 6mg

6 medium Bartlett pears

¼ cup dry white wine such as sauvignon blanc

Finely grated zest of one lemon

1 tablespoon fresh lemon juice

¾ cup sugar

2 orange slices

1 lemon slice

2 whole cloves

1 vanilla bean, split lengthwise

1 cinnamon stick

¼ teaspoon ground cardamom

Pinch sea salt

Place vanilla bean pods in granulated sugar to make vanilla sugar. Use this sugar when making cakes, pies, and cookies for an extra flavorful twist.

1. Rinse, peel, and core the pears and cut them into 1" dice. Add the pears, wine, zest, and lemon juice to the pressure cooker. Lock the lid into place and bring to low pressure; maintain pressure for 8 minutes.

2. Remove from heat and allow pressure to release naturally for 10 minutes. Quick-release any remaining pressure and remove the lid. Transfer the fruit and juices to a blender or food processor and purée.

3. Return the purée to the pressure cooker. Add the sugar. Stir and cook over low heat until sugar dissolves. Stir in the remaining ingredients. Increase the heat to medium and boil gently, cooking and stirring for about 30 minutes or until mixture thickens and mounds slightly on spoon.

4. Remove and discard the orange and lemon slices, cloves, and cinnamon stick. Remove the vanilla pod; use the back of a knife to scrape away any vanilla seeds still clinging to the pod and stir them into the pear butter. Cool and refrigerate covered for up to 10 days or freeze for up to 4 months.

Lemon Glacé

 Serves 6

1⅓ cups sugar

3 large eggs

1 egg yolk

¼ cup butter, softened

¼ cup fresh lemon juice

1 teaspoon lemon zest, grated

2 cups water

Serve this refreshing lemon dessert in a martini glass topped with fresh berries. Yum!

1. Add the sugar to a blender or food processor. Process to create superfine sugar. Add the eggs, egg yolk, butter, lemon juice, and lemon zest. Process until well-mixed.
2. Prepare a 3-cup heatproof casserole dish that will sit on the rack of the pressure cooker by treating it with nonstick spray or coating the inside with butter. Strain the mixture from the blender or food processor into the dish. Cover tightly with aluminum foil.
3. Pour the water into the pressure cooker and insert the rack. Place the foil-covered casserole dish on the rack. Lock the lid into place and bring to low pressure; maintain pressure for 18 minutes. Remove the pressure cooker from the heat, quick-release the pressure, and remove the lid. Remove the casserole dish and place it on a wire rack.
4. Remove the foil from the casserole dish, being careful not to let any moisture clinging to the foil drop into the lemon curd. Use a small whisk or a fork to whisk the lemon curd.
5. The lemon curd can be served warm, but it will be somewhat runny. Cool, and then refrigerate covered for at least 4 hours to thicken the curd.

Lemon Filling

This delicious lemon treat also works well as a filling for baked pastry shells or as a pie filling. Make a rich lemon angel food cake by creating finger-sized holes in the angel food and pouring the lemon glacé over the top, dripping into the holes and down the sides of the cake.

INDEX

Note: Page numbers in **bold** indicate recipe category lists.

Apple dishes, 318, 326

Apricot or peach dishes, 12, 17, 323, 325

Artichoke Hearts and Quinoa, Salad of, 261

Asparagus with Olive Oil and Shallots, 301

Banana Cream "Pie," 324

Beans and legumes: Black Bean Soups, 185, 203; Cannellini Bean Salad with Dried Cranberries and Asian Chilies, 251; Cannellini Bean Soup with Kale, 182; Chickpea Pasta with Cabbage Sauce, 233; Chickpea Pilaf with Lemon, 245; Classic American Baked Beans, 252; Curried Chicken Salad with Lentils, 254; Lentil Chili with Black Beans, 234; Lentil Soup with Spinach, 183; New Orleans Red Beans and Rice, 253; Pork and Beans with Cayenne, 112; Quick-Cooking Pork and Beans, 105; Salad of Bell Peppers and Garbanzo Beans, 258; Southern Black-Eyed Peas, 274; Southern Lima Beans with Bacon, 295; Spiced Black Beans and Rice, 140; Spiced Split Pea Purée on Pita Crisps, 22; Spicy Black Bean Purée with Monterey Jack, 24; Spicy Red Beans, 246; Split Pea Soup with Bacon, 181; Stew of Lima Beans, Okra, and Chicken, 216; Tortilla Chili, 238; Traditional Hummus, 18; Vegetarian Chili, 232; White Bean Soup with Chicken and Chilies, 212; Wild Rice with Soy Beans, 239

Beef, **116**–51; African-Style Stew, 208; Barbecue Chuck Roast, 121; Barley Soup, 184; Beer-Braised Ribs, 117; Bell Peppers Stuffed with, Rice, and Herbs, 136; Browned, with Onions, 123; Cabbage with, and Caraway, 137; Casserole of, Bell Pepper, and Tomato, 287; Classic Open-Face Meatball Sandwich with Mozzarella, 135; "Corn" Corned, 128; Corned, and Cabbage, 122; Creamy Enchiladas, 124; German Sauerbraten, 151; Hearty Bolognese Sauce, 33; Hungarian-Style Stew, 144; Meatball Soup

with Potatoes, 187; Meatloaf of, and Pork, 129; Mexican Meatballs, 138; Minestrone with, 186; Old-Fashioned Pot Roast, 118; Onions Stuffed with Spicy, 139; Purple Cabbage Rolls with Beef, Mint, and Tarragon, 23; Quick Stew with Mixed Vegetables, 205; Roast, with Yukon Potatoes, 127; Root Vegetable Soup with, 147; Shredded, Tacos, 125; Shredded Cabbage with, and Tomatoes, 134; Simple Swiss Steak, 120; Sirloin Burger with Mushrooms, 131; Soy Pepper Steak, 148; Spicy, with Jalapeño Cheddar, 281; Spicy BBQ, 119; Star of Texas Stew, 217; Steak Fajitas, 126; Stew with Apricots and Almonds, 141; Stew with Mushrooms and Dumplings, 221; Stroganoff Soup, 192; Swedish Meatballs, 146; Traditional Sloppy Joes, 130; Vegetable Beef Stew, 207; Vietnamese Pho Noodles with, 179–80

Beet dishes, 292, 293

Beet Greens with Shallots and Balsamic, 310

Berry dishes, 14, 34, 319, 322

Breads: Bread Pudding "Parfait," 49; Breakfast Bread Pudding with Apples and Raisins, 48; Southern Sausage Gravy over Buttermilk Biscuits, 42

Breakfast, **36**–56

Broccoli dishes, 198, 296, 297

Brussels Sprouts with Parmesan, 305

Cabbage: Chickpea Pasta with Cabbage Sauce, 233; with meat. See Beef; Pork; with Merlot Apples, 294

Carrot, Purée of, with Turnip and Nutmeg, 315

Cheese dishes, 52, 195, 260

Chicken: Alfredo with Mushrooms, 255; Barley Soup with, and Mushrooms, 190; Basic Stew, 206; Basil Pesto, 60; Beer-Brewed Stew, 219–20; Brandied Casserole, 142–43; with Carrots and Herbs, 86; Cayenne, with a Hint of Cinnamon, 67; Chili Pepper, with Fresh Ginger, 63; Citrus Spice, 65; Curried Salad, 62; Curried Salad with Lentils, 254; Curry Yogurt, 71; Ginger Honey, with Olives, 87; Grand Marnier, with Sweet Potatoes, 64; Indian, Masala, 58; Jalapeño Chili, 218; Lemon

Herbed, 68; Mexicali Dip of, and Bacon, 26; Mexican Jalapeño Stew with, 210–11; Mushroom, with Potatoes, 69; with Mushrooms in White Wine, 61; 'n' Dumplings, 209; No-Fuss, Piccata, 70; Paprika, with Bell Peppers, 66; pasta or rice with. See Pasta, rice, and grains; Satay-Flavored, 72; Simple Stuffed Grape Leaves, 19; Soup with Corn, 196; Soup with Egg Noodles, 188

Corn/polenta dishes, 15, 44, 196, 202, 215, 244, 247, 299, 302

Desserts, **317**–29

Dips, spreads, appetizers, and sauces, **10**–35, 31–32, 60, 235

Egg dishes, 47, 54, 55, 56, 321

Eggplant dishes, 21, 230, 236

Fennel, Poached with Onion, 309

Fig Sauce, 76, 89

Fish and seafood, **152**–75; Calamari with Marinara, 153; Creamy Crab "Dip," 159; Curried Tuna with Potatoes, 169; Fish Burritos, 171; Fish Chowder, 154; Fish Chowder with Potatoes and Leek, 214; Gulf Grouper with Peppers and Tomato, 164; Hard Tacos with Shrimp and Potatoes, 167; Herbed-Seasoned Whitefish with Tomatoes, 155; Jambalaya with Chicken, Sausage, and Shrimp, 133; Manhattan Clam Chowder, 223; New England Clam Chowder, 222; New Orleans–Style Shrimp with Black Beans and Rice, 173; Paper Poached Whitefish, 158; Paprika Catfish with Fresh Tarragon, 160; Parslied Trout, 161; pasta with. See Pasta, rice, and grains; Poached Salmon with Black Peppercorns and Red Wine, 165; Red Snapper in Rice Wine and Miso, 157; Red Snapper Risotto, 168; Risotto with Crab and Spinach, 175; Risotto with Shrimp and Fennel Seed, 263; Seafood Stew with Coconut Milk, 162; Southern Grits with Shrimp, 172; Tilapia with Black Olives, 163; Tuna with Swiss Cheese and Gemelli Pasta, 166; Whitefish Steamed in White Wine with Veggies, 156; Whitefish with Corn, Celery, and Lima Bean Medley, 170

Grape Leaves, Stuffed, 19

Kale, Pressure-Braised with Potatoes, 308

Mangoes, in Jalapeño Mango Chutney, 13

Mushroom dishes, 227, 240, 280

Onion dishes, 193, 264

Parsnip Purée with Nutmeg, 306

Pasta, rice, and grains, **249**–76. *See also* Beans and legumes; Breads; Corn and polenta; Barley Soups, 184, 190, 231; Barley with Ham and Bell Pepper, 284; Brown Rice Risotto with Fontina Cheese, 275; Cajun-Style Chicken with Rice, 272; Cheese Tortellini with Chicken, 262; Chicken Alfredo with Mushrooms, 255; Chicken and Brown Rice Salad, 268; Chicken and Rice Casserole with Vegetables, 270; Chicken with Mushrooms and Rice, 266; Chickpea Pasta with Cabbage Sauce, 233; Cinnamon Brown Rice with Dried Apricots and Plums, 269; Curried Wild Rice with Apple Chutney, 242; Farfalle with Italian Sausage, 256; Fresh Vegetable Risotto with Basil, 267; Green Onion Rice Pilaf with Carrot and Toasted Almonds, 264; Indian-Spiced Rice Primavera, 248; Jambalaya with Chicken, Sausage, and Shrimp, 133; Linguini with Clams, 174; Long-Grain Rice with Mixed Vegetables and Lemon, 273; Oatmeal with Dried Fruits, 46; One-Pot "Paella," 283; Pasta Fagiole, 229; Pasta with Potatoes, 241; Penne Chicken Cacciatore, 59; Red Snapper Risotto, 168; Rice Pilaf with Cauliflower, Peppers, and Almonds, 276; Risotto of Barley and Mushrooms, 259; Risotto Primavera, 228; Risotto with Crab and Spinach, 175; Risotto with Shrimp and Fennel Seed, 263; Salad of Artichoke Hearts and Quinoa, 261; Smoked Salmon Fettuccine, 257; Spiced Rice with Coconut, 271; Steamed Vegetable Salad with Wheat Berries, 250; Swiss Chard with Brown Rice and Water Chestnuts, 265; Three-Cheese Mac 'n' Cheese, 260; Toasted Oats with Dates, 38; Tuna with Swiss Cheese and Gemelli Pasta, 166; Wild Mushroom Risotto, 240; Wild Rice with Soy Beans, 239; Ziti and Summer Sausage Casserole with Cream Cheese, 282

Peaches. *See* Apricots and peaches

Pear dishes, 320, 327, 328

Pineapple Cilantro Pesto on Crostini, 20

Pork, **88**–115; Acorn Squash with Pork Vegetable Stuffing, 132; Asian Ribs, 150; and Beans with Cayenne, 112; Beer BBQ Sliders with Apple, 93; Boneless Chops with Plums, 92; Breakfast Rolls of Sausage and Pear Chutney, 51; Cabbage with Bratwurst and Beer, 110; Casserole of, with Black Beans and Jalapeño Taco Sauce, 111; Casserole of Eggplant with, 102; Chop Cabbage, 107; Chops with Apricots Three Ways, 108; Chops with Figs and Balsamic, 90; Curry, 149; Dijon Chops with Pear, 106; Double Dijon Chops with Horseradish, 114; Ginger Soy Chops with Broccoli, 103; Ham and Cabbage Casserole, 289; Ham and Swiss "Panini," 53; Ham Stuffed with Potato, Spinach, and Red Bell Pepper, 286; Jalapeño, over Long-Grain Rice, 113; Maple-Glazed Ham with Raisins, 100; Meatloaf of Beef and, 129; Melt-in-Your-Mouth Barbecue Ribs, 89; Mexican Soup with, 194; Quick and Easy Fajitas, 109; Quick-Cooking, and Beans, 105; Roast with Fresh Rosemary and Granny Smith Apples, 91; Roast with Potatoes and Leeks, 101; Root Beer, 97; Sauerkraut Chops with Red New Potatoes, 94; Sausage with Bell Peppers and Onions, 95; sausage with hash browns. *See* Potatoes; Sesame, with Pineapple, 98–99; Shredded Barbecue, on Whole-Wheat Buns, 104; Smoked Ham Sausage Soup, 145; Smothered Sausage with Corn and Potatoes, 40; Sweet Ham with Red-Eye Au Jus, 43; Sweet Potato, with Cranberry, 96; Three-Cheese, with Potatoes, 115

Potatoes: Breakfast Sausage with Tri-Color Bell Peppers and Hash Browns, 45; Creamy Potato Soup, 200; Garlic Mashed Potatoes with Chives, 303; Hash Browns of Sweet Potato with Bacon and Pecans, 50; Hash Browns with Country Sausage and Eggs, 37; Herbed New Potatoes, 291; Pasta with Potatoes, 241; Potato Chowder with Chicken and Fennel, 213; Potato Sausage Casserole, 279; Red Potato Casserole with Ham, 278; Scalloped Potatoes with Ham and Onion, 285; Smoked Sausage Hash Browns with Apples and Walnuts, 41; Sweet Potatoes and Bell Pepper with Coconut, 298; Two-Potato Soup, 199; Veggie Breakfast Burrito, 39; Yam and Potato with Curry, 290

Pumpkin Ginger Soup, 197

Radishes with Italian Parsley, 312

Rutabagas, Creamed, with Parsnips, 316

Savory casseroles and side dishes, **277**–316. *See also specific main ingredients*

Soups, 145, 147, **176**–203, 237. *See also* Stews and chowders

Spinach Sauce with Chicken, Curried, 35

Squash dishes, 201, 243

Stews and chowders, 141, 144, 154, 162, **204**–23. *See also* Soups

Tomatoes: Basil and Sun-Dried Tomato Soup, 177; Cream of Tomato Soup, 189; Curried Green Tomatoes, 307; Fresh Herb Marinara, 27; Fresh Marinara with Beef and Herbs, 30; Fresh Tomato Salsa, 20; Plum Tomato Sauce with Spicy Italian Sausage and Mushrooms, 28–29; Tomato-Based Broth, 226; Tomato Chutney with Fresh Ginger Root, 11; Torta of Sun-Dried Tomato, 25

Turkey: à la King, 82; Breast with Citrus Cranberry Chutney, 78; Breast with Herbs and Port Wine Sauce, 77; Breast with White Wine Tarragon Sauce, 83; Five-Spice Chili, 73; Fresh Herb Blend and Romano Cheese, 80; Louisiana Gumbo with, and Sausage, 81; with Mixed Vegetables and Potatoes, 288; Petit Meat Loaf, 84; "Pot Pie," 74–75; Spiced Mustard-Glazed Breast, 79; Thighs with Balsamic Fig Glaze, 76; with Zucchini and Eggplant, 85

Turnip dishes, 311, 313, 314

Vegetables: Classic Minestrone, 237; Creamy Root Vegetables, 300; Indian-Spiced Rice Primavera, 248; Risotto Primavera, 228; Vegetable Beef Stew, 207; Vegetable Broth, 225; Vegetable Soup with Chicken, 178; Vegetable Soup with Turkey, 191

Vegetarian favorites, **224**–28

the hungry Editor

Foodies Unite!

Bring your appetite and follow The Hungry Editor who really loves to eat. She'll be discussing (and drooling over) all things low-fat and full-fat, local and fresh, canned and frozen, highbrow and lowbrow. . . When it comes to good eats, The Hungry Editor (and her tastebuds) do not discriminate!

It's a Feeding Frenzy—dig in!